Romanticism and Postmodernism

D0407813

Romanticism and Postmodernism

The persistence of Romantic thought and literary practice into the late twentieth century is evident in many contexts, from the philosophical and ideological abstractions of literary theory to the thematic and formal preoccupations of contemporary fiction and poetry. Though the precise meaning of the Romantic legacy is contested, it remains stubbornly difficult to move beyond. This collection of essays by prominent critics and literary theorists explores the continuing impact of Romanticism on a variety of authors and genres, including John Barth, William Gibson, and John Ashbery, while writers from the Romantic and Victorian period include Wordsworth, Byron and Emily Brontë. Many critics have assumed that the forms and modes of feeling associated with the Romantic period continued to exert a powerful influence on the cultural history of the first half of the twentieth century. This is the first book to consider the mutual impact of Romanticism and Postmodernism.

EDWARD LARRISSY is Professor of English Literature in the University of Leeds. He is the author of *William Blake* (1985), *Reading Twentieth-Century Poetry: the Language of Gender and Objects* (1990) and *Yeats the Poet: the Measures of Difference* (1994), and editor of The Oxford Authors *Yeats* (1997).

ROMANTICISM AND POSTMODERNISM

EDITED BY

Edward Larrissy

CAMBRIDGE
UNIVERSITY PRESS

PUBLISHED BY THE PRESS SYNDICATE OF THE UNIVERSITY OF CAMBRIDGE
The Pitt Building, Trumpington Street, Cambridge CB2 1RP, United Kingdom

CAMBRIDGE UNIVERSITY PRESS
The Edinburgh Building, Cambridge, CB2 2RU, United Kingdom   http://www.cup.cam.ac.uk
40 West 20th Street, New York, NY 10011–4211, USA   http://www.cup.org
10 Stamford Road, Oakleigh, Melbourne 3166, Australia

First published 1999

Printed in the United Kingdom at the University Press, Cambridge

Typeset in Baskerville 11/12.5 pt   [CE]

A catalogue record for this book is available from the British Library

Library of Congress cataloguing in publication data

ISBN 0 521 64272 8 hardback

Contents

Illustrations

Notes on contributors

J. DRUMMOND BONE is Professor of English Literature and Vice-Principal in the University of Glasgow. He is a co-editor of the journal *Romanticism* and a past editor of *The Byron Journal*. He has written and lectured widely on Romanticism and on literary theory.

FRED BOTTING is Lecturer in English at the University of Lancaster. He is the author of *Making Monstrous: Frankenstein, Criticism, Theory* (1991) and *Gothic: New Critical Idiom* (1996). He has edited *Frankenstein: a New Casebook* (1995) and (with Scott Wilson) *The Bataille Reader* (1997).

STEPHEN CLARK is British Academy Fellow at the Centre for English Studies, School of Advanced Study, University of London. He is the author of *Paul Ricoeur* (1990) and *Sordid Images: the Poetry of Masculine Desire* (1994). He has edited a selection from Akenside, Macpherson and Young and, with David Worrall, two volumes of essays on Blake: *Historicizing Blake* (1994) and *Blake in the Nineties* (forthcoming).

JOHN FLETCHER is a Lecturer in the Department of English and Comparative Literary Studies, University of Warwick. He is the editor, with Andrew Benjamin, of *Abjection, Melancholia and Love: the Work of Julia Kristeva* (1990); of *Jean Laplanche: Seduction, Translation and the Drives* (1992), with Martin Stanton; and of Jean Laplanche's *Essays on Otherness* (1998).

EMMA FRANCIS is a Lecturer in English and Feminist Thought in the Centre for the Study of Women and Gender, University of Warwick. She has published essays on Amy Levy and Letitia Landon and is currently at work on a variety of projects studying nineteenth-century British literature and culture, including a monograph study, *Women's Poetry and Woman's Mission: British Womens' Poetry and the Sexual Division of Culture, 1824–1894.*

PAUL HAMILTON is Professor of English at Queen Mary and Westfield College, University of London. He is the author of books on Historicism, Coleridge, Wordsworth and Shelley. Currently he is completing a book on Metaromanticism.

EDWARD LARRISSY is Professor of English Literature in the University of Leeds. He is the author of *William Blake* (1985), *Reading Twentieth Century Poetry: the Language of Gender and Objects* (1990) and *Yeats the Poet: the Measures of Difference* (1994). He has edited *The Oxford Authors Yeats* (1997). He is currently working on a book on the idea of blindness in the Romantic period.

MARJORIE PERLOFF is Sadie Dernham Professor of Humanities at Stanford University. She was President of the American Comparative Literature Association from 1993 to 1995, and is a Fellow of the American Academy of Arts and Sciences. Her many publications include *The Poetics of Indeterminacy: Rimbaud to Cage* (1981), *The Dance of the Intellect: Studies in the Poetry of the Pound Tradition* (1985), *Poetic Licence: Studies in Modernist and Postmodernist Lyric* (1990), and *Wittgenstein's Ladder: Poetic Language and the Strangeness of the Ordinary* (1996).

ANDREW MICHAEL ROBERTS teaches English at the University of Dundee. His publications include books on *The Novel* (1994) and *Conrad and Masculinity* (1999), as well as articles on Wordsworth, Yeats, Conrad, Mina Loy and Geoffrey Hill. Forthcoming work includes books on *Literature and Psychoanalysis* and on *Geoffrey Hill*, as well as an edited volume, *Poetry and Contemporary Culture.*

WILLIAM VAUGHAN is Professor of the History of Art at Birkbeck College, University of London. He is editor in chief of *Computers and the History of Art*. His principal publications are *Romanticism and Art* (2nd edn, 1994) and *German Romantic Painting* (2nd edn 1994). He is the editor, with Andrew Hemingway, of a collection of essays, *Art in Bourgeois Society* (1997). He gave the Paul Mellon lectures on British Art in the National Gallery in autumn 1998. He is currently preparing a survey book on British Art *c.* 1714–1837. On the computer side, he is completing work on the EC-funded Van Eyck project for the visual searching of picture archives.

GEOFF WARD is Professor of English at the University of Dundee. His publications include *Statutes of Liberty: the New York School of Poets* (1993) and *Language Poetry and the American Avant-Garde* (1993). He has edited *The Bloomsbury Guide to Romantic Literature* (1994) and, with John Brannigan and Julian Wolfreys, *Re:Joyce: Text, Culture, Politics* (1998).

Acknowledgements

This collection grew, in part, out of a conference, 'From Romanticism to Postmodernism', held in 1992 in the European Humanities Research Centre, University of Warwick. The editor is grateful for the assistance rendered by the Centre and by the British Academy. He is also deeply indebted to the co-organizer, Dr Rolf Lass, of the Department of English and Comparative Literary Studies at Warwick, in consultation with whom the original title was devised. Although some of the essays gathered here are substantially revised versions of papers delivered there, there are also several fresh contributions. The collection has been much enhanced by the helpful comments and suggestions of the Press's readers. The editor is very grateful for the patience and encouragement of Josie Dixon, the Press's editor.

William Vaughan's 'Turnabouts in Taste: the Case of Late Turner' is a development from the lecture he gave at the Turner Society's 11th Kurt Pantzer memorial Lecture at the Clore Gallery, Tate Gallery on Wednesday 25 April 1995. The text of this lecture was subsequently published in *Turner Society News*, no. 55, pp. 10–12, and no. 56, pp. 12–14, 1990. The author and the editor are grateful to the Turner Society and to Cecelia Powell, editor of *Turner Society News*, for permission to re-use material from this publication in this revised and expanded form.

'Postmodernism/*Fin de Siècle*: Defining Difference in Late Twentieth-Century Poetics' is reprinted in slightly different form from *Poetry On & Off the Page: Essays for Emergent Occasions* by Marjorie Perloff published by Northwestern University Press in 1998. Copyright © 1998 by Marjorie Perloff. All rights reserved; used by permission of Northwestern University Press.

The editor is grateful for permission to quote from the following authors:

John Ash, from *The Goodbyes* (1982), *The Branching Stairs* (1984) and *The Burnt Pages* (1991) to Carcanet Press Limited, Manchester.

John Ashbery, 'Europe' from *The Tennis Court Oath* © 1962 by John Ashbery, Wesleyan University Press, by permission of University Press of New England.

John Ashbery, 22 lines from *Flow Chart* (New York: Alfred A. Knopf, Inc., 1991). Copyright © by John Ashbery 1991. Permission granted by Alfred A. Knopf, Inc. and Georges Borchardt, Inc. From *Flow Chart* (Manchester: Carcanet New Press, 1991), permission granted by Carcanet Press Limited.

From 'The Songbook of Sebastian Arrurruz' (38 lines from pp. 92, 95, 96, 97 and 98) first published in *Kong Log* from *Collected Poems* by Geoffrey Hill (Penguin Books, 1985) copyright © Geoffrey Hill 1968, 1985. Reproduced by permission of Penguin Books Ltd. To Dufour Editions Inc. for permission to reprint quotes from Geoffrey Hill's 'The Songbook of Sebastian Arrurruz', from *King Log* (1968).

Steve McCaffery, from 'Staged Dialogue with Failed Transit Actiant Opposition' from his *Theory of Sediment* (Vancouver: Talon Books, 1991). Permission granted by the author.

CHAPTER I

Introduction

Edward Larrissy

I

The title of this collection refers to two separable but closely related topics. One is a genetic thesis about the persistence of Romanticism in the present, both in thematic and stylistic tendencies: just as it has often been claimed that Modernism is essentially a remoulding of Romanticism, so this volume addresses the proposition that Postmodernism is also yet another mutation of the original stock. But the title also refers to the problem of interpreting the past: to the ineluctable capture of definitions of Romanticism in current interests and ideologies. It could thus be seen as referring specifically to the typically postmodern discovery of Postmodernism in Romanticism, or whatever is taken to be Romanticism. There might appear to be a dubiety here: is the tendency of this volume genetic, or is it about a hermeneutic problem? But the dubiety is only an apparent one. The questions of what influence the past may have on us, and how that influence may operate, must be closely bound up with the question how we decide what the past is, and whether the interpreter's view is altering the evidence.

The first matters to address are those about terms, and their definition. Patricia Waugh has written about how, by the early eighties, the term Postmodernism 'shifts from the description of a range of aesthetic practices involving playful irony, parody, parataxis, self-consciousness, fragmentation, to a use which encompasses a more general shift in thought and seems to register a pervasive cynicism about the progressivist ideals of modernity'.[1] Marjorie Perloff, below (pp. 180–4), identifies a similar shift, and links it with the work of Lyotard, who asserts that Postmodernism means the death of 'grand narratives';[2] which chiefly means, because of the epoch in which we live, the grand narratives of Enlightenment and modernity. But whatever about the shift, it does seem likely that most could agree on a combination of self-consciousness, the tendency to parody and the tendency to cynicism as included in the contemporary reference of the word. But how widespread is the contemporary reference? Perloff also suggests a doubt about the ability of the postmodernist idea to generate new vitality in art, overwhelmed as it now is by theory and theorisers. Yet despite the undoubted presence of a theory industry on the subject, the irony, parodic tendencies and cynicism appear to be persisting long after the first forecasts of the death of Postmodernism were made. The theory serves to answer a hunger to understand these undeniable features of the cultural production of the late twentieth century, both in popular and high art.

There are also questions to be answered about the use of the term Romanticism. A relevant point to make is that the tendency nowadays is to think in terms of Romanticisms in the plural, as Stephen Clark points out below (p. 158). That tendency, it might be argued, is itself an example of a typically postmodern piece of de-essentialising. Yet it has long been recognised that Romanticism is a dubious essence. Arthur O. Lovejoy's paper, 'On the discrimination of Romanticisms', first appeared in *PMLA* in 1924, but its thesis is more radical even than its title implies, for it claims that Romanticism resists all categorisation; and many authors have alluded to the conflicting definitions offered by so-called Romantics themselves of a word which, in the English language, did not even refer to the notion of an artistic movement until 1844. Although few would now subscribe to the view of a unified Romantic discourse expounded by Wellek in his response to Lovejoy,[3] there is, nevertheless, a marked propensity to recognise (and deconstruct) a 'Romantic ideology', in Jerome McGann's celebrated usage, which comprises a series of related tendencies, and which has bequeathed its prejudices and misprisions even to our own belated generation. McGann sees this bequeathal as founding a dangerous collusion of latter-day critics with their Romantic objects, though his point can be seen as a refinement of the theoretical Marxist attack already mounted by Macherey and Eagleton on critical collusion in general.[4]

But one might see the latter-day Romantic ideologist not only as colluding with the objects of enquiry, but as constituting them as Romantic. And in that case a question arises: which comes first in the hermeneutic moment: the inheritance that makes the critic a latter-day Romantic, or the latter-day criticism that decides what constitutes 'Romanticism'? Such are the circles to which discussion of interpretation are prone in a postmodern universe. And of course this is the same circle with which we began.

There are further ironies attending this question. Contemporary historicist, feminist and post-colonial criticisms seek to explode the Romantic canon, partly under the pressure to de-essentialise, though admittedly for other, political motives as well. But the canon they explode is itself very far from comprising those writers who were celebrated in the 'Romantic period'. Few today read, for instance, the poetry of Scott, Rogers, Moore or Campbell, yet it is they who, in the early nineteenth century, dominated the poetic scene in the estimation of their contemporaries, as Byron recorded in his journal.[5] If we are to speak of canons, it is only fair to conceive this rough grouping as a major component in an initial Romantic poetic canon which has subsequently ceased to exist. Can it then, in any simple way, be a Romantic ideology which has ended up by relegating them and giving us, instead, Blake, Wordsworth and Coleridge as canonical figures? In fact, the canonisation of this group can be seen as part of a complex process involving also the development of late nineteenth-century tendencies that were to issue in Modernism. So the current impetus to go *Beyond Romanticism* (the title of a widely disseminated collection of recent essays, edited by Stephen Copley and John Whale) can be seen as part of a post-modern swerve away from the Modernist constitution of Romanticism. On this reading, Modernist images and immediacies are not so much descendants of Romantic organicism and symbolism as developed in tandem with a particular reading of Romanticism which emphasised these aspects. This phenomenon is something that may itself be subject to study and criticism: William Vaughan's essay in this volume shows how contemporary accounts of Turner, based on a thorough historical scholarship, are questioning the notion of a 'late Turner', a conception seized on by earlier modern critics as anticipating Modernism. To be very explicit: this is an example of the creation of a Romanticism which is fit to act as a precursor for Modernism. One would be inclined to expect that contemporary readings of Romanticism would emphasise types of writing that do not accord with the idea of Romantic lyricism or sublimity, even while recognising and questioning the continued influence of those modes. Indeed, questioning in the present is bound up with reconstituting the past. That reconstitution includes the poetry, prose fiction and journals of women writers, and the finding has tended to be that women's writing of the period does not participate in the fashion for the sublime (which is seen as a male preserve), as in the case of Dorothy Wordsworth: the particulars in her writing, not constantly under pressure to fold themselves into a scheme of sublimity, can be seen in partial but strong contrast to the poetry of her brother, even though it is also true, as Paul Hamilton subtly points out, that the particulars in the literature of the Romantic sublime are both more evident to postmodern critics, and are seen by them as palpably failing to support the sublime framework proposed for them by the Romantic writer. Hamilton himself refers to Dorothy Wordsworth, and so does Anne Mellor in *Romanticism and Gender* (1993).[6] A pointed example of the conscious way in which female writers might question the pretensions of the male sublime is provided by the work of Anna Laetitia Barbauld, who questions Coleridge's immersion in 'metaphysic lore' in a poem addressed to him. The 'feminine tradition', as Margaret Homans calls it, in work discussed here by Emma Francis (pp. 56–8), thus piquantly undermines one of the key categories mooted as providing a continuity, or at least a parallel, between Romanticism and Postmodernism – namely, the sublime – and does so as early as the Romantic period itself.[7] This is not to say that women poets did not essay sublimity: Charlotte Smith's *Beachy Head* and portions of her *The Emigrants* provide good contrary examples. But there is an abundance of concentration on the poetry of sensibility. Indeed, one of the revisionist points made by contemporary criticism is the extent to which women poets pioneered new modes in that kind: both Wordsworth and Coleridge acknowledged their indebtedness to Smith's *Elegiac Sonnets* (first edition 1784), though not perhaps with sufficient emphasis: I would claim, though, that the facts are eloquent enough, when properly read. Smith's title, with its avowal of mixed modes – elegy and sonnet – predates by some years a work with a similar title: *Lyrical Ballads*, by Wordsworth and Coleridge.

The salience of discussion about the sublime in debates about Romanticism and about the relationship of Romanticism and Postmodernism, evident in this very collection, is itself worthy of comment – as is its natural concomitant: the renewed interest in German Romantic philosophy in advanced theoretical discussion in the English-speaking world. That salience also derives from Lyotard's work, the key connection being the notion of attempting to 'present the unpresentable'. Once the matter is put in that way, it is not difficult to sketch in another related topic: the heroic, experimental artist who makes the attempt. The artist as hero, and as male hero, is not a nineteenth-century conception only; and there is work enough on the gender-preconceptions of Modernist writers to suggest that the 'masculine tradition' continues into the twentieth century, despite notable innovators such as Woolf. But does it continue into the Postmodern? That seems a more problematic thought. An empirical survey would hardly demonstrate that women artists tend on the whole to exclude themselves from ambitious experiment and innovation. But at the same time, it often seems to matter less: what is left of the sublime is ironic, self-conscious, lacking in metaphysical confidence, and thus more easily prone to enter into dialogue with the popular and accessible.

But this dialogue is also reflected in the way the Romantic period is now constructed. To see the recently fashionable array of texts from the Romantic period as another canon, recognised in the Postmodern, must seem like a joke in a period so cynical about canon-formation and all social consensus. So to put it no more strongly: this array not only broadens the range of reading, but also supports a study of the interaction in the period between the more and the less 'Romantic'.

II

What does the new array of texts represent? Nothing that would have seemed like an acceptable anthology to readers of the period, nor to Victorian or early twentieth-century readers. A compilation such as McGann's *New Oxford Book of Romantic Period Verse*, which contains, for instance, ample selections of Blake alongside anonymous ballads and small but judicious selections of Rogers and Campbell, represents a view of the period which never was on sea or land, but one which conscientiously seeks to offer something nearer to the 'truth' of the period than could have been offered before, while at the same time connecting the effect of 'truth' to the operation of twentieth-century interests. In order to go beyond the postmodernist cynicism which runs parallel to such beliefs, McGann – or a writer such as Alan Liu – has to believe that the values informing current emancipatory political interests should be approved, and that the broadly Marxian analytic tools employed in criticism by those interests have real scientific validity. What one often finds is a strange combination of postmodern, post-deconstructionist scepticism with the culturally approved leftism which provides the last, if substantial, tatters of value and veridicality. This amalgam, 'deconstructive materialism' as Marjorie Levinson has called it,[8] is by no means risible in what it has offered in terms of new analyses conscious of the aporias and supplemental logic governing the political texts and sub-texts of 'Romanticism'. But in confronting the fundamental questions raised by its own method it frequently offers a kind of bleak hand-wringing. Alan Liu, who identifies himself as a deconstructlve materialist, sets down these thoughts in the 'Epilogue' to his book on Wordsworth: 'No one can know the differential relation between history and literature, or any other register of mind, with full certainty. This is why, after all, I say "I believe." I treat not of certainty but of credibility.'[9] One has to be far more confidently Marxist than this to be able to place postmodernist scepticism, however sympathetically, as part of 'the cultural logic of Late Capitalism', as Fredric Jameson does. But the post-modern sceptic may reply by questioning not only the veridical claims of Marxist dialectics, but also the humanist, Judaeo-Christian values which provide (it may plausibly be maintained) a matrix for orthodox Marxist thought. The question whether one either can or should invoke such a core of value is, perhaps surprisingly, very much on the agenda again. Eagleton, for instance, in patently invoking the concept of species-being, is unapologetic about the basis of Marxism in human nature, even if he is wary about some of the implications of that phrase.[10] Stjepan Mestrovic, picturing the despair entailed by the absence of value, finds the answer in a new *fin de siècle* of unabashed and confident subjectivism.[11] A conference at Cambridge on Postmodernism and Religion, evokes the persistence of the 'Shadow of Spirit', which is to suggest a continued efficacy for Spirit even if one believes in the unlikely proposition that a shadow can exist without something to cast it.[12] The extent to which Spirit can continue to have an effect when it is thought to have died is raised, in specific relation to Romanticism, by Lyotard's famous essay, 'What is Postmodernism?', appended by his translators to *The Postmodern Condition*. Here, both modern and postmodern (he does distinguish) are seen as operating under the sign of the sublime, in that the sublime is what attempts to represent the unrepresentable.

The distinction between modern and postmodern is supposed to turn on the notion that Modernism remains nostalgic for the transcendence that underlay the notion of sublimity, while Postmodernism does not. The thesis of 'What is Postmodernism?' is in fact related to the rather differently conceived treatise on *The Postmodern Condition*. The language games in which, *Just Gaming*, we are supposed to delight are conceived in terms recognisable from other attempts to define Postmodernism: the emphasis is on the difference of specific formal features of types of discourse and communication. But the absence of a transparent discourse is a notion here relegated in favour of a formulation of deeper resonance: the 'absence of a grand narrative': that is, of a narrative accepted as grand because founded in transcendence. But even if one is disposed to accept this, the question how far one can completely cut such a Postmodernism adrift from the transcendent persists, if its techniques and impulses have in fact emerged from a Romantic matrix. Even if we feel difficulty in believing in a grand narrative founded in the transcendent, we are perhaps inclined to believe in – or at least have nightmares about – one that is controlled by a shadowy sector of multinational capital, or by a conspiracy of Mafia and corrupt state agents. And it is the persistence of Gothic which most obviously points to the paranoid fear that, having expunged the transcendent, the inheritors of the Enlightenment may find that they are acting in an obscure Satanic narrative, though possibly one that is very much of this world. From a psychoanalytic perspective, John Fletcher considers below not only the significance of the persistence of Gothic, but also its uncanny power:

Preoccupied always with the question of limit, of residues and archaisms, with what resists the modern and remains both active and unsurpassable within it, perhaps it is only with the proposed obsolescence of modernity itself, that the traditional vocation of Gothic will converge with the dystopian fantasies of a science fiction concerned with the unsurpassability of a Dark Future rather than a Dark Past. (pp. 139–40)

In Fletcher's account the return of the repressed is figured as the return of the fascist in a world where the enlightened project of modernity is itself seen as naive, uneducated in the persistence of the dark dreams of power. Yet it could be said that the spectre of this return matters less in the flattened perspective and sceptical point of view of Postmodernism: popular culture offers an increasing number of examples of the apocalyptic becoming a matter of mundane and heavily stylised entertainment, *The X-Files* being the rather too obvious example. One of the uncanny effects of reading Fletcher's essay is to find the fascist more likely to appear because it matters less. Another is to find it understandable that the Gothic erosion of enlightened value should be the most enduring and inexorable progeny of Romanticism. Yet this darkness may be only one side of the story, for the contemporary cybernetic fantasy also continues the Romantic tale of endless human potential, and links back to the more radiant versions of the sublime. As Fred Botting points out, the wavering between dark and light versions of the fantasy is itself a Romantic inheritance.

III

Of course, sceptical and ludic Postmodernism in its various forms can itself be given a plausible Romantic ancestry, and a number of essays in this volume make that point. Drummond Bone is able to find analogies between the Romantic and the postmodern attitude to endings and what they imply. His title, 'A Sense of Endings', pays homage (with a significantly postmodernist transformation) to Frank Kermode's book. It seems worth recalling that in *Practising Postmodernism* Patricia Waugh also feels impelled to refer to this work several times, noting Kermode's perception that 'people with no clear sense of ending will always fabricate one'.[13] Bone makes the necessary point that the fabrication – or, better, fabrications – will bear the ironic imprint of the lack of faith, the lack of a grand narrative. An antecedent for such irony can be found in the work of Byron. Yet, as he observes, critics of Romanticism remain mesmerised by Wordsworth and Shelley; and he ventures the thought that the tradition of deconstruction and the Levinson-Liu type of New Historicism, far from eschewing transcendence, is a late descendant of Romantic tradition. This is a view which detects, in the realm of criticism, a remote echo of Lyotard's findings.

If an ending is the embodiment of an ordered view, modelled on some idea of how narratives, grand or petty, should end, then syntax may, at least in a poem, embody the way a narrative should go. It is, so to speak, another kind of upholstery button in the undisciplined fabric of experience. Geoff Ward, paying particular attention to Wordsworth and Ashbery, examines the way in which the syntax of

Wordsworth's *Prelude*, though gesturing at control, meanders and qualifies its course away from confident assertion, and thus reveals its own attempt to 'suture over trauma' (p. 90). Ashbery's endless qualifications are seen as exacerbating the sense of trauma, but Ward also makes a useful distinction between the earlier Ashbery and the Ashbery of the 1990s, who has become far more markedly a particular kind of poet of syntax.

On the important topic of Romantic irony, Andrew Roberts's essay is a good example of a piece of the rewards that can derive from the kind of self-consciousness with which we began this introduction. He shows how Geoffrey Hill is both aware of his Romantic antecedents and of the need to encompass that awareness in his irony. Yet certain kinds of postmodernist irony can seem profoundly frivolous. Stephen Clark, in his unexpected essay on John Ash and Ashbery (an undoubted postmodernist, if ever there was one) sees the latter's Romanticism as an ironic private lyricism which colludes with the American imperium. This essay has the effect of finding a significant value in the work of Ash, but that value is seen as residing in a deliberate recuperation of elements of Ashbery's style, originally moulded along with his vertiginous scepticism, to a view which can accommodate a degree of realism and political critique. This could be seen as another example of the way in which generic boundaries are everywhere becoming insecure. There is another way of being indebted to Romanticism, and that is by continuing to be indebted to Romantic ideology. Marjorie Perloff (pp. 198–20) offers a principled reminder of the seriousness of Modernist experiments, and a warning against the adoption, in a complacently relativist universe, of some of the more tired and belated forms of Romantic discourse, which are still very much in circulation in our culture.

IV

The Romantic irony of a Friedrich Schlegel is often found to have its correlates in the attacks on system in Byron's *Don Juan*, but less playful authors such as Blake and Wordsworth, inhabit the same universe: Wordsworth's 'something ever more about to be' may have a German ancestry, but least of all can one deny it the title of Romantic for that reason. As for Blake, he can now be seen as an ironic parodist in no frivolous sense, for whom the chief question is:

how avoid the limitations of influence as imposed and thus redeem influence as creative. This is the true sense of his self-injunction: 'I must create a System or be enslaved by another Man's.' There is no escaping system, and to escape enslavement is not to escape influence but to harness it. But seeing premonitions of postmodernism in canonical texts may merge with constituting a new postmodernist's Romanticism. We are back in another circle, which is arguably where Diane Elam is in her *Romancing the Postmodern*. The radical claim of this book goes beyond definitions of Romanticism by identifying an atemporal Postmodernism, though an unstable one that always 'differs from itself'.[14] She does not, however, feel impelled to look at pre-Romantic writing, though Chrétien de Troyes is mentioned. On the other hand, Scott, George Eliot and Kathy Acker are considered at length in this work, though not, of course, in chronological order. 'For, Postmodernism is not a perspectival view on history; it is the rethinking of history as an ironic coexistence of temporalities, which is why this book cannot be structured as a chronological survey.'[15] According to Elam we can now see that Romance is postmodern and that Postmodernism is Romance. This mode, so to call it, defies 'historical boundaries' and 'also makes impossible the taking hold of what Lyotard calls the "now" or "the present from which we can claim to have a right view over the successive periods of our history"'.[16] Indeed the idea of an identifiable historical present is also likely to be questioned by deconstruction as are other notions of presentness or context. The analytic considerations which may buttress this kind of argument may be well illustrated from the case of Blake. A student who has studied Pope, Young, Gray and Macpherson, and also the Hermetic tradition, has a better chance of properly understanding Blake's strategies and terms than one who has not. Yet from this list only Macpherson makes regular, though by no means reliable, appearances on 'Romanticism' courses. And again, when did Blake first find a wide readership? From the point of view of the study of reception Blake is a late nineteenth-century and twentieth-century poet, important to the understanding of Swinburne, Yeats and Joyce, Ginsberg and Ted Hughes. In fact, if only in these precise senses, Blake is not a poet of the Romantic period. This kind of multiple temporality certainly problematises the rather shabby question, 'Are you a real Romanticist?' Yet the question is becoming more common in an age when scrutiny of research by funding councils requires the application of easily-grasped criteria. Of course, many 'historicist' critics would argue strongly that they assume good scholarship can only be produced in the willingness to confront complex temporalities such as the above. Nevertheless, much historicist criticism depends on a privileging of the idea of context, and the assumption that the best literature of a period is essentially engaging with contemporary political realities. A basic epitome of this cast of mind is to be found in McGann's anthology, where the poems selected are printed not by author but by date of publication. This fascinating volume is illuminating about the whole period, and much of the illumination derives from the wide range of non-canonical texts printed, well-chosen to illustrate connections. Immediate contextualisation is often revealing, but not always in an especially striking way. Printing, next to Blake's *Marriage of Heaven and Hell*, a relatively insignificant poem, the anonymous 'Humble Petition of the British Jacobins to their Brethren of France', is indeed mildly interesting, in the way that a lecturer's adverting to context might be. More interesting (as of course it was intended to be) is the reprinting of some of Sir William Jones's translations of Sanskrit mythological poems at various points in the volume. But simply by virtue of being what they are, as well as by virtue of occurring at different dates, these cannot be said to benefit from the same straightforward concept of contextualisation as governed the choice of the 'Humble Petition'. Elam and McGann might seem to represent opposite poles in a system which nevertheless revolves around questions of historicity. But the real critical opposites in our period, are, if anything, even further apart than that. Clifford Siskin, in a rigorous version of anti-collusionism, castigates the 'lyric turn' of criticism of Romantic writing, a lyric turn which mirrors the movement of its object.[17] Yet much of the poststructuralist thought which has influenced Postmodernism has been devoted to the attempt to demonstrate that it is almost impossible for language to escape a lyric turn, whether because 'there is no metalanguage' (Lacan), or because there is no escape from metaphor (Derrida, 'Mythologie blanche'). Indeed, the work of Julia Kristeva attributes an emancipatory power to a poetic language which itself derives from a dimension of language in general. It is precisely because of the destabilising inheritance of poststructuralism that the historicists are so chary of grand claims, and yet they seek to don the mantle of scientificity. It is arguable that no theorist has yet proved adequate to the complex questions raised by this encounter. Yet as far as the criticism of Romanticism is concerned, both positions are indebted to poststructuralism and to Romanticism at the same time. It is in this light that the essays which follow should be read, for part of their claim to attention resides not only in the fact that they reflect the current conjuncture, but that they were commissioned to do so in full consciousness of what was at stake.

CHAPTER 2

From sublimity to indeterminacy: new world order or aftermath of Romantic ideology

Paul Hamilton

I

A chiasmus is oddly reassuring to a modern Romanticist, and the unwieldy but chiasmic form of this paper's title is intended to be a propos. Let me try to unpack it. The Romantic trope of sublimity recasts failures of understanding as the successful symbolic expression of something greater than understanding; Postmodernism rereads this success as indicating only the indeterminacy of meaning. Our occasional inability to get on terms merely highlights the condition under which our understanding labours anyway, were we only to examine it more closely: sublimity is more of the same, not the sign for something qualitatively different. Nevertheless, much postmodernist thinking does not regard itself as merely demythologising Romantic pretensions, deconstructing back into understanding the Kantian postulate of a faculty of Reason capable of apprehending metaphysical reality. Postmodernism has its own agenda, one intended to replace former agendas like that of Romanticism. Far from being the aftermath of Romantic ideology, bound to it in its role of debunker, Postmodernism proposes initiatives. Its unseating of the grand, emancipatory narratives of science, history, philosophy and so on proposes an alternative to the failed Enlightenment which Romanticism endeavoured to replace in its turn. The postmodern alternative does not rest in Adorno's melancholy disillusionment. The Postmodernism of, say, Jean-François Lyotard, advances a new liberalism in which diagnosis of the indeterminacy of meaning will lead to a proper respect for cultural difference. A freedom inherent in our inability to define will replace the freedom traditionally aimed at by thought and action.

Post-colonial and feminist criticism have undoubtedly benefited from postmodernist scepticism. But in this aspiration towards a new world order, something qualitatively different from that symbolised in Romantic discourse, the Romantic ambition or Idea returns. Postmodernism reconsiders its Romantic starting point, and we find Lyotard poring over Kant's writings on judgement and the sublime. Sublimity, then, is deconstructed by Postmodernism into indeterminacy; yet, in its escape from the task of mere translator, Postmodernism doubles back on the Romantic pretension from which it originally differed. A becomes B, and B, however redescribed, becomes A: a chiasmus.[1]

The dialectical structure of the figure of chiasmus suggests transcendence of some kind; its strict containment of that impulse, though, makes sure that the aspiration is securely anchored in the here and now. This is all we know on earth and all we need to know; no temple to Apollo stands at this cross-roads, and so on. The figure is involuted; it gestures outwards, but is crucially impaired, drawing attention to its own figurality or the calculated design by which it simulates what it cannot do. Its grounding is in itself, the repetition or traverse of its own structure; the identity it asserts cannot stand as a fact discovered or as a step forward in any grand narrative. Despite first appearances, in other words, it strives for analytical rather than dialectical truth. Relieved of the embarrassment of a full-blown Romanticism, with its accompanying religious or mystical overtones, postmodern Romanticists can, with proper modesty, scepticism and self-reflexivity, address the lesser problem of whether or not their chiasmus coheres. They check that in this case the chiasmus follows the pattern, A is B and B is A, with the assumption that if a real difference has crept in they have made a mistake; above all, they have *not* discovered a new grounding for A or B. Or maybe mistake is too strong: at best they have committed a catachresis, expressed themselves in another figure of speech, and so continued the rhetorical activity which, for a second, they might have thought they had disrupted by the intrusion of something else.

The name, Postmodernism, sounds like where we are at, rather than the indication of a methodology, such as poststructuralism, which we might or might not adopt. However, since so much of our criticism, not only of Romanticism, is concerned with showing that where people are at is where they choose to be, perhaps this distinction is illusory. We see what we need to see, even when that is unpleasant. I would like to suggest, here, that from a postmodern perspective, looking at Romanticism takes on the chiasmic character

I have just been describing. There are two main points to be made. First of all, this is what postmodern readings do to Romantic discourse. Dialectical theories which distinguish between appearance and reality or between different orders of being are collapsed into chiasmus. This way of reading is typical both of deconstruction and of historicism. In the former, apparent crossings-over are shown to be crossings-back; A and B mean differentially, in relation to each other and not because they refer to different things; B does not denote something on the other side of a threshold from A. In the latter, historicist readings, the Romantic sublimation of practical, political issues is detected by the cool glass of a criticism on whose surface the supposedly unfathered vapour condenses or solidifies. Again, an apparent transformation into something else turns out to contain its own reversal into the same. The second main point is that postmodernists repeat this groundlessness in their own discourse. That, on most descriptions, is just what Postmodernism is about: the failure to ground any story of what is happening is the failure to legitimate any explanation in terms other than those already belonging to it. It can hardly be a coincidence that the postmodernist reads this absence of foundations into Romantic literature and philosophy.

In this scenario, Romanticism cannot anticipate Postmodernism: since the postmodernist cannot see it any other way, it must always have been like this. But, equally, Romantic refinements of the theoretical set Postmodernism must think it shares show a theoretical initiative of their own. For example, postmodern criticism seems to reiterate Hegel's phenomenological critique of Kant. Hegel's *Phenomenology of Mind* does away with the distinction between Kant's two worlds, the world of things as they appear to us and the world of things in themselves in which appearances are grounded. Hegel argues that the second, noumenal world is nothing more than the mirror image of the first. In this inversion, we encounter the familiar turn around in which transgression is demystified, and the voyage out becomes the voyage home; the noumenal world only retraces the outline of the phenomenal world in a different direction. We get the 'others' we deserve, opposites tailored to our images of the normal, the ordinary and the sane. For the postmodernist, the price of this epistemological xenophobia is that we never learn anything new. Like Satan in *Paradise Lost*, our journeys are never original, only perverse, and the country into which we travel has already been mapped by a moral orthodoxy we can refract or invert in various ways, but never escape. Nevertheless, as I have already recalled, Lyotard looks to Kant's aesthetics rather than Hegel's phenomenology for his model of philosophical judiciousness. Hegel's philosophy appears much more like a grand narrative in this context, whatever its success in ungrounding Kant's thought. In Kant's aesthetics, Lyotard finds a championing of the recalcitrance of particularity to abstraction, the resistance of specificity to universals; Kant's aesthetic judgements remain indeterminate, judgements made prior to the imposition of concepts enabling us to generalise about the experience in question. Indeterminacy, Lyotard seems to be implying, produces differences in the definitions of things which ought to be tolerated in the way that we accept differences in how people might paint things, or tell stories about them. The act of artistic expression may well be an attempt to win our assent, to get us to see something in the artist's way, but it is not an attempt to universalise, produce a rule or define the world through representation. We want other people to accept our judgements of taste, and would feel these judgements needed reconsideration if they did not succeed in winning agreement. But the sureness of touch demonstrated in sound aesthetic judgement is, for Kant, a cultural norm rather than a logical axiom. The *sensus communis* Kant argues is displayed in aesthetic agreement is indeed the sense of a community, a polis, which is why Hannah Arendt regarded Kant's aesthetic writings as the core of his political thought. Where Lyotard's politics differs from Kant's and Arendt's is in its emphasis on the individual *sensus* over the *communis* which validates or accredits it. Provided it still makes sense to talk of a judgement whose rationale is *still to be argued for*, Lyotard has all that he wants. Having got rid of Kant's grounding of knowledge in a noumenal world of Reason, Lyotard also gets rid of his grounding of aesthetic judgement in cultural consensus. For him, such consensus is a kind of cultural indifference, callous as capital, shadowing the tyrannical grand narratives he is at such pains to refute. Lyotard spells out the political consequences, as he sees them, of this privileging of the aesthetic particular over the cultural unanimity which, for Kant, guarantees that the particular *is* aesthetic rather than plain peculiar or eccentric.

Within the tradition of modernity, the movement towards emancipation is a movement whereby a third party, who is initially outside the *we* of the emancipating avant-garde, eventually becomes part of the community of real (first person) or potential (second person) speakers. Eventually, there will only be a *we* made up of *you* and *I*. Within this tradition, the position of the first person is in fact marked as being that of the mastery of speech and meaning; let the people have a political voice, the worker a social voice, the poor an economic voice, let the particular seize hold of the universal, let the last be first! Forgive me if I over-simplify. It follows that, being torn apart between the present minority situation in which third parties count for a great deal and in which you and I count for little, and the future unanimity in which the third parties will, by definition, be banished, the *we* of the question I am asking reproduces the very tension humanity must experience because of its vocation for emancipation, the tension between the singularity, contingency and opacity of its present, and the universality, self-determination and transparency of the future it is promised.[2]

Lyotard's overriding sense of cultural relativism leads him to prioritise 'singularity, contingency and opacity' over 'universality' or a welcoming consensus. However emancipatory its plans for the 'self-determination' of minorities, the consensus will, he thinks, efface the cultural difference, the particularity which defines each minority and it alone.

But doesn't this break with Kantian aesthetics also break open the chiasmus which I was arguing explained the relation between Romanticism and Postmodernism? The new world order implied by Lyotard's pluralism dispenses with exactly what makes it possible for Kant to call aesthetic experience a judgement, and so to have a philosophy of it. Isn't the new world order of Postmodernism not a return to Kantian aesthetics, but its deconstruction? Well, I think Lyotard has not broken completely from Kant; his model, after all, is Kant's judgements of the sublime rather than of the beautiful, and it is in his account of sublimity that Kant accords most to the cultural construction of aesthetic experience. Sublimity, for Kant, is certainly a pretty *recherché* experience, to be clearly distinguished from the gawpings of the uneducated. Kant then needs his account of 'genius' to show how it might ever be possible for so unique an experience to filter down to the rest of the community. Yet the fact that it does become assimilated distinguishes genius from irrational raving or fanaticism. In *The Postmodern Condition* Lyotard focuses on the tense-logic of the sublime: in sublime experience, our judgement of what is happening is always one of what 'will have been', future-perfect, never one which provides a rule for the present. The particularity of the experience does seem to predominate, and all rationalisations of it look belated. Only afterwards can we tell that the genius was not raving; that his source was an Idea of Reason which he could not, by definition, represent directly; that the eccentric particularity of his discourse was after all symbolic. There is, in other words, a Kantian cue for Lyotard's ideal of a kind of judgement, and so a philosophical position, which emancipates particularity from any general rule.

However, what this continuing link with Kant's theory of sublimity shows is also something typical of Romantic discourse. The Romantic dislike of abstraction and distrust of rules fosters a cult of individual genius which constantly threatens to explode the Romantic aesthetic from within. But the scope allowed to ordinary, unexceptional particularity by Kant's theory of the sublime was also exploited at the time. Romanticists nowadays, alert to the prescriptions of Romantic ideology, are constantly looking for different kinds of writing in the period, writings which exceed ideological prescription, or, in falling short of what Romanticism requires, remain significantly recalcitrant. The cutting edge of this internal difference from Romantic ideology is an explicitly anti-symbolic writing. Many recognisably new developments in Romantic criticism at the moment, I would suggest, come from attempts to find a critical vocabulary for those writings of the period which fail to satisfy the dominant aesthetic. The critic wishing to defend or champion these writings must decide if they work on *different* aesthetic lines. Within the canon, Jerome McGann's Byron or John Barrell's Clare provide successful examples; outside, the most persistent pressure for a revised aesthetic comes especially from the writing of women.

But I am arguing that Postmodernism helps us see how some non-standard Romantic writings might also be widening a fault in the *prevailing* aesthetic at its most presumptuous and exalted: that is, in the Kantian theory of sublimity. The scandal of this writing, then, would lie in its immanence within the dominant aesthetic, not its alterity. It circumscribes the pretensions of symbolic writing with a relish for particularity which simply pushes the implications of sublimity that bit further. John Clare, and the difficulty of writing about him, is perhaps the best canonical example; women's poetry and journals in the period furnish others. Both popularity and unpopularity were reasons for subsequent critical exclusions, perhaps showing that consensus culture had as heavy and selective a hand as Lyotard suspected. In due course I should like to focus on Dorothy Wordsworth's *Journals* as examples of anti-symbolic particularity, but first I will summarise where I think my comparison of Postmodernism and Romanticism has reached.

On the one hand, postmodernists like Lyotard are attracted to Romantic aesthetic theory because it provides the model of a groundless judgement. It allows a review of experience in which objects are savoured in their particularity and agreement about their character is solicited by an openly collaborative, cultural activity. An accurate judgement, in this context, is achieved through a consensual activity about which one can be more or less cynical. Lyotard is extremely cynical, and I shall have more to say about postmodern cynicism and its reprise of Romantic cynicism in the last part of this paper. However, I have so far been stressing the positives claimed by Lyotard's approach, principally how the freedom he detects in indeterminacy allows for an exemplary respect for the particular. Here, he again takes off from a Kantian model of sublimity, but implies that the time-lapse between the sublime experience and the critical recognition or judgement of its sublimity allows the particular experience a distinct preeminence and authority of its own. Quotidian particularity, on this theory, is privileged prior to judgement, and is no longer necessarily part of a larger narrative, as it is in *The Prelude* or in William's figurings of his sister in 'Tintern Abbey', articulated and valued only by the maturity into which it grows.

Dorothy Wordsworth was one of the principal Romantic dealers in quotidian reality. Her critics and biographers have always had to cope with the symbiosis of her writing and her relationship with her brother, William Wordsworth. There have been two main lines of interpretation. Her journals either occupy a helpfully ancillary position to her brother's poetry: in Mary Moorman's edition of the *Alfoxden* and *Grasmere Journals* it is a nice point as to which is the primary, which the secondary text, the journals or the poems of William Wordsworth listed at the end. The other main critical view is that the 'self-baffling' De Quincey detected in Dorothy Wordsworth's life is repeated in her writings. Her readers witness an embryonic poet failing to rise to the highest aesthetic challenges. Dorothy's frequent literary downgradings of her own work show that she shared a Romantic ideology in which journal entries become highlighted where they are demonstrably the occasional stuff out of which lasting poetic transformations can be made. Recent criticism, though, has read her journals as unconsciously opposing this kind of ideology. Far from 'baffling' her literary self, Dorothy's prose threatens the aesthetic hegemony of Romantic poetry and proposes an alternative model for understanding the individual's place in nature and the community.[3]

Feminist critics, such as Margaret Homans, Susan Levin and Susan Wolfson have taken the lead here, emphasising in different ways and to varying degrees the extent to which Dorothy's failure to sustain the Romantic sublime in fact succeeds in defining sexual difference. Once that success is acknowledged, a new stylistics comes into play, and different critical criteria must be invoked to judge Dorothy's rendering of her quotidian reality. Her writing shrugs off the verdicts of those who praise or detract by discussing its relation to William's poetry or to poetry in general. Instead, it challenges readers to become aware of the options with which literary particularity confronts them: to realise the possibilities for judgement raised by the individual character or scene when presented in a mode which initially appears to prevaricate over which judgement is solicited – aesthetic, social, political, economic and so on. Or, perhaps more accurately, we should say that we experience as prevarication representation whose lack of fit with a prevailing, historically expected literariness makes its readers hang judgement temporarily. As I have claimed already, this experience leaves the reader with two options: to find a non-hegemonic aesthetic which *does* fit, or to understand the recalcitrant writing as combatively engaged with the prevailing taste which seems to exclude it. The fact that the idea of the aesthetic gained unprecedented prominence during the Romantic period dovetails with Dorothy's relation to one of its main English constructors. Dorothy's attempt to establish her own discourse – however unwilling, unconscious or inadvertent – allegorises her life as spinster sister with the married couple, William and Mary, whose interests she then served with such devotion and apparent self-effacement as to attract the pity of De Quincey and the eventual dismissal of Coleridge. Had she written novels, Dorothy might have ridden the crest of a wave of success in women's writing which already had its allotted place in the contemporary economy of taste. Her early journals, though, and the critical problems they raise, are just those arising from their match with her domestic subordination and with her assimilation as groundwork for the conventionally superior, sublime poetic project of her brother.

In other words, one can first of all look around for another rationale for Dorothy's writings which might remove them entirely from the artistic hierarchy in which they occupy so low a position.

John Barrell, Michael Rosenthal and others have written persuasively about the presence of a Virgilian, Georgic ethic in some late
eighteenth- and early nineteenth-century painting and literature.
Kurt Heinzelman has successfully fed these perceptions into the
reading of Dorothy. The aesthetic potential of her writer's interest in
a domestic economy which, despite its lack of obvious pattern or
symmetry, retrieves artistic value from labour itself, becomes highlighted. It infiltrates her descriptions of Lakeland characters, foregrounding their work and interests in an unusually collaborative
way, striking because those she meets are not prized as the symbolic
motivators of a separate literary activity but as co-workers in a way
of life which Dorothy's literature indifferently records. The possibility that writer and worker are doing the same or analogous or
mutually illuminating things is not at issue, as it always is for
William. Rather, Romantic criticism must be repositioned so as to
appreciate that it is this kind of writing, the *Grasmere Journals*, say,
which is produced by various modes of production, from the
industrious to the beggarly, the residential to the transient, in
Cumbria at this time. Labour has its art, as much as reading,
musing, or learned lucubration, and is exhibited in the kind of
writing required to describe it adequately and the critical exercise
required to read it with propriety.[4]

My free expression here of a kind of Georgic materialism clearly
reverses the idealist aesthetic usually associated with Romanticism.
But, allied with the first is the second stage of reading I have been
arguing for which sees that Dorothy's kind of writing is possible
within the idiom of the sublime when that idiom is given the
inflection Postmodernism foregrounds: one in which materialist
particularity is at odds with its idealist, judgemental endpoint. In a
tellingly reflexive incident of March 1802 in the *Grasmere Journals*,
Dorothy reads to William an earlier episode, 'that account of the
little boy belonging to the tall woman', which she had written about
two years previously. William is composing a poem anyway about
the incident, but this re-reading of his supposed source material
stops him in his tracks. Dorothy writes of the effects of her reading,
'and an unlucky thing it was, for he could not escape from these very
words, and so he *could not write the poem*'. Clearly there is an integrity
or propriety to Dorothy's literalism which resists poetic translation.[5]

William is halted temporarily, but after a night's sleep he *can* write
the poem. His judgement is suspended, for a while, but then, after

having slept on it (badly), he can reorganise the details of Dorothy's account in such a way as to demonstrate that, finally, his aesthetic judgement stuck. But the hiatus is symptomatic: Dorothy's writing no longer need be understood merely as a source for William's poem. It speaks in its own character through its power to delay judgement; in that pause we become aware of other possible judgements, judgements different from the aesthetic one producing William's poem. Dorothy's writing thus contrives a twin critique of the Romantic aesthetic. Its symbolism is bypassed by her miscellaneous record of a life which permits natural objects and people their own ordinary, unsymbolic existence without thereby forfeiting connection with them. Secondly, this relish for the particular forces a way through the passage of sublimity into a space which solicits comparable approval, recognition and agreement. But the judgement formed is one whose imagined community need not be poetic.

Let us look at an example in more detail. The *Grasmere Journal* is periodically symbolic; it plots the story of an unmarried woman anxious that her brother's impending marriage will not affect her life and relationship with him adversely. In the shadow of these fears landscape, incident and person can unsurprisingly wear a psychological or emotional character. Nevertheless, by far the main substance of the *Grasmere Journal* is its circumscription of these symbolic distillations, demystifying their portentousness and lodging the significance of what is described in a labouring social and domestic context. Here is almost all the entry for 14 February 1802:

After dinner a little before sunset I walked out about 20 yards above Glowworm Rock. I met a Carman, a Highlander I suppose, with 4 Carts, the first 3 belonging to himself, the last evidently to a man and his family who had joined company with him, and who I guessed to be Potters. The Carman was cheering his horses, and talking to a little Lass about 10 years of age who seemed to make him her companion. She ran to the wall, and took up a large stone to support the wheel of one of his carts, and ran on before with it in her arms to be ready for him. She was a beautiful creature, and there was something uncommonly impressive in the lightness and joyousness of her manner. Her business seemed to be all pleasure – pleasure in her own motions, and the man looked at her as if he too was pleased, and spoke to her in the same tone in which he spoke to his horses. There was a wildness in her whole figure, not the wildness of a Mountain lass but a *Road* lass, a traveller from her birth, who had wanted neither food nor clothes. Her Mother followed the last cart with a lovely child, perhaps about a year old, at her back, and a good-looking girl, about 15 years old,

walked beside her. All the children were like the mother. – She had a very
fresh complexion, but she was blown with fagging up the hill, with the
steepness of the hill and the bairn that she carried. Her husband was
helping the horse to drag the cart up by pushing it with his shoulder. I got
tea when I reached home, and read German till about 9 o'clock. Then
Molly went away and I wrote to Coleridge. Went to bed about 12 o'clock.
Slept in Wm.'s bed and I slept badly, for my thoughts were full of William.[6]

The anxious ending reminds us that Dorothy is writing in the year of
William's marriage. Dorothy sleeps badly thinking of her brother, as
we saw him doing thinking, if not of Dorothy's person, then of her
untranslatable words. They might well have posed him the same
problem here. The description of the Scottish Carman, little lass,
mother, children and husband looks a picture but inventories hard
work. 'There was a wildness in her whole figure' – the light and
joyous manner of the 'little lass' echoes the register of William's
poetic celebration of Dorothy. John Barrell has alerted us to 'the
Uses of Dorothy', principally the use in 'Tintern Abbey' of the figure
of Dorothy to engineer various kinds of poetic legitimation for
William. But here we have the 'uses of William' put to work in her
writing. Dorothy is not attributing any preeminence to this incident,
nor, by implication, to the mind alive to its symbolic potential. But it
is as if we read her passage through the pattern of William's 'obscure
sense of possible sublimity' to arrive somewhere else by the same
road.

Can I make clear that in this reading of Dorothy I am not
claiming something daft, nor, I hope, shamelessly dabbling in
opportunistic anachronism. I am not saying that Dorothy Wordsworth is a proto-postmodernist. Rather, I am saying that postmodernist interpretations of the Romantic sublime allow it to include a
sheer particularity usually thought to be inimical to its symbolic
discourse. I do not think one can find this possibility considered by
earlier critics of the sublime, even those as exploratory of its
structures as Thomas Weiskel and Neil Hertz. Were Dorothy Wordsworth, wonderful to relate, to be a postmodernist, then she would
also be a cynic. It would not be enough for her to see sublimity and
particularity, the exalted and the quotidian, as connected means of
constructing culture or consensus. It would not even be enough for
her to suspect the truth of her observations because they were
constructed; she would have to suspect them especially when they were
consensual. She would have to possess a cynicism concerning con-

sensus, one which led her to doubt that any consensus could, at bottom, be anything other than the temporary imposition of a particular group's views, disguised under the title of the common interest. Yet even this cynical stance recrosses a Romantic path.

A 'hypermystical, hypermodern, hypercynic' – who is being described? Jean Baudrillard? No, Friedrich Schlegel, caught in the words of a Novalis worried about the reception that Schlegel's novel, *Lucinde*, was going to attract, a novel subtitled 'Cynical fantasies or Satanisms'. But Schlegel's cynicism is of course part of his Romantic irony, a detachment from what he professes, powered by a sense of inner reserve far in excess of any outward show it might make. In the service of irony, Schlegel's wit produces a heroic cynicism. Its refusal to accept material values and definitions allies it with a Christianity which Schlegel calls 'universal cynicism' (*AF*, 16).[7] In one of the *Athenaeum Fragments*, Schlegel and Schleiermacher co-author an aphorism in which the dazzle of cynicism belies its bad faith: 'A *cynic* should really have no possessions whatever: for a man's possessions, in a certain sense, actually possess him. The solution to this problem is to own possessions as if one didn't own them. But it's even more artistic and cynical not to own possessions as if one owned them' (*AF*, 35). In this heroic mood, the cynic can politicise the Kantian aesthetic of particularity, turning its resistance to rules into a democratic programme: 'Poetry is republican speech: a speech which is its own law and end unto itself, and in which all the parts are free citizens and have the right to vote' (*CF*, 65). The pronounced spin given to Kantian aesthetics here by Schlegel can be measured by contrasting statements of Romantic organicism by his brother and a host of other Romantics. In *Biographia Literaria*, Coleridge famously compares Shakespeare's choice of words to bricks integral to a building; in this Burkean analogy, aesthetic particulars are reciprocally means and ends, as Kant prescribes. But Schlegel's adaptation suggests that Kant might have left it open for the autonomy of his aesthetic citizens to generate a centrifugal rather than a centripetal force, thus symbolising an as yet unrealised order rather than cementing the propriety and fitness of the present one. Schlegel's irony rather prefigures Walter Benjamin's aesthetics of history, learned from Paul Klee's 'Angelus Novus', which imagines strategies for blasting historical particulars out of the progressive narratives in which they have been imbedded. Benjamin, famously, is intent on the task of politicising aesthetics; but it is questionable whether or not he ever envisages a republic in which these particulars, liberated, as Lyotard wants them to be, from grand interpretations, would speak with individual voices. The Messianic moment in which he conceives the shedding of explanatory contexts, this tiger's leap in the dark, is obscure and apocryphal in comparison to Schlegel's confident scepticism. For Schlegel, 'skeptical method would more or less resemble a rebellious government' (*AF*, 97). Taking on the conventions of his day and locating freedom in the resulting indeterminacy is, for him, immediately suggestive of political action in the likeness of the recent French Revolution – one of the main 'tendencies of the age', impossible to escape. Unlike Lyotard, and perhaps Benjamin, Schlegel's revolution does have a model.

Yet Schlegel happily develops irony to the cynical extremes that worried Novalis, 'Only cynics make love in the market place' (*AF*, 119), he claims, meaning that for the true ironist public and private can never coincide. No scandalous exposure of self is involved. But his dismissal of authenticity perhaps leaves nowhere to make love in except the market place. Schlegel seems to think that the private can only be expressed in debased images because the *consensual* is always devalued by its provisional, constructed nature. But, in this case, how long can the private experience's notional independence of the public survive? Does not it gradually drop out of consideration like the beetle in the box which Wittgenstein used to allegorise the redundancy of private sense-data to any theory of meaning? Don't we have to admit that we are obliged to live our life in public images, and Schlegel's contrasting inner richness becomes merely an act of faith? Or, since we *never* have authentic expressions of the private alternative to the market place, perhaps all we can do is live a life of false consciousness, but a life of knowing false consciousness, unhappy but not taken in by the straits to which we are reduced. Schlegel is sure such disillusionment evinces 'superiority', analogous to that of the Goethian artist hovering over his creations or the Fichtean philosopher brimming with his own egotistic reserves. But why should not such alienation rather produce an irony which looks more like the last recourse of the inner city slum-dweller or the victim of a poverty trap? Sometimes Schlegel looks like a philosophical slummer.

This is what Novalis feared, carried to its logical, postmodern conclusion. Similarly, Benjamin's exploded histories, no longer a part of any progressive, logical sequence, have to sink or swim in competition with each other for our attention. Market forces may again become the final arbiter. Benjamin's apparent democratisation of historical facts frees them from the hierarchies of privilege or repression through which traditional historical narratives supposedly conferred on them significance. But a postmodernist could argue that he only succeeds in leaving history vulnerable to a cynical eclecticism. This would be to simplify Benjamin, and simplification is one of the main tagets of Peter Sloterdijk when he investigates postmodern cynicism at great length in his *Critique of Cynical Reason*. If, when carried to extremes, the groundlessness of Romantic aesthetics leaves us with nothing except a knowing reflection of our unauthentic state, then Schlegelian superiority does indeed degenerate into the 'enlightened false consciousness' which Sloterdijk excoriates in his book. Symptomatically, Sloterdijk's starting point is Kantian. In his Preface, he describes the 'occasion' for writing a critique of cynical reason:

This year (1981) is the 200th anniversary of the publication of Immanuel Kant's *Critique of Pure Reason* – a date in world history. Seldom has there been a jubilee as dull as this one. It is a sober celebration; the scholars keep to themselves. Six hundred Kant experts gathered in Mainz – that does not produce a carnival atmosphere ... Is it not a sad festival where the invited guests secretly hope that the person being celebrated is prevented from appearing because those who constantly invoke him would have to be ashamed on his arrival ... Who could bring himself to give Kant a summary of history since 1795, the year in which the philosopher published his essay *On Perpetual Peace*? Who would have the nerve to inform him about the state of the Enlightenment – the emancipation of humanity from 'self-imposed dependency'? Who would be so frivolous to explain to him Marx's 'Theses on Feuerbach'? I imagine that Kant's splendid humour would help us out of our stunned state.[8]

Humour is important to the alternative which Sloterdijk's book goes on to propose. A 'cheeky' tradition of what he calls 'low theory' or different versions of carnival, from Diogenes to the film MASH, is called in to reinvigorate the cynicism of the *conférenciers*. Although he does not mention Friedrich Schlegel, it is as if Sloterdijk tries to restore the optimism and rebellion to Schlegelian irony in order to close up its fatal trajectory towards a cynical postmodernism deprived of any agenda. Reading Kant becomes funny, like Musil's description of the young Torless's attempt: 'When he stopped in exhaustion after about half an hour, he had only reached the second page, and sweat stood out on his brow'.[9] And the rest of Sloterdijk's complex book evokes a multitude of such apparently naive or ingenuously physical responses to the philosophical texts which have produced our contemporary mental set, doing so in order to rehabilitate the language of ideology-critique. The targeted mental set is

Cynicism ... *enlightened false consciousness.* It is that modernized, unhappy consciousness, on which enlightenment has laboured both successfully and in vain. It has learned its lessons in enlightenment, but it has not, and probably was not able to, put them into practice. Well-off and miserable at the same time, this consciousness no longer feels affected by any critique of ideology: its falseness is already reflexively buffered.[10]

Sloterdijk's critique of this cynical reason is his 'attempt to enter the old building of ideology critique through a new entrance'.[11] He thinks that the tradition of ideology critique which he inherits is disabled by the ubiquity of ideology. Ideology, after all, has been *the* intellectual growth industry of recent times. In his recent book, *Spinoza and the Origins of Modern Critical Theory,* Christopher Norris emphasises the ancestry of Spinoza in recent all-embracing definitions of ideology. He is especially convincing in his description of Althusser's debt to various of Spinoza's ideas, and sensitive to the degree to which Spinoza is read through a Romantic interpretation.[12] The most notorious characteristic of the Romantic adaptation was pantheism. Commentary on the Romantic pantheistic tradition, such as Thomas McFarland's, has stressed the doctrinal problems which pantheism posed for Christian poets who, like Coleridge, were specially alive to the symbolic possibility pantheism opened up to the poet of nature. But the monism resulting from pantheism, in which, since you cannot find God 'outside' you must find him everywhere, has all sorts of other implications. Fundamentally, it makes all critique immanent. It leads to that equality of particulars, which temporarily silenced William Wordsworth, and a potential democracy of subject-matter which so troubled Coleridge about Wordsworth's own 'Immortality Ode'. In other words, it sets up the opposition we have seen at work between a cynical refusal to believe in appearance, and a rebellious celebration of the destructive effect this has on received hierarchies of meaning. A footnote in Sloterdijk suggests that he thinks this ideological consciousness leads to a kind of Jacobinical sublime. He quotes the famous words of the Abbé Sieyès – 'What is the Third Estate? Nothing. What does it want to be? Everything' – and finds in this 'all-or-nothing logic' a cynical lack of objectivity in need of critique.[13]

Sloterdijk tries to find a legitimate role for cynicism which takes account of the postmodern condition but does not connive at it. As I tried to show was the case with Romantic sublimity, and its privileging of particularity, Romantic cynicism also contains an inner, destabilising dynamic which undoes its pretensions. A quotidian individuality, a varied relish for 'minute particulars' often celebrated by Romantic writing, goes against the idea of sublimity, but it can be seen through postmodern eyes to be a consequence of the most thoroughgoing rationale provided for sublimity, that expounded by Kant's *Critique of Judgement*. In the case of Romantic cynicism, Schlegelian ebullience also exposes a perspective different from the one in which it ostensibly places its reader. The ego's scepticism of the adequacy of public institutions to represent it either produces a Wordsworthian sublimity in need, I suggest, of Dorothy's correctives. Or else what takes over is a cynical flouting of convention which acknowledges that it has no new language to substitute for a public sphere assumed, by definition, to be debasing. The particularity promoted by Lyotard and Sloterdijk as exceptions to the rule of ideology do seem a far cry from Dorothy Wordsworth's records, but all re-work the same structure of sublimity in similar ways. Perhaps I can be cheekily sure that my initial chiasmus is more plausible now: the postmodern championing of particulars undetermined by any rule exceeds its Romantic heritage but only as it reworks Romanticism to serve different historical uses. I should, in justice, though, end a paper like this with Friedrich Schlegel's warning in the *Athenaeum Fragments* about the uses of Kant:

The Kantian philosophy resembles that forged letter – which Maria puts in Malvolio's way in Shakespeare's *Twelfth Night*. With the only difference that in Germany there are countless philosophical Malvolios who tie their garters crosswise, wear yellow stockings, and are forever smiling madly. (*AF*, 21)

CHAPTER 3

Turnabouts in taste: the case of late Turner

William Vaughan

A familiar concept in the history of art is that of particular painters and sculptors having a 'late style'. Coming (by definition) at the end of a practice this style is usually held to have a particular profundity, its perceptual richness compensating for any weakening of manual dexterity. Not all artists have a 'late style', of course. Many (like Thomas Sydney Cooper – for seventy years a painter of near identical cows) continue in the same old line until infirmity strikes them down. It is only the greatest – artists like Michelangelo, Titian, Rembrandt and Cézanne – that are held to reach this higher level.

Turner is one of the artists for whom this distinction has been claimed. Indeed, in the current hang of the Turner bequest in the Clore Gallery, there is a sizeable room devoted to 'Late Turner', in which his broadest and most painterly pictures – such as 'Norham Castle' (ill. 3.1) – are hung. There is far more behind this claim than a mere description of stylistic change. It has come to stand for his primary significance as an artist. In the twentieth century advanced critical opinion has tended to focus on such works, seeing them as being prophetic of the modern movement. Their broad painterliness is held to represent an early stage of that movement towards the triumph of abstraction over representation. Perhaps the most distinguished elaboration of this position is that given by Sir Lawrence Gowing in his Introduction to the New York exhibition *Turner: Imagination and Reality*. Here Gowing asserts that Turner, in his later works 'isolated an intrinsic quality of painting and revealed that it could be self-sufficient, an independent imaginative function.'[1]

Gowing's comments firmly place Turner in the Modernist tradition. Like others of that persuasion before him, he saw the key to this Modernism in a particular phenomenon that is associated particularly with the artist's later years. This is, of course, his habit of

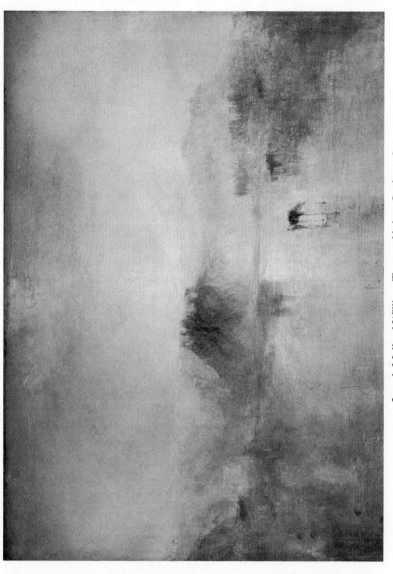

3.1 Joseph Mallord William Turner, *Norham Castle, c.* 1840

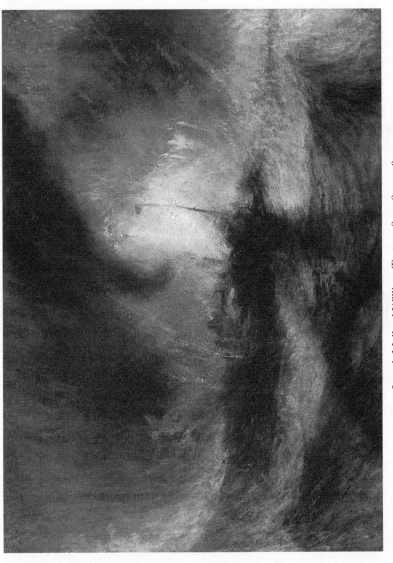

3.2   Joseph Mallord William Turner, *Snow Storm*, 1842

creating works that were apparently unfinished, and that were never exhibited in the artist's lifetime.

Such works – found in their hundreds in the artist's studio after his death – are regarded by Gowing as the fundamental part of Turner's achievement. The finished and exhibited pictures – such as the *Snow Storm* of 1842 (ill. 3.2) – are in his opinion marred by their elaboration into unnecessary detail: 'To complete the product, he was apt to add synthetic details; we do not always find them convincing.'

In recent decades, such a reading of Turner has stimulated increasing opposition. By and large, it is the historians who have led the attack. Those concerned with seeing Turner in terms of his engagement with his own society have pointed out that such 'abstract' Turners tell us little about the artist's complex intellectual world or of his wish to address the issues of his age. John Gage – in his recent excellent study *J. M. W. Turner: 'A Wonderful Range of Mind'* has gone so far as to challenge the whole relevance of the concept of 'late Turner'. While not denying the evident stylistic development of Turner's art, he sees this as part of a continuum, in which ideas and interests are developed. Perhaps most tellingly of all, he points to the fact that much of what is associated with Turner's 'late style' can in fact be found in his works decades earlier. Even the much vaunted 'abstraction' of the later unfinished works can be found in earlier sketches and studies – sometime from as far back as the 1790s, when the artist was in his early twenties – as in the case of certain watercolour studies in the 'Wilson' sketchbook of 1797.

The growing critique of the 'specialness' of Turner's later style has been matched by an increasing interest in his early works and a general tendency throughout to place greater emphasis on iconographical readings – something that tends to favour the exhibited works, where some complex intention can be seen to have been worked through.

On the face of it, this might seem like something of an academic quibble – the consequence of a change in intellectual fashions. But I think there is more to it than that. In a very real sense the artist's reputation is at stake. There is no doubt that the immense prestige that Turner currently enjoys has been largely due to the popularity of the 'Modernist' reading of his pictures in this century. Indeed, one might go so far as to say that that remarkable achievement of the 1980s – the final establishment of a whole gallery dedicated to works he bequeathed to the nation – would not have been possible had it not been for the status that Turner had gained as a precursor of the modern movement. Nor should we be lulled into thinking that – once this gallery has been achieved – the artist is secure. Many of us can recall the melancholy experience of going to visit a gallery dedicated to the works of an artist who was once revered but who has since fallen out of favour. We walk alone in halls where thousands once had trod. The Clore Gallery is, of course, attached to a busy and important gallery – namely, the Tate. But this is no guarantee of lasting status. For if Turner's popularity declines, how long will it be before the spaces set aside for the exhibition of his works are given over to other purposes?

Fortunately, we do not seem to be approaching a position yet where this is the case. For while historians have been questioning the nature and status of 'late Turner', critical opinion has been moving against the Modernist readings that made this phenomenon seem so central. As the recent rehang of the Tate Gallery suggests, there is now far more sympathy for setting up an interaction between the historical and the modern – something that in itself, of course, is evident in current 'postmodern' artistic practice. It is not just the academic world that is questioning 'late Turner'. Artistic taste in general is more prepared to give time and space to the historicist side of Turner. Admiration of his pictorial brilliance has not abated. But this is seen within the context of larger historical structures.

But where does this leave 'late Turner'? Is it a concept that – as John Gage hints – should be more or less abandoned. Not according to the Clore Gallery, where, as we all know, the collection culminates in the largest space of all being given over to 'Late Works'. While other areas are designated by theme – such as the 'Classical Vision' or 'Venice' – this room is designated by a chronological division. It is one that assumes, of course, a specialness about the late career.

It is the question of this specialness that I will be addressing in the rest of this article. First, I will consider the way in which the concept of 'late Turner' developed in the century following the artist's death. Then I will see what it has to offer us in the current critical climate.

In one sense, one might say that 'late Turner' was anticipated by the critics of Turner's early works. For the accusation that the indistinctness in his work was comparable to that which one would expect to find in one enfeebled by old age can be found as early as the time when he exhibited *Crossing the Brook* in 1815, at the age of forty. This was the occasion on which the celebrated connoisseur – and opponent of Turner – Sir George Beaumont told the academician Joseph Farington that the picture 'appeared to him *weak* and like the work of an Old man, one who had [*sic*] no longer saw or felt colour properly'.[2] This was also the period in which Hazlitt issued his celebrated epigram on Turner's art: 'Pictures of nothing – and very like.'

To make sense of such criticism one has, of course, to view Turner's style in terms of the position from which it had started off, and from which his critics were still viewing it. They were taking as their yardstick the standard of representation established by the great landscape masters of the seventeenth century. Beaumont was seeing Turner's idyllic representation of the Devon countryside in *Crossing the Brook* very much in terms of the work of his own Claude.

No picture was closer to Beaumont than the small painting by Claude, *Hagar and the Angel*. The work – which is now in the National Gallery – was then in his collection. He was reputed to have been so fond of it that he took it with him in his coach on his travels. Turner is, of course, explicitly referring to the Claudian tradition in *Crossing the Brook*. He is providing what is in his eyes an updated version – one that represents the modern world (that of Devon, which he had visited two years before) with a modern sensibility – one that gave pride of place to the representation of the effects of light.

The idea of Turner's increasing move away from detailed naturalism as being an enfeeblement of powers became in subsequent decades a well-recognised trope amongst critics. Even when power of conception, or brilliance of particular effect, was recognised, there was still a regret at what appeared to be a failure due to deviation.

At first sight it might seem that Ruskin's celebrated defence of Turner, which first began to reach the public with the publication of the first volume of *Modern Painters* in 1843, marked the beginning of a new perception. He did, it is true, liberate Turner from the need to be judged in terms of the Old Masters. In what was still then a remarkably bold strategy, he set out to demonstrate that Turner's art was actually superior in its representation of nature to that of the Old Masters. Against Beaumont's charge of Turner's 'feebleness' in comparison to Claude, Ruskin argued that the reverse was the case. In such works as *Crossing the Brook*, he said, Turner showed a much clearer understanding of the way forms are modulated by atmospherics. He saw Turner's greatest strength, however, as being those pictures in which the artist had moved away altogether from the model of the Old Masters, offering instead innovations of his own. It was Ruskin's opinion that *Ulysses Deriding Polyphemus* of 1829 (National Gallery, London) was 'the *central Picture* in Turner's career', one in which his full brilliance of colouring was put to work to represent one of the most glorious spectacles in nature. For, while other critics might grudgingly accept such violent effects as those of the sunrise as long as they were described as 'gorgeous visions of the imagination', Ruskin made a point of insisting that they be seen as representations of the observed world.

All this might be seen as a vindication of 'late Turner'. But in fact Ruskin's 'late Turner' is also the Turner of enfeeblement. For what other critics might see as being late was seen by Ruskin as being the artist's *middle* career. For Ruskin true late Turner began around 1839, the year in which he painted the *Fighting Temeraire*.

In fact Ruskin described the *Fighting Temeraire* as 'the last thoroughly perfect picture [Turner] ever painted'.[3] It was the last picture, he later explained, in which Turner's execution is 'as firm and faultless as in middle life'. All later pictures, while sometimes (up to 1843 at least) maintaining a grandeur of vision, nevertheless displayed 'some failure in distinctness of sight, and firmness of hand'.[4] This means in effect that such works as *Snow Storm, Peace, Burial at Sea* and *Rain, Steam and Speed* are all partially products, in Ruskin's eyes, of declining powers. To understand this it is important to remember how central the natural aesthetic was to Ruskin as a basis of his criticism. He might allow full space for the power of imagination to enhance perception. But the goal had still to be the narration of the world of experience.

Ruskin codified his distinctions in the *Notes* that he provided for the first display of the works that Turner bequeathed to the nation which opened at Marlborough House in 1856. Here he named the three phases of Turner's career as 'studentship', 'mastery' and 'decline'. The 'studentship' period lasted up to 1819 and was characterised by his shadowing and eventually (in Ruskin's eyes) surpassing the styles of the Old Masters. The 'mastery' period lasted from then until the painting of the *Fighting Temeraire* twenty years later. That of 'decline' took in the rest of the artist's career. It showed in a gradual decline first in executive powers and then after 1843, the year in which he painted one of Ruskin's favourite last pictures, *The Sun of Venice Going to Sea*, in mental powers as well.

Ruskin's tripartite schema follows, of course, an archetypal cyclical model familiar since antiquity, and closely mirrored by the image of the ages of man. It was one that was widely copied by other commentators in the nineteenth century. The only points of disagreement were in establishing the precise time at which the decline of the 'late' style occurred. For Turner's early biographer, Thornbury, the decline took place relatively early. But then he, as he confessed in his book, had a decided preference for Turner's early style and did not follow Ruskin in his adulation of the 'higher' style of naturalism.

It was not, in fact, until the publication of Walter Armstrong's comprehensive oeuvre catalogue and survey of Turner's art in 1902 that a distinctly different view of late Turner emerged. Armstrong, who kept to the Ruskinian division of styles, unequivocally retained his greatest enthusiasm for the work of Turner's last period. Recognising that such a stance would have been unacceptable twenty years previously, he soon makes it clear that the main reason for his ability to see late Turner in such a positive light is because of his abandonment of a naturalistic aesthetic. He sees the later works as poems of light, providing at best 'equivalents' to the effects of nature.

It is not difficult to see where Armstrong has got his new aesthetic from. For he belonged to the generation of British connoisseurs whose values had been transformed by Impressionist art. Armstrong supported the argument that saw 'late Turner' as being essentially impressionist in nature. Like so many others of the period, he drew a comparison between Turner and Monet.

The comparison was almost an inevitable one, both because of Monet's position at that time as the most important living French painter and impressionist in nature – and because of Monet's interest in English atmospherics. At the time that Armstrong was writing, Monet was still making visits to London to paint his series of Thames views.

Like so many British, Armstrong found in favour of Turner on account of that artist's supposed greater imaginative range. For he saw Monet as being rooted to an 'objective' form of representation, whereas Turner could go beyond this.

It is, I think, worth emphasising, that this perception of Turner the 'impressionist' was being propagated before the 'unfinished' pictures that we now associate with the argument were generally known. Armstrong does not in fact include any of them in his oeuvre catalogue and they were not at this time catalogued or on exhibition.

THE UNFINISHED WORKS

Since there is some confusion about the early history of Turner's unfinished works, it is perhaps worth looking briefly at this issue now, before going on to consider how their emergence affected the subsequent conception of the artist's later style.

As has been frequently remarked, Turner appears at the end of his life not to have wished to have these pictures as part of the permanent record of his work. For in the last codicil of his will in 1849, in which he left his works to the nation, he specified that this should only be his 'finished' works. There is some tantalisingly indistinct evidence that he might have thought of having them as part of the display, but in the end he turned against it. Owing to the difficulties with the will, however, the full contents of the studio were in fact acquired by the nation following a judgement of 1857. But those charged with drawing up an inventory of the full contents maintained a firm distinction between 'finished' and 'unfinished'. Of the oil paintings, they identified 100 'finished' works. These were the pictures that were put on view at Marlborough House in 1856. There were five 'unfinished' works. They were clearly marked as such. Accounts of what was displayed as 'unfinished' vary. But the clearly identifiable ones are ones that were in fact quite close to completion, such as *Fire at Sea*.

The wish expressed in the will that only 'finished' works should be shown was fairly strictly observed. Of the oils, only exhibited works and a handful of highly worked unexhibited and 'unfinished' ones were put on view.[5] The total came to 105. They were exhibited first at Marlborough House and then at a number of other locations during the nineteenth century, ending up largely at the National Gallery itself. While watercolour sketches were included in exhibitions in this period, the only oils to be shown were those from the original selection. The rest of the Turner Bequest remained without classification – beyond the rudimentary description of them that had been given in the schedule of 1858. They stayed in the vaults of the National Gallery, uncatalogued, uncounted and unconsidered.

It was in fact in 1901 – the year before the publication of Armstrong's book – that the first signs of a reconsideration occurred. For in this year four more paintings from the unclassified part of the Bequest were given accession numbers.[6] *River Scene with Cattle, c.* 1809 (Tate Gallery no. 1857); *Christ and the Woman of Samaria, c.* 1830 (Tate Gallery no. 1875); *Sunset, c.* 1830–5 (Tate Gallery no. 1876). The last three of these are in fact mentioned in Armstrong's catalogue.

Yet over the next forty-three years further sections of the unclassified part of the bequest were given accession numbers until by 1944 the whole of it had been accounted for. It is not difficult to tell which works were accessioned in this way, or the sequence in which they were processed. This can be learned from the size of their accession numbers. Briefly any Turner in the Clore Gallery whose accession number is between 458 and 562 is part of the original selection. All the other pictures from the Turner Bequest have numbers running from 1857 onwards. Those with numbers between 1857 and 2707 were accessioned between 1911 and 1932; those with numbers from 5473 to 5546 were accessioned in 1944.

In other words, it is only in the twentieth century that many of the works that we regard as major productions by Turner actually became regarded officially as being pictures. More than this, they did not even become known until this century, for the reason that they were unclassified and unshown. Such striking pictures as *Norham Castle, Sunrise* and *Interior at Petworth* (both Clore Gallery), for example fall into this category. Both were first put on show in 1906.[7]

The process of selecting and accessioning 'unfinished' pictures from the Turner Bequest was most active during the Edwardian period. Between 1901 and 1908, seventy-one such works were accessioned.[8] After that there was a slower process. By 1932 a further thirty-eight had been accessioned. Then there was a gap until the discoveries of Lord Clark completed the collection in 1944.

When viewing these accessions chronologically the impression gained is that there were two principles at work behind the selection. The first was a gradual tendency to accept more and more 'abstract' works as pictures. The Edwardian acquisitions focused largely on works that were clearly 'studies', such as *The Thames near Walton Bridges*[9] and those that had recognisable locations, such as the *Norham Castle, Sunrise* – mentioned above. The aesthetic that guided such choices was clearly 'impressionist' in inspiration – as will be suggested in more detail in a moment.

In the 1920s this taste gradually widened until it was possible, by 1932, to see such glorious atmospheric and topographically impenetrable hazes as *Sun Setting over a Lake* (*c.* 1828; Clore Gallery) as a picture. The other tendency was a greater tolerance toward those areas of Turner's art where he was not considered to have excelled, namely his figure compositions. Such a detailed and finished figure subject as *George IV at St. Giles Edinburgh* (*c.* 1822; Clore Gallery) was not considered worthy of an accession before 1911. Those pictures that had the double disadvantage of being both figurative and indistinct had to wait a lot longer. The ethereal *Scene in a Church or Vaulted Hall* – which is related in 'style and general composition'[10] to the painting of *George IV at St. Giles Edinburgh* was not given an accession number until 1944, the point when, as I have suggested, anything touched by Turner was accessioned without demur.

Behind these two tendencies we might discern the activities of two pressure groups. One is the 'aesthetes', who found in the unfinished Turners evidence of that Modernism that British art seemed to be lacking elsewhere. The other group is the scholars, who wished more simply to keep a record of all the great man's productions.

It was the aesthetes who seem to have been foremost in bringing about a call for a revaluation of the unexhibited Turners. Significantly, evidence of the appreciation of this side of the painter's art came first from works that had mysteriously 'disappeared' from his studio while his bequest was still going through the lengthy process of obtaining probate.

A notable example is the *Landscape with a River and Bay in the Distance*[11] now in the Louvre, which had arrived in Paris in 1890. Praised by Edmond de Goncourt and (it would seem) by Camille Pissarro,[12] such works gained a new significance from the comparison that they suggested with the works of the French Impressionists. In a period when English art was undergoing a crisis, it was highly welcome to unearth works by artists which might suggest there was a national tradition of Impressionism to set against that of the French. This tendency had already reached a high point by 1903, when the distinguished critic Charles Holmes edited a collection of essays entitled *The Genius of J. M. W. Turner.* 'Turner was the first of the Impressionists', wrote one of the authors, 'and after a lapse of eighty years he remains the greatest.'[13] As if to emphasise this point, the one late picture reproduced in colour in this book – *A Seapiece* in the collection of James Orrock[14] – was given the superscript 'Oil-Colour

Impressionism, Late Period, about 1842'. As so often in the discussion of these unexhibited Turners during the Edwardian period, the assumption is that these were direct, *plein-air* paintings. It is significant too, that to make the point about Turner being an Impressionist it was necessary at that time to go to the handful of unfinished works that had seeped out of Turner's studio before its contents were handed over to the nation, for by 1903, as has already been said, no more than a handful of the 'unfinished' oils in the Turner Bequest had ever been on show.

Pressure for a revaluation of the unexhibited works of Turner was added to by the scholar E. T. Cook in his polemical *Hidden Treasures at the National Gallery*, published by the *Strand Magazine* in 1905. Cook – best known as one of the editors of the magisterial library edition of Ruskin's works[15] – published his work to expose the scandal of the 'remarkable accumulation of Turners' which 'had been allowed to lie for 50 years' in the basement of the National Gallery.

It is interesting to see that it was precisely at the time of these publications that the curators of the National Gallery began to look in their vaults again and start recounting their Turners. As has already been mentioned, the newly numbered works tended to be those which could most comfortably be fitted into an Impressionist aesthetic. Some were put on show in the National Gallery itself – the *Thames near Walton Bridges* was one of these. But most were shipped off to the 'National Gallery of British Art' where they were housed in Gallery XVIII, the last of the rooms built by Henry Tate as part of the original foundation.[16]

Undoubtedly the decision to move these Turners to the Tate was part of a familiar policy – active until the separation of the Tate from the National Gallery in 1955 (on St Valentine's Day, as it happens) – of moving pictures of insecure aesthetic status out of the main institution to the lesser one on Millbank. In fairness it must be said, too, that the National Gallery was suffering from hideous overcrowding and could not cope with finding space for the growing brood of Turners it was gradually discovering that it possessed. Whatever the reasons, however, the effect was clearly remarkable. For by having the traditional 'finished' Turners still on show at the National Gallery – where such tried favourites as *The Fighting Temeraire* had long assumed the status of national institutions – and the new 'unfinished' works at the Tate, they were able to emphasise the distinction between the two.

'It is most interesting today to go to and fro between the two greatest Turner collections, that in Trafalgar Square and that near Vauxhall bridge', wrote the art historian Josef Stryzgowski in the *Burlington Magazine* in 1907. 'In the early period the idea of objective representation pre-dominates; later the pronounced desire for a definite subjective effect.'[17]

Stryzgowski brought some unfamiliar central European psychologising to the issue. Indeed, he is almost on the point of making Turner an expressionist when he calls *Interior at Petworth*, a 'private confession of faith', adding 'we moderns break down these barriers and seek the artist by preference in his intuitions'. But his reaction is in other ways typical. Not only does he see the 'unfinished' Turners as being a distinct entity on their own. He also considers them to be quintessentially related to the latter part of Turner's career. The assumption is an interesting one because it has been so unquestioningly followed. Since Turner was productive up to the end of his life, it is hardly surprising that most of the 'unfinished' works found in it would relate to his later years. But it is worth pointing out that many of the 'unfinished' pictures do come from early periods. Some of the most indistinct, indeed, date from the 1790s.[18] We should also remember that the dates currently ascribed to these works are largely arrived at from stylistic analyses based on the assumption of a growing haziness in his manner.

The argument that Turner was an artist who moved into a more and more 'indefinite late career' had been supported first of all by Ruskin. But Ruskin promoted the concept that such late work was still really deeply involved in the representation of nature. Ruskin himself did not countenance the idea that 'unfinished' Turners were a serious part of the oeuvre – something that is clear in his activities in relation to the Turner Bequest.[19] But the idea that 'unfinished' Turner represented his apogee rapidly gained credence in the Edwardian period. Charles Holmes returned to this theme in an article in the *Burlington Magazine* of 1908,[20] where he compared Turner to Rembrandt in this respect and talked of him being one of those really great artists who manifest a 'late' style. But he also notes that Turner is less consistent in this than are other artists who achieve such a style. What bothers him is the fact that, while painting his broader works, Turner still went on exhibiting pictures of relative detail. He is scornful of such work, claiming that *The Fighting Temeraire* was 'limited' by its subject-matter.

The success of the room of 'unfinished' Turners at the Tate led to an important sequel. This was the funding of a suite of Turner rooms by Lord Duveen and the removal of a far greater collection of Turners from the National Gallery to the Tate in 1910. The result of this was the 'finished' and 'unfinished' Turners were now hung together; though for a long time some division was still made between the two categories. The Impressionist reading of Turner still gained credence in most quarters. Often this was to the detriment of the French, as when Clutton-Brock claimed in 1910 that: '*Norham Castle* compared with the most brilliant sun-piece by Monet, is like lyrical poetry compared with prose, that is to say it leaves a stronger image upon my mind because it is a more highly organised means of expression.'[21] The high evaluation of Turner against the Impressionists was partly due to nationalism and partly to ignorance. While Impressionist paintings were turning up more frequently in the salerooms and galleries (not least in Roger Fry's famous Post-Impressionist exhibitions) it was not until 1917, with the Hugh Lane Bequest, that any such works entered the national collection. With this bequest, and with subsequent purchases, talk of Turner as the greatest of the Impressionists declined. It received its *coup de grâce* with the onslaught meted out by Roger Fry in his celebrated attack on British Painting in 1934.[22]

But 'Impressionist' Turner was replaced by other Turners – notably 'abstract' Turner who received an impetus after the full accessioning of the contents of his studio at the end of the Second World War. In the aesthetic underpinning of this concept attention moved from the idea of Turner as the creator of 'equivalences'. This nearly got over the objection raised by defenders of French Impressionism that Turner was not truly analytical in his work. There was even an attempt to suggest that Turner had been striving in his later works to create a public for his 'abstract' works; something most ingeniously argued by Lawrence Gowing.[23] Gowing perhaps contributed more than anyone in the presentation of late Turner as a complex though coherent aesthetic entity. It is perhaps significant that this was most persuasively argued in his essay *Turner: Imagination and Reality* which accompanied an exhibition of Turner's works at the Museum of Modern Art in New York.[24] For this image of Turner as an expressive character emerged at this time and place where abstract expressionism had recently reached its apogee as a contemporary artistic movement.

It is also interesting to note that many of the pictures around which Gowing based his arguments – for example the *Yacht Approaching the Coast* (*c.* 1835; Clore Gallery) – were those that first went on exhibition in the 1920s and 1930s.

ROMANTICISM AND THE AESTHETIC OF THE SKETCH

I would like to conclude with some thoughts about this issue, to see, in fact, if there is any historical – as opposed to critical – construction that can make sense of the concept of 'late' Turner. In approaching such a problem, I am aware that there is a question of precisely what kind of historical perspective I am suggesting. Broadly speaking, one might divide historical modes of interpretation into three kinds: discovery, projection and dialogue. The discovery theory sees history as a bed of facts to be uncovered. It assumes an objective process of exhumation. Projection theory, on the other hand sees the past as essentially the construct of the present, mirroring and reinforcing whatever prejudices exist in our own world. Dialogue theory sees an interaction between the present and the past, in which the present – and by extension the future – is being constantly guided and shaped by what is uncovered from the past. We may, it is true, only hear one side of the dialogue, but it is an interaction, all the same. It is the dialogue theory that I myself prefer, and which I want to use to bring together some of the strands that I have been scattering in this essay.

First, one might say that while the concept of 'late' Turner loses value when it is imposed too rigorously as a historical period, it does gain strength as an indication of pictorial practice that – while it certainly does not have its origin in his later work – indisputably grows in prominence then. This growth has traditionally been shown as a kind of personal pilgrimage, a private maturing. Yet it is underpinned at least by aesthetic practices of the day.

'Late Turner' is, in fact, something that can be understood in terms of the Romantic movement of which he forms a part. In aligning Turner with Romanticism, I do not mean to suggest that he was a card-carrying member of a movement. Rather I want to imply that he is intimately connected with the dominant tendency of his time; that tendency that, for want of a better name, we characterise as Romantic but which does in any case represent a coherent and extensive body of practice.

The particular area of Romantic thought that Turner's art connects with is that of allusiveness. This had, indeed, been a central part of the overt definition of Romanticism, first made by the German critic Friedrich Schlegel when he talked about Romantic poetry as being eternally in the process of becoming, and of never being complete. To some extent in self-conscious opposition to Classicism, Romanticism represented itself as the art of incompleteness made necessary by the ineffable and eternally evolving processes of the universe. There are many examples of incompleteness within the Romantic canon – for example, Coleridge's 'Kubla Khan'. It is striking, too, that the distinction between intentional and unintentional completeness is being constantly blurred by such writers.

In the visual arts, images of incompleteness abound. An early example is the drawing by Fuseli, which shows the artist in Rome in 1778 overcome by the thought of the Colossus that he must reconstruct in his mind.[25] Such visual manifestations found their counterpart in the aesthetic theory of the time. There was the famous launching of what has become known as 'association aesthetics' by Archibald Alison in his *Essay on Taste* of 1790. This publication coincided with that of the *Critique of Judgement* by Immanuel Kant in Germany. Although the two studies are very different in approach and interests, they share the emphasis on the beholder's share in aesthetic apprehension, and the essentially symbolic and associative nature of aesthetic appreciation. In both countries, too, these books stimulated a mode of aesthetic appreciation in which allusion and association are emphasised. It was for this reason that the critic A. W. Schlegel argued that painting was the quintessential Romantic visual art. For it was the one that was most dependent on illusion for its effect – something that was to be contrasted with sculpture, which was nearer to the classical idea of embodiment. In a bold stroke, Schlegel even thought about the redefinition of Outline. He did this when reviewing the most famous outlines of the period – the illustrations by the English sculptor John Flaxman to Homer and Dante that first appeared in Rome in 1793.[26]

Previously Outline had been seen as being particularly prized in classical art as representing the embodiment of the essential form. Schlegel, by contrast, read it as a technique for allusion which 'incited the imagination to expand' and complete the form. This is a reading that Flaxman himself did not accept – and indeed it may be inappropriate for his particular style of Outline drawing. But it certainly made an impact on other artists and encouraged the development of the allusive line. Might it not be too fanciful to see some such concept at work in Turner's use of line? Such linear elaborations of this subject have been dismissed as 'scrawls'. But I see them as a means of getting allusive subject-matter into the late works. This is the way in which ideas get associated with the magnificent displays of colour. And, indeed, in the skilful dislocation between the line and the colour areas one sees precisely those spaces in which the imagination can expand.

But more important than the precise indication of the use of line is Schlegel's assumption of the significance of the beholder's share in the reading of a picture, and of the virtue of incompleteness in pictorial representation. Here we see a more general Romantic principle which might be called 'the aesthetic of the sketch'.

The aesthetic of the sketch is something that is shared in both German and English versions of associative aesthetics. It can be found in the highly important *Analytical Enquiry* of Richard Payne Knight where he states that 'superior taste', as he terms it, will 'prefer the sketch' to the finished work on the grounds that it will have 'Something of character and expression, which may awaken sympathy, excite new ideas, or expand those already formed.'[27] Payne Knight was an important figure in Turner's development particularly around the time when he produced the *Analytical Enquiry* and when he encouraged Turner to take an interest in Rembrandt. Later, as we know, Turner's interest in Rembrandt focused particularly on the allusiveness of his 'mystic veil of colour'.

It is typical of the situation in England, that Payne Knight should refer to the taste for the sketch as being the domain of 'superior taste'. For in this country – unlike contemporary Germany – the management of culture was the domain of the upper classes. Payne Knight is typical of his class in annexing a Romantic principle, and seeing it as being the prerogative of people with a certain class and education. This is, I think, important too in assessing Turner's response to associative Romantic Aesthetics. For as he grew wealthier and more secure, he himself began to behave more like the leisured classes – as in fact did other 'nouveaux riches'. Turner's later patrons belong very much to the aristocratic class (like Munro or Novar) or those elements of the bourgeoisie (like Ruskin's father) who aped them. Perhaps particularly important is the fact that he could himself exercise his 'superior taste' by having patrons – as

John Gage has recently pointed out – who were themselves amateur artists and could share his growing sophistication of representation. The growing gap between such 'informed' approval of his work and the baying of the 'vulgar' critics in the exhibition reviews is an important feature. The existence of this sympathetic circle is, I think, important for understanding the development of Turner's allusive approach in his later pictures.

In this last section I have attempted to offer a contemporary practice that would at least present a context for Turner's allusive manner. Within the context of Romantic representation – I would like to argue – there is space for both 'finished' and 'unfinished' works. Indeed, there is a positive aesthetic for the 'unfinished' works. I have also sought to suggest that the particular appropriation of Romantic aesthetics by a leisured class in Britain helps to explain the privacy of the most allusive part of Turner's late career – the so-called 'unfinished' works. For they exist within that private sphere of the 'superior' observer of which Turner increasingly became part in later life. It is striking in this context that he seemed at one time to have been toying with the idea of including these 'unfinished' works in his public oeuvre and then turned against it. For the aesthetic in which he operated had no public forum. It was in France that such innovative structures were given a public context, by a very different socio-political system. This system in the end produced the means whereby it was possible to recover the 'unfinished' Turner – but only at a price. The price was the reading of them in an alien aesthetic that was more interested in the primacy of paint than in the process of association. But association is at the heart of all Turner's work whether 'finished' or 'unfinished'. Only by seeing this can we gain a context in which the late – or perhaps one should say the 'private' – Turner can be profitably seen.

CHAPTER 4

'Conquered good and conquering ill': femininity, power and Romanticism in Emily Brontë's poetry

Emma Francis

In one of those moods that everyone falls into sometimes, when the world of the imagination suffers a winter that blights its vegetation; when the light of life seems to go out and existence becomes a barren desert where we wander, exposed to all the tempests that blow under heaven, without hope of rest or shelter – in one of these black humors, I was walking one evening at the edge of a forest. It was summer; the sun was still shining high in the west and the air resounded with the songs of birds. All appeared happy, but for me, it was only an appearance. I sat at the foot of an old oak, among whose branches the nightingale had just begun its vespers. 'Poor fool,' I said to myself, 'is it to guide the bullet to your breast or the child to your brood that you sing so loud and clear? Silence that untimely tune, perch yourself on your nest; tomorrow, perhaps, it will be empty.' But why address myself to you alone? All creation is equally mad. Behold those flies playing above the brook; the swallows and fish diminish their number every minute. These will become, in their turn, the prey of some tyrant of the air or water; and man for his amusement or his needs will kill their murderers. Nature is an inexplicable problem; it exists on a principle of destruction. Every being must be the tireless instrument of death to others, or itself must cease to live, yet nonetheless we celebrate the day of our birth, and we praise God for having entered such a world.

During my soliloquy I picked a flower at my side; it was fair and freshly opened, but an ugly caterpillar had hidden itself among the petals and already they were shriveling and fading. 'Sad image of the earth and its inhabitants!' I exclaimed. 'This worm lives only to injure the plant that protects it. Why was it created, and why was man created? He torments, he kills, he devours; he suffers, dies, is devoured – there you have his whole story. It is true that there is a heaven for the saint, but the saint leaves enough misery here below to sadden him even before the throne of God.'

I threw the flower to the earth. At that moment the universe appeared to me a vast machine constructed only to produce evil. I almost doubted the goodness of God, in not annihilating man on the day he first sinned. 'The world should have been destroyed,' I said, 'crushed as I crush this reptile, which has done nothing in its life but render all that it touches as disgusting as itself.' I had scarcely removed my foot from the poor insect when, like a censoring angel sent from heaven, there came fluttering through the trees a butterfly with large wings of lustrous gold and purple. It shone but a moment before my eyes; then, rising among the leaves, it vanished into the height of the azure vault. I was mute, but an inner voice said to me, 'Let not the creature judge his Creator; here is a symbol of the world to come. As the ugly caterpillar is the origin of the splendid butterfly, so this globe is the embryo of a new heaven and a new earth whose poorest beauty will infinitely exceed your mortal imagination. And when you see the magnificent result of that which seems so base to you now, how you will scorn your blind presumption, in accusing Omniscience for not having made nature perish in her infancy.

God is the god of justice and mercy; then surely, every grief that he inflicts on his creatures, be they human or animal, rational or irrational, every suffering of our unhappy nature is only a seed of that divine harvest which will be gathered when, Sin having spent its last drop of venom, Death having launched its final shaft, both will perish on the pyre of a universe in flames and leave their ancient victims to an eternal empire of happiness and glory.[1]

'The Butterfly' is a translation of a French language exercise written by Emily Brontë whilst she was studying in Brussels in 1842. It is structured around a series of contrasts and contradictions between different ontologies, different epistemologies and the different languages which speak about them. The essay travels through (at least) two sets of oppositional accounts. It begins with the extraordinary vision of life, nature and creation enlisted to the performance of a theatre of death, insanity and destruction: 'All creation is equally mad … it exists on a principle of destruction.' The agony of this realisation is sharpened by the refusal to retreat into atheism. The narrator is confident of the existence of God and elaborates the vision in the light of this knowledge, creating an irony which becomes increasingly bitter as the description proceeds. The nightingale's song, articulated as the Christian ceremonial of vespers, is perverted from a recommendation of the supplicant to God's protection into an advertisement for predators of the location of easy prey. In the face of this logic of destruction the rituals of praise for the creation of the earth enjoined by orthodoxy become gross. Even the promise of Heaven cannot provide comfort, but is instead cause for further dread, because the misery of earth is so huge it is bound to find continuance and will haunt even the saint contemplating the full presence of God. It is an account of a theistic order from which the concepts of redemption and salvation are absent. However, the essay ends with a completely contrasting account of life as essentially good and overseen by a wholly benevolent creator who can make intelligible the apparent insanity of nature and who will eventually abolish the logic of destruction which presently seems to govern it. Redemption is the organising dynamic of this universe. The earth in the first account is a microcosm of and metaphor for the fully developed mechanism of the universe 'constructed only to produce evil', an order which is governed wholly by repetition and is unamenable to transformation. In the second, nature is read according to the metonymic conventions of Christian typology. It speaks a prophecy of transformation, of something more splendid than itself. It is a symbol of 'a new heaven and a new earth', unimaginably beautiful, which has yet to come into being.

The text makes another journey. It begins with a narrator whose interpretation relies completely upon individual perception. In the early parts of the essay the narrator's convictions result in an outrageous, blasphemous analysis, presented as self-consciously transgressive and idiosyncratic, with full knowledge of its place outside of conventional teleology and its implication in a poetics of evil. But by the end, the narrator has relinquished the self and rearticulated a commitment to a collective, archaic belief system and vocabulary which is recognisable as Christian orthodoxy. The 'I's which litter the first two thirds of the text vanish completely in the final section which elaborates the optimistic account of the cosmos, indicating the way in which the narrator has relinquished individual perception in favour of participation in collectively generated knowledge. This shift involves an alteration in the narrator's relationship with language. The contemplation of the caterpillar provokes a commentary upon the violence of the world located within the narrator's direct speech: ' "Sad image of the earth and its inhabitants!" I exclaimed.' By contrast, the vision of the butterfly prompts the appearance of a voice located beyond, or at an unconscious level of the self, which supersedes the narrator's own voice: 'I was mute, but an inner voice said to me, "Let not the creature judge his Creator..." '. In the final section of the essay, the narrator abandons his or her own voice entirely and becomes amanuensis for the prophecy of the 'divine harvest'.

The essay does nothing at all to synthesise these oppositions but it is also constructed in a way which makes it impossible for us to prioritise or legislate between the two accounts. We cannot be satisfied with the first because it follows the metaphor around which the text is constructed only half way. The deeply conventional nature of the image – the most usual function caterpillars have within literature and myth is to turn into butterflies – means that even if we stop reading at the end of the first paragraph we cannot but intuit a good deal of the content of the second. But if Brontë's metaphorical structure sends us out of the first account into the second then, equally, her dislocation of the text away from individual philosophical speculation into a quite different register of anonymous theistic orthodoxy propels us away from the second account and back to the first. The heretical imagination to which Brontë has appealed in the first half of the essay cannot possibly be contented with the conventional Christian orthodoxy of the final section. We search for the subjectivity with which we formed a relationship in the early parts of the essay, which outlined such astonishing ideas about the world. The erasure of this voice makes us suspicious of the comforts of the theology outlined in the final section. Equally, however, as we return to the first account we bring with us a suspicion about the status of the subjectivity which produced it, which admits its commentary quite openly to be the effusions of melancholia. The dis-ease and derangement of this subjectivity is thrown into relief by the celebration and satisfaction of the voice speaking at the end of the essay.

The incomplete or idiosyncratic punctuation of the essay increases the indeterminacy. There is no terminal speech mark to indicate the ending of the utterance of the 'inner voice' and the reader is left to guess where and whether it ceases to speak and where and whether the voice of the original narrator re-enters the text (Sue Lonoff, the translator of the version I am using, is faithful to Brontë's original manuscript in her refusal to supply the 'missing' punctuation here). The content of the final paragraph of the essay, which is consistent with the philosophy of the previous sentences, praising God and justifying His power, suggests that it is a continuation of the utterance of the 'inner voice'. However, this reading means that another speech mark is missing – the additional opening speech mark at the start of the final paragraph. The other possibility, requiring only one missing speech mark, at the end of the penultimate paragraph, means that the voice speaking at the end of the essay is that of the first narrator. Again, it is difficult to be fully convinced that he or she has, in such a short space of time, conformed so completely to an account utterly divergent from her or his initial views. Lonoff does depart from Brontë's manuscript in an attempt to provide a measure of closure for the essay by supplying a full stop at its end. Brontë's original uses a dash: '—', making stronger the implication that this is not the end of the story, that the voice speaking at the end of the essay (whichever voice it is) has more to say and might just as easily revert to the pessimism of the opening as continue the hymn of praise in progress when the essay breaks off.

This essay poses the stake of Brontë's poetry. Her poetics are elaborated around a series of anomalies and contradictions. Between texts and, in many cases, within individual poems themselves Brontë opens a space into which she unleashes a profound warfare which rages between different accounts of power, gender and language and between different ways of conceptualising the relations between them. Just as in 'The Butterfly' we are denied any position of rest or interpretative security, but instead are continually propelled back into the cyclical structure of the essay, so the poetry holds off political closure even in the places where it seems to achieve narrative closure or imagistic completion. The strain which Brontë's investigations impose upon her poetic language becomes so acute that the text fragments, multiplies and throws up the mirror image of itself as a separate poem. Isobel Armstrong has identified 'doubleness' as a characteristic mode of Victorian poetry, and particularly of nine-teenth-century women's poetry.[2] Brontë pushes the structure of the 'double poem' up to and beyond its limits as she releases into it the conflicting energies of early nineteenth-century accounts of the political articulations of gender.

My essay, which explores the nature of the conflicting energies which structure and strain Brontë's poetry, has a two-fold and very simple purpose. First, I wish to re-open the question of the woman writer's and particularly the woman poet's relationship with Roman-ticism. Strangely, given that the majority of her surviving poetry was written in the late 1830s and 1840s, Brontë has been read almost solely in terms of a supposed relation to Romanticism. Many, perhaps the majority of readings of Brontë's poetry to be produced between the publication of Hatfield's edition of the complete poems in 1941 and the early 1980s when feminist criticism intervened, concentrated on the traces of Blake, Wordsworth, Coleridge, Shelley, Keats and Byron which critics claim can be discerned in Brontë's poetry.[3] It is an argument or assumption of this strand of criticism that Brontë shares aspects of the aesthetic and political radicalism of Romanticism, that her poetry is primarily committed to an exploration of the transgressive energies of the Romantic sublime. I shall focus in detail on the reading of Brontë made by Georges Bataille in his study of 1957 *Literature and Evil* which makes precisely this move.[4] This account argues or assumes that Brontë's work bypasses both the agendas governing other women's poetry written in the mid-nineteenth century and that, therefore, the most meaningful comparisons of her work are to be made with male-authored texts of the Romantic period. In its higher flights of fancy, critics concerned to trace Brontë's implication within mainstream Romanticism go so far as to argue or assume that she actually transcends femininity itself.[5]

By contrast, it has been precisely Brontë's femininity which the exponents of the second major strand of criticism I want to point to have seen as the central determining factor of her poetry. Brontë survived as a poet by masquerading as a man throughout the majority of the twentieth century, only to emerge as a woman again with the advent of Anglo-American feminist criticism, which rediscovered the femininity the earlier accounts effaced in order to read it as a problem. This second account of Brontë's relationship with Romanticism has been developed from the early 1980s in the work of American feminist critics, chiefly Margaret Homans in her seminal *Women Writers and Poetic Identity* and more recently by Irene Taylor in *Holy Ghosts: The Male Muses of Charlotte and Emily Brontë*.[6] In different ways, these critics pursue the argument that the single most important determinant of Brontë's poetics is her awareness of and confinement to her femininity. Romanticism in these feminist accounts, far from being transgressive and emancipatory, a discourse which sweeps away social and sexual restriction, is a prison-house for women writers, a recalcitrant aesthetic, structured, in the words of another feminist critic of women's poetry of the early nineteenth century, Marlon B. Ross, by the 'contours of masculine desire'.[7] In this account, creativity, and particularly poetic identity, is identified with masculinity to such an extent that the woman poet finds it virtually impossible to find a foothold within it.

So Brontë's poetry has been read as both a radical refusal of femininity in favour of the transgressive energies of Romanticism and as a drama of the agony of the woman's subjection, because of her femininity, to the sexual violence of Romanticism. The strength of Brontë's refusal to legislate within and stabilise her poetics – and her relation to and repudiation of Romanticism – is in exact proportion to the refusal of many readers of her poetry to comprehend her commitment to anomaly and anarchy and the virulence of their attempt to locate her poetics on one side or the other of a range of binary oppositions. Each strand fastens, I would argue, onto one of the conflicting energies we saw Brontë exploring in 'The Butterfly'. The other is either ignored, or is understood as a manifestation of the incompleteness of Brontë's poetic gift, her inability to sustain the energy of her vision throughout the corpus.[8] These two tendencies produce accounts of Brontë's poetics, their gendering and their politics, which are almost mirror images of each other. The clash and contradiction between the two positions throws into relief the questions about the conceptualisations of power, language and gender which Brontë's poetry raises, which I will pursue through the remainder of this essay.

The second aspect of my project in this essay, intimately linked with the first, is to pose the question of the extent to which Brontë's conflictual and overdetermined relationship with Romanticism – and with the Romanticisms envisaged by the strands of twentieth-century criticism – can and should be elucidated by aspects of the conceptual framework provided by Postmodernism. I want to ask whether what I will seek to demonstrate is a profound refusal and interrogation of essential and stable accounts of the relationship between gender and power in Brontë's poetry necessitates the designation of her poetics as a postmodern Romanticism. Several of the essays in this collection pursue in different ways the thesis that Romanticism has within itself a critique of grand narrative, essence and monolithic accounts of power, that aspects of Postmodernism are already implicit within the projects of Romanticism. However, it is notable that a good deal of the work which has sought dialogue with or inclusion into the category 'Romantic' for women's writing has not replicated this move. In the feminist criticism I discuss below, Romanticism is reinscribed as a repressive grand narrative disciplined by a vigorous sexual division. At stake in my reading of Brontë's poetry and the way in which it has been read by feminist and non-feminist critics in the twentieth century is the issue of women writers' relationship with the politics of Romantic canonicity. To what extent can women writers have a postmodern Romanticism? Will the rediscovery of women's role within literary culture within and around the Romantic period destabilise and complicate our understanding of the relationship between gender and power within Romanticism, or is it dependent upon the stabilisation and memorialisation of an oppressive equation between them?

'CONQUERING ILL': MAINSTREAM ROMANTICIST READINGS

Perhaps the most famous statement of the ascription of Brontë to Romanticism and the one which lays bare most completely the theoretical presuppositions which underlie it is Georges Bataille's account of Brontë's novel and poetry in *Literature and Evil*. Bataille's essay on Brontë opens his study which 'attempts to extract the essence of literature'.[9] Bataille's literary theory elaborates the dialectic formed out of the encounter of Romanticism with Modernism, as two movements which in his view articulate moments of profound break with and repudiation of previous literary and moral configurations. For Bataille, literature is 'an acute form of Evil ... [it] is not innocent' and yet 'literature is a return to childhood'; the Evil expressed by literature 'has a sovereign value for us ... does not exclude morality: on the contrary, it demands a "hypermorality"'.[10] It is easy to see how Brontë's negotiation with Romanticism, in particular the way in which in *Wuthering Heights* and in some of her poems she pushes the Romantic account of the child up to its limits and over them into a ghoulish travesty, speaks to Bataille's project. He argues that *Wuthering Heights* is primarily an exploration of the asocial and amoral aspects of childhood and the way in which its transgressive energies continue to haunt the adult lives of Heathcliff and the first Catherine.

The investment which Bataille makes in Brontë is enormous. His essay is a *tour de force*, packed full of many of the arguments and aphorisms for which he is most famous. Through his exploration of Brontë's heterodoxy and blasphemy, her refusal of conventional accounts of sexuality and subjectivity, he pursues his thesis, drawn from Freud's account of the role of the death drive in psychic life, of the intimate connection of sexuality and death, that 'eroticism is the approval of life up until death'.[11] He finds in the incongruity of Brontë's morally exemplary life with the acute comprehension of evil her work contains a perfect illustration of the dynamics of 'hypermorality', that evil 'is not only the dream of the wicked: it is to some extent the dream of the Good'.[12]

Central to Bataille's account of Brontë, and to his wider thesis about evil, is his understanding of the mysticism which he finds in her poetry. Mysticism, he argues, is cognate with the content of literature because both break the law, both are 'asocial aspect[s] of religion'.[13] He quotes a stanza from the poem he calls 'The Prisoner' (torn out of its context within the poem and without any indication of the content of the text as a whole) as an illustration of the 'indescribable anguish' and unassimilable savagery her mysticism could comprehend at its climax.

> 'Yet I would lose no sting, would wish no torture less;
> The more that anguish racks, the earlier it will bless;
> And robed in fires of hell, or bright with heavenly shine,
> If it but herald death, the vision is divine!'[14]

The triumph of Brontë's vision is achieved, for Bataille, solely by virtue of it antecedents in Romanticism. He calls *Wuthering Heights* the 'late masterpiece'[15] of Romanticism and reminds us of her debt to 'Byron, whom she certainly read'.[16]

Bataille legitimates the enormous stake he is placing in Brontë by arguing that Brontë's own stake in a poetics of evil was even more profound. He claims (choosing not to dwell upon evidence that Brontë, in common with a large number of the other inhabitants of the earlier nineteenth-century Haworth, was consumptive) that she 'died for having experienced the states of mind she described',[17] just as Heathcliff's fury (and not a poorly supervised pregnancy and childbirth) 'is the remorseless and passionate cause of Catherine's disease and death'.[18] Bataille's own essay replicates the Romantic excess which he celebrates in Brontë's work. The company which Brontë keeps in Bataille's study – with Baudelaire, Michelet, Blake, Sade, Proust, Kafka and Genet – indicates the provenance of his interest in her. And yet Brontë stands as example to all his other subjects, reaching heights of evil and transgression to which none of them attain.

Bataille, in fact, follows Brontë's poetics as far as the first section of 'The Butterfly'. He celebrates her violation of social, sexual and religious orthodoxies, her construction of a vision of evil rare in its clarity and unique in its intensity. He has no interest in anything in Brontë's work which would contradict this account, such as the political narrative framing the account of mystical experience in the poem he calls 'The Prisoner', which challenges the valorisation of transgression which Bataille extracts from the poem, or the recuperative close of *Wuthering Heights* where the novel tries to argue that the violent energies of Heathcliff and the first Cathy's relationship are laid to rest by the love of Hareton and the second Cathy.[19]

Bataille's essay has inspired other readings which explore Brontë's link with the Romantic sublime further and replicate the emphases of Bataille's account, notably J. Hillis Miller's discussion of Brontë in *The Disappearance of God* (1963), in which Miller quotes the same stanza from 'The Prisoner' as Bataille, to make a similar point about the centrality of the death drive to Brontë's vision: 'Anything which leads to death is divine, for death is an absolute transformation of our earthly state.'[20]

One of the most striking aspects of this critical approach is the fact that it occurs to neither Bataille nor its other exponents to take any account of Brontë's femininity. For both, she functions symbolically as a man, bypassing the concerns and prescriptions of nineteenth-century femininity in producing a vision of power, violence and transgression to rival the sublimest moments of Romanticism. For Bataille, Brontë's femininity has absolutely no purchase on or relevance to her poetics.

'CONQUERED GOOD': FEMINIST READINGS

Margaret Homans's analysis of Brontë is an application of her general thesis about women's problematic relationship with the Romantic account of poetic identity which has been enormously influential, and even hegemonic, for feminist criticism since its first publication in 1980. She argues that Brontë, like all other nineteenth-century women, writes in the shadow of the demarcation which Homans sees as central to Romanticism, between nature identified as feminine and the writing self which takes nature as its subject, identified as masculine. Caught in this way between a rock and a hard place, Brontë has to take extraordinary measures to break her identification with silent, objectified nature, to which Romanticism would relegate her, and reach a position from which she can write. At the sharp end of the conflict, she constructs a foothold in poetic identity by means of 'borrowing an identity'. Homans sees the beginnings of this borrowing in Brontë's imaginative identification with the characters of the Angria and Gondal sagas during her childhood, but argues that in the poetry written in her adulthood 'this pattern of supplanting identity ... begins to produce sinister effects'.[21] Brontë has to generate a relation to and stake in masculinity in order to legitimate her poetic identity, but, paradoxically, this borrowing of masculinity constitutes the most serious threat to that identity.

> Brontë is troubled by the apparent otherness of the mind's powers which she imagines as a series of masculine visitants who bring visionary experience to her ... The visionary visitant of later poems takes many forms, but he is always masculine, and he is threatening as well as inspiring, dangerous as well as beloved ... because, being external, he can withdraw her poetic powers at will.[22]

Rather than being, as it is for Bataille, the source of her power, Brontë's commitment to visionary experience is for Homans the source of her vulnerability. She argues that Brontë's poetry is fractured by the strain of the attempt to negotiate the anomaly of being a woman, trying to establish a secure writing subjectivity in the shadow of Romantic tradition and avoid the objectification and disempowerment inherent in her identification with nature which Romanticism would dictate.

Irene Taylor develops Homans's thesis with the observation that Brontë wedded her poetry to Romanticism because it provided a way for her to memorialise and explore the trauma of the bereavement she suffered when her mother died in her early childhood. Taylor argues that feminised nature has a significance for Brontë over and above that which it would have for any other woman writing poetry in the shadow of Romanticism. She claims that Brontë came to identify nature with the realm of plenitude and pleasure her lost relationship with her mother represented. This psychobiographical twist makes Brontë's grasp on poetic identity seem even more fraught and problematic than it is even in Homans's account. For Taylor, Brontë has an impossible investment in her own poetry, it represented for her a way of preserving her relationship with her lost mother but necessitated that Brontë create and commit herself to a male muse in order to sustain her writing, because of the emphasis within Romanticism upon the masculinity of creative genius. Brontë's poetry for Taylor, then, is as much a repudiation of the feminine – the mother – as a memorialisation of her, writing poetry a deeply ambivalent activity oscillating between introjection and abjection of both femininity and masculinity, which each both compel and prohibit poetic production.

Taylor maps the Romantic notions of language and creativity

through a psychoanalytic account of the way in which subjectivity and the entry into language are produced by the forced separation from the mother. She argues that Brontë's poetry enacts a struggle between the 'mother world' of silence, plenitude and privacy and the 'father world' of 'bustling business, goal-oriented rivalry, ambition and achievement'.[23] Taylor finds the reason for Brontë's cessation from writing poetry in 1846, and what she sees as her willing embrace of her own death, in the choice Brontë made to allow the claims of the mother world to triumph over those of the father world, her abandonment of the attempt to negotiate the impossible relationship with the contradictions of female poetic identity.

Both Homans and Taylor present an account of Brontë's poetics as occupying a position something like that of the speaker of the second half of 'The Butterfly'. Homans argues that Brontë is not in full control of her own poetic language. Like the speaker of the second half of the essay, whose voice is colonised by the prophecy of cosmic transformation, she is struggling against being spoken by the conventions of masculine Romanticism, which would seek to wrest her from writing subjectivity and into an identification with objectified and silent nature. Taylor sees Brontë's poetry as an elaborate process of dialogue with and resistance to the kind of violence and destruction of the first vision, which she represents as the 'father world' of ambition and aggression, and the attempt to recuperate a lost realm of plenitude and bliss, of reintegration with a benevolent other, the 'mother world', analogous to the second.

The absolutely symmetrical opposition of these two accounts – between the mainstream Romanticists on the one hand and the feminists on the other – is striking. In the first account, Brontë is powerful and transgressive because structurally, aesthetically and ideologically she is *not* a woman; she is liberated by her refusal or evasion of femininity. In the second, she is powerless and entrapped because biologically, aesthetically and ideologically she *is* a woman; her poetic identity is disrupted by her accession to her femininity. I believe that each of these arguments identifies a crucial aspect of Brontë's poetics, but that neither constitutes a fully adequate description of them. Moreover, rather than it being possible to identify Brontë completely with either of these positions, it should be recognised that her poetry holds each of them up for scrutiny. Brontë's poetry offers the kind of contradictory structure we saw in

'The Butterfly', by positioning alongside each other completely incompatible accounts of power, gender and language. The opposition and contradiction between the two accounts I have just described is anticipated and analysed by Brontë herself. Brontë is a fierce analyst and critic of her own Romanticism, generating strategies of friction and exploration of it, two of which I now wish to examine in detail.

ROMANTIC OR VICTORIAN POET?: 'FAITH AND DESPONDENCY'

One of the most significant reasons for the lack of comprehension of the state of warfare which governs Brontë's poetry, is the emphasis which has been placed on positioning Brontë as a Romantic. Oppositional as the two accounts I have just outlined are, they share the conviction that it makes sense to discuss Brontë's poetry in terms of its relationship with Romanticism. It is certainly the case that in many places Brontë explores some of the central thematics of Romanticism and that she is, in particular, concerned with the way in which gender is articulated by the Romantic matrix (I go on to discuss this issue in my next section), but this by no means exhausts the scope of her poetics. It has been suggested much less frequently that Brontë's poetry also shares many of what have come to be understood as the central features of Victorian poetry.[24] Many of the poems explore diseased subjectivities, whose philosophies and analyses are certainly not to be trusted, from the inside, in a manner analogous to Browning or Tennyson. Moreover, the process of reflection and interior dialogue itself is sometimes regarded by Brontë's texts with the suspicion first voiced by the contemporary reviewers of early Victorian poetry and given its most famous expression in Matthew Arnold's diatribe against the 'dialogue of the mind with itself'.[25]

For example, the poem which Brontë published under the title of 'Faith and Despondency' exemplifies the move made by many of her poems, which seem to articulate themselves into classic Romantic paradigms but then destabilise them and veer away into problematics which are much more recognisable as early Victorian.[26] As an encounter between an adult and a child, in which the adult is educated and enlightened by the child, the poem invokes the Romantic, Wordsworthian account of the child, as the repository of cultural innocence, moral value and inspiration. As a conversation about alternative conceptions of death, it owes a good deal to Wordsworth's Lyrical Ballad 'We Are Seven'.[27] It is worth comparing Brontë's poem with its precursor text, as this reveals Brontë's characteristic perversion of the Romantic project.

The spatial situation in which the conversation in Wordsworth's poem takes place is not specified, but in the course of her narrative, the little maid imaginatively occupies the external space of the graveyard ' "Twelve steps or more from [her] mother's door" ' (line 39). Both her own account and that of the poem's speaker emphasise her free movement outside, and are consonant with Romanticism's account of the child's healthful unity with nature. She remembers her play beside the graves of her sister and brother and the speaker's attempt to convince her of the difference between her condition and that of her dead siblings is staked upon the contrast between her movement and their stasis: ' "You run about, my little maid, / Your limbs they are alive; / If two are in the church-yard laid, / Then ye are only five" ' (lines 33–6). By contrast, 'Faith and Despondency' opens with the father compelling his child's stasis, within an enclosed domestic interior, which locates the poem within the preoccupation of Victorian domestic ideology with situating and stabilising the family within domestic space. Her father urges Iernë to relinquish her play, to sit beside him where ' "Not one faint breath can enter... / Enough to wave my daughter's hair" ' (lines 8–9).

The two poems differ significantly in their ascriptions of innocence and knowledge and the inspirational and instructive value of each. The child in the classic Romantic account represented in Wordsworth's poem is able to provide an enlightened vision because of her innocence, her lack of knowledge of the conventions of culture, including the significance accorded to death: 'A simple child, dear brother Jim, / That lightly draws its breath, / And feels its life in every limb, / What should it know of death?' (lines 1–4). The adult tries unsuccessfully to educate her in the comprehension of death. The implicit project of the poem, to offer an alternative, optimistic account of death which will ease the pain of bereavement, is predicated on a simple division between the innocence of the child and the knowledge of the adult. In Brontë's poem this division is rejected. Iernë not only has full knowledge of death and can conceive of the absence of the dead from their physical bodies in the grave, but has achieved conscious control of her emotional response to bereavement by means of an optimistic theology.

'Oh! not for them, should we despair,
The grave is drear, but they are not there;
    Their dust is mingled with the sod,
    Their happy souls are gone to God!

'But, I'll not fear, I will not weep
For those whose bodies rest in sleep, –
    I know there is a blessed shore,
        Opening its ports for me, and mine;
    And, gazing Time's wide waters o'er,
        I weary for that land divine,
    Where we were born, where you and I
    Shall meet our Dearest, when we die;
    From suffering and corruption free,
    Restored into the Deity.'   (lines 38–41 and 53–62)

The educative process at work here is very different from that of 'We Are Seven'. It is Iernë's knowledge rather than innocence which enables her to cope with death and to urge her father to a similar outlook. Moreover, behind this encounter is another scene of instruction. Iernë does not speak a natural philosophy, which Wordsworth's Romanticism sees as the special gift of the child, but is returning to her father the knowledge and philosophy he has previously imparted to her.

'You told me this, and yet you sigh,
And murmur that your friends must die.
Ah! my dear father, tell me why?
For, if your former words were true,
How useless would such sorrow be;'   (lines 42–6)

The opposite of knowledge is represented not by the innocence of a child, but by the father's forgetting or repression and is the result not of mental and emotional purity but of mental and emotional corruption, caused by trauma.

Just as Iernë has a more complex educational history than the little maid of Wordsworth's poem so she also has a more complex emotional history. Wordsworth's chid has no knowledge of grief, her emotions have no temporality, she has not entered in to any kind of emotional process which would allow her to make a distinction between her experience before and after her bereavements. But Iernë has a history of depression and despair, caused by her father's desertion of her in the past, which she has had to work through in order to achieve her present enlightenment.

'Father, in early infancy,
When you were far beyond the sea,
Such thoughts were tyrants over me!
I often sat, for hours together,
Through the long nights of angry weather,
Raised on my pillow, to descry
The dim moon struggling in the sky;
Or, with strained ear, to catch the shock,
Of rock with wave, and wave with rock;
So I would fearful vigil keep,
And, all for listening, never sleep.'   (lines 25–35)

The condition of insomniac melancholia in which Iernë spent her early childhood is in stark contrast with the felicity which the child of Wordsworth's poem has enjoyed. Iernë's inspiration of her father cloaks her recrimination with him, for his desertion of her and for reneging on the philosophy he educated her within.

Perhaps the most striking difference between the texts lies in their accounts not of death but of life. 'We Are Seven' works to affirm and celebrate life, the little maid repudiates the knowledge of death because of the integrity, purity and joy of her experience of life before her bereavements, which she wishes to preserve. The adult's capacity to comprehend death in this poem is a mark of his relative corruption. But in 'Faith and Despondency' Iernë is optimistic about death because it promises release from the pains of life: ' "this world's life has much to dread, / Not so, my Father, with the dead" ' (lines 36–7). It is death, not childhood innocence which is ' "From suffering and corruption free" ' (line 61). Brontë's poem is almost a parody of Wordsworth's, giving a sinister gloss to the Romantic accounts of 'We Are Seven'. In its fixation upon the intimacy of parent and child inside domestic space it is exploring one of the conventions of Victorian poetry, and this text, like several of Brontë's other poems about private interiors – and like early Victorian poems such as Browning's 'Porphyria's Lover'[28] – problematises domestic felicity. The inside does not offer exclusion of and protection from the sufferings of the outside, rather, it is the scene in which they are most completely apprehended.

It seems to me that a recognition of the critical and parodic elements of Brontë's engagement with Romanticism is vital to understanding her poetics. Like much women's poetry written in the second quarter of the nineteenth century, Brontë's work throws the conventional critical demarcation between Romanticism and Victorianism into crisis. For all the comparisons which have been drawn between her writing and Byron's, Brontë does not commit herself to a Byronic, hydraulic account of poetry as the 'lava of the imagination whose eruption prevents an earth-quake' originating from the poet's 'deepest self' (this would approximate to the account of Romantic poetry which underlies Bataille's account).[29] Several poems dramatise a collapse of faith in this innocent, enthusiastic, violent account of expression. Rather, Brontë is a poet who often interrogates the conditions of being of expressive utterance. She is keenly aware of the way in which language refracts and distorts, making unmediated, innocent expression impossible and, conversely, of the strain which language comes under when urgent political and functional demands are placed upon it. She can also be sceptical of those speakers who themselves lack scepticism and commit themselves to a unitary analysis or coherent politics. It is the central irony of Brontë's poetry that some of its most expressive cries are disciplined by the most elaborate systems of interrogation. I want to move finally to a text where this analytic dialectic structure is used to open up questions about gender and power within Romanticism.

FEMININITY, ROMANTICISM AND POWER: 'STARS'

The preoccupation in Brontë's poetics with the articulation of gender into the accounts of vision and power central to Romanticism comes under scrutiny in 'Stars'.[30] Rather like 'The Butterfly', the poem juxtaposes two contrasting forms of power experienced by the speaker as the different lights shed by the stars and the sun. The early stanzas of the poem are an elegy for the departed stars, whose effects are remembered as wholly benign and pleasurable.

> All through the night, your glorious eyes
>   Were gazing down in mine,
> And with a full heart's thankful sighs,
>   I blessed that watch divine.
>
> I was at peace, and drank your beams
>   As they were life to me;
> And revelled in my changeful dreams,
>   Like petrel on the sea.
>
> Thought followed thought, star followed star,
>   Through boundless regions, on;

> While one sweet influence, near and far,
> Thrilled through, and proved us one!   (lines 5–16)

The relationship the speaker enjoyed with the stars created a state of plenitude which permeated every aspect of this subjectivity. The emotional plenitude of the 'full heart' was matched by an intellectual plenitude as the 'boundless' space the stars traversed inspired the multiplication of the speaker's thought, in parallel with the stars' expansion. The speaker also compares this state to one of physical satiation in the image of drinking the life-giving light of the stars. In turn, this is intimately linked with a sense of spiritual bliss, as the peace the stars bring allows the speaker to imagine them as divine.

Irene Taylor argues that this state of glorious reciprocity should be understood as Brontë's memory of a lost state of physical and psychic unity with her mother. Taylor understands the personified, physical image of the drinking of the stars' beams as a fantasy of the experience of the infant during breastfeeding and links the pleasure of the visual relationship with the stars the speaker enjoys with the emphasis within a particular strand of psychoanalysis on the crucial role eye contact between mother and child during the process of feeding plays in the formation of the child's identity. Utilising the work of Bertram Lewis, who has argued for 'a relationship between ecstatic states and fantasies of return to the breast', Taylor argues that this account of visionary experience should be read as 'a tender evocation of herself as an infant nestled in her mother's arms, nursing at her breast'.[31] She contends that this reading of the stars as feminine and maternal seems to be confirmed and thrown into sharper relief by the terms of the description of the breaking of the day which follows from stanza five.

> Why did the morning dawn to break
>   So great, so pure, a spell;
> And scorch with fire, the tranquil cheek,
>   Where your cool radiance fell?
>
> Blood-red, he rose, and, arrow-straight,
>   His fierce beams struck my brow;
> The soul of nature, sprang, elate,
>   But *mine* sank sad and low!   (lines 17–24)

The intervention of the sun, explicitly gendered male, is described in terms which it is very easy to read into the kind of psychoanalytic narrative with which Taylor is concerned. The speaker inflects the account of the rising of the sun through an image of tumescence and represents its effects as an aggressive, phallic assault. The first two lines of stanza six are over-burdened with stresses so that they stand out from the more mellifluous, predominantly iambic rhythms which govern the rest of the poem, reinforcing the sense of the brutality of the sun's beams. These images can be mapped neatly onto an account of the disruptive intervention of the father into the pre-oedipal unity of mother and child. Taylor argues that the speaker's resentment of the sun signifies Brontë's equivocal relationship with her father who survived after her mother's death.[32]

Taylor is right to say that images of masculinity and femininity are a crucial part of the poem's investigations. However, I would dissent from her argument that they constitute a stable system, which regulates a fixed power structure and coherent moral economy. As the poem proceeds it produces points of dislocation within the terms it has set up which challenge the kind of systematic reading Taylor wants to make of it.

Taylor's argument rests upon the assumption that the poem is a lyric, whose speaker is to be identified with Emily Brontë. She is convinced that the speaker is both feminine and innocent, passive and blameless recipient of the forces of the feminine stars which, because she is feminine, she experiences as sympathetic and benevolent, and the masculine sun, which, because she is feminine, she experiences as oppositional, violent and damaging. For the most part, other critics of this poem have made the same assumption. Robin Grove, for example, argues that the poem describes a woman in a state of 'psychological unpreparedness' who is unready to receive 'masculine demands'.[33]

However, the poem, in fact, holds back from the direct ascription of femininity either to the stars or to the speaker. What *is* made explicit is that the aggressive conflict it describes is enacted not between masculinity and femininity, but between different masculinities. The only gender to be named in the poem is masculinity. Its ascription occurs twice, for the first time, as we have just seen, in the description of the sun and for the second in the final stanza, when the speaker describes the way in which the sun 'drains the blood of suffering men' (line 45). It is with these 'suffering men' that the speaker's suffering is identified. In a poem which is so consciously engaged with images of gender as the mode of its investigations, an innocent use of 'men' as a generic at its climax seems unlikely.

Moreover, the word is granted especial prominence by the fact that the line ending which it creates bears the most distant phonetic relation to the ending of the third line of the same stanza of any in the poem. Throughout the poem, the first and third lines have agreed in more or less perfect rhyme, except in stanza five, where the violent intervention of the day is signified in the para-rhyme of 'break' with 'cheek' (lines 17 and 19), and in stanza nine, where the disrupted and surreal experience of the speaker, suffering the assaults of the day, is figured in the lack of agreement between 'glowed' and 'wood' (lines 33 and 35). The even more distant relationship between 'men' and 'reign' (lines 45 and 47) throws the use of the masculine into sharp relief.

By contrast, there are no direct references to femininity at all. We construct the femininity of the stars and of the speaker purely by inference, from a series of assumptions about what constitutes femininity – passivity, lack of aggression, capacity to nurture, vulnerability – and from what we think we know about the gender of the author of the poem. Brontë frequently deploys male speakers in her poems and I see no reason to retain an absolute commitment to the femininity of the speaker of this poem. The point is not that characteristics generally ascribed to the feminine do not appear in the poem; they clearly do. But the fact that the poem refuses explicitly to name femininity and concerns itself only with the naming of masculinity throws into relief what is at stake in the ascription of femininity. In a sense, Taylor falls straight into the trap the poem sets up, and exemplifies the process which it is examining, by assuming the femininity of the stars and the speaker. The psychobiographical strategy which she brings to the poem obscures a crucial aspect of its complexity. 'Stars' is, in part, an exploration of the means by which femininity is constructed around categories of passivity, victimisation, sensibility and privacy. It is an analysis of how power and powerlessness become gendered within Romanticism. The poem dislocates its sexual symbolism just sufficiently, produces just enough space within itself, to throw the logic of this symbolism into question.

Moreover, the moral economy of the poem, which seems to be based upon the demarcation of masculinity and femininity, is disrupted by its later stanzas, which raise suspicions about the speaker's integrity in a number of ways. In other poems, notably 'Julian M. and A. G. Rochelle',[34] speakers deliberately enclose themselves within domestic space in order to resist the assaults of

cold or violent weather, but here the external world which tries to
force an entrance is benign and attractive.

> It would not do – the pillow glowed,
>   And glowed both roof and floor;
> And birds sang loudly in the wood,
>   And fresh winds shook the door;   (lines 33–6)

I find John Hewish's observation that 'Stars' is a poem of the
1840s, written during a period when the increasing industrialisation
and mechanisation of production in Britain was becoming the cause
of serious concern for cultural commentators, very suggestive.[35]
Hewish notes that the poem was composed at a time when Brontë
was regularly scrutinising the newspapers in order to check on the
status of the investments of her own and her sisters' capital which
she had made in the railways. His suggestion that the speaker of the
poem may dread the day because its arrival means a return to the
suffering of industrial labour, that the poem 'reveals the human cost
exacted by the society of the 1840s' is important.[36] Indeed, it is
possible to extend Hewish's materialist reading and argue that the
flies in the speaker's room suggest the presence of physical disease or
degeneration, caused, perhaps, by industrial or newly mechanised
and reorganised agricultural labour, or due to the conditions of
poverty in which the workforce lived.

But this reading only takes us part of the way through the poem.
'Stars' is not a Romantic repudiation of industry and human culture
in favour of nature in any simple sense. Like 'Faith and Despondency' the text swerves away from the Romantic trajectory on which
it seems to be set. The external world the speaker rejects is anything
but a landscape of industrial horror. The speaker is insistent that it is
the prospect of nature itself which is unbearable. The brightness and
freshness outside, which the speaker finds intolerable, throw into
relief the insanitary environment inside. That the speaker should be
addicted to such an unwholesome situation and should feel no
attraction for nature, which the poem makes clear is healthful and
pleasurable, raises doubts about her or his psychological integrity.

If the gender and the sanity of the speaker are thrown into doubt
by close examination of the language of the poem then, equally,
when we look at the detail of the text the speaker's innocence also
becomes a matter of dispute. The speaker's presence within and
apparent addiction to a vermin-infested environment, in themselves

cast aspersions upon his or her moral integrity. But the poem goes further and insists that this interior is a scene of domination, where the speaker is the perpetrator rather than the victim of oppression. Powerless as the speaker is in the face of the assaults of the sun, he or she can still exercise power within the domestic environment. The speaker understands that the flies inside the room are '[i]mprisoned' (line 39), and in need of the speaker's permission and action to be released. However, although the speaker can comprehend her or his own implication to this extent, he or she refuses to acknowledge the much more serious proposition that the violence of the sun has been prefigured in her or his own behaviour. The speaker complains that the sun 'drains the blood of suffering men; / Drinks tears, instead of dew' (lines 45–6) but will not admit that she or he has already performed a similar act of vampirism, described earlier in stanza three: 'I . . . drank your beams / As they were life to me' (lines 9–10). The relationship with the stars, which the speaker represents as the moral opposite of the encounter with the sun, is in fact structured by the same process of vampiric consumption (the speaker's fear of sunlight and day and attraction to night and darkness have already raised the issue of vampirism) this time with the speaker, instead of the sun, as the one who drinks and drains. The poem refuses to grant to the speaker absolute passivity and innocence, but instead, insists upon his or her implication in the structures of violence and oppression it explores.

Taylor is quite right to find images of masculinity and femininity in 'Stars' and to argue that they are mapped onto notions of power and powerlessness, aggression and vulnerability, but she misses a crucial aspect of the poem's significance by ignoring the way in which it worries away at the symmetry it sets up. It is wrong to ask 'Stars' for a definite pronouncement upon the nature of the political articulation of gender within the Romantic paradigm. The poem is concerned, instead, to re-open the question of the relationship between gender and power. 'Stars' undermines the security of the identifications it tempts us to make within it, so as to throw the binary oppositions we are using to construct our account into relief.

A discussion of 'Stars' forms the climax of Margaret Homans's account of Brontë's poetry. She argues that the terrifying vision of nature it contains is a representation of the horror the woman poet, writing under the shadow of Romanticism, feels at her identification with nature, which threatens to undermine her poetic identity and cast her into the realm of silence.[37] As we have seen, at the poem's climax the speaker experiences a profound dislocation and is unable, or refuses, to identify either with the masculine sun or with the implicitly feminised nature which responds to it. To this extent we might argue, as Homans does, that it is a study of the woman poet's exclusion from, or refusal of, poetic identity as it is conceptualised by Romanticism. But close examination also reveals that the poem will not allow us to be sure either that this is a feminine response, or that the alternative economy of inspiration and vision the poem postulates or the speaker who stakes her or his innocence on the experience of this realm, themselves escape implication in the dynamics of oppression and violence. Quite simply, the poem argues that it is impossible either to conceptualise a position outside of power or to stabilise gender identifications within it. In this poem, perhaps more than any other, Brontë demonstrates that she is not subjected by Romantic paradigms, but is an analyst of them.

'Stars' demonstrates the profound political and aesthetic agnosticism which structures Brontë's poetics. It is a 'double poem' in several senses: it oscillates between lyric and dramatic modes; it engages both with the concerns of Romanticism with the nature of vision and influence and with the obsession of early Victorian poetry with deranged and diseased subjectivities; it produces a radical destabilisation and interrogation of the sexual division it stakes itself upon. The metre of the text recalls nothing so much as that of the eighteenth- and early nineteenth-century protestant hymn. As we have seen, in its early stanzas, the poem flirts with religious terminology and experiments with placing its understanding of the visionary encounter within the conventions of religious experience. Yet this regulation and apparent accession to orthodoxy contains a text which is profoundly amoral in its refusal of a demarcation between guilt and innocence, aggressions and vulnerability, power and powerlessness. In this and other poems concerned with the nature of visionary influence, Brontë is exploring a structure in which neither force or account can triumph over its opposite. Brontë is insistent that an intensification of one force, of one side of the equation produces a parallel strengthening of the other.

In his Introduction to this volume Larrissy identifies two kinds of pressure which conceptualisations of the history and historicity of 'Romanticism' have come under from critical Postmodernism. First there is the collapse of historical boundaries between the Romantic and the postmodern (and sometimes anything preceding or in between them), and 'discovery' of an 'ironic coexistence of temporalities' superintended by an 'atemporal Postmodernism'. In this account the deconstruction of the grand narratives of Romanticism which Postmodernism would seek to enact is already implicit or explicit in Romanticism itself. Second there is the hyper-historicity (the overdetermination of history?) evident in the attempt to transgress and challenge the grand narratives of canonical Romanticism by devoting attention to the complexity of the context in which they were produced and signified: by challenging the strict chronological limits of the period and by studying texts by a range of women (not simply those related to male canonical figures), working-class writers, texts leaking in various ways across cultural boundaries from non-Western societies, political propaganda and other 'popular' forms, alongside those of the established canon.

I would argue that Brontë's poetry needs to be elucidated by both of these positions. To take the second kind of pressure first, 'Faith and Despondency', I have argued, needs to be read as very much a poem of its moment, the mid 1840s. It is not sufficient to compare it only with Romantic precursors. It enacts a collision between the 'Romantic' and the 'Victorian'. If we are to continue to consider Brontë as a Romantic or a post-Romantic (and I think that it does make sense to do so) we need to find ways to describe her complication and interrogation of Romanticism with early Victorian poetics and ideology, with the preoccupations of English poetry of the 1840s. 'Stars', one might argue, exemplifies the relevance of the first kind of postmodern pressure on Brontë's Romanticism. Although I am more wary of a Postmodernism which celebrates the collapse of history, which identifies any critique of essence, identity or common-sense assumptions about power in texts of any period as 'postmodern', it is clear that 'Stars' does produce an interrogation of femininity and the means by which it is constructed in relation to power which offers a profound challenge to the monolithic grand narrative of oppression of femininity and the woman writer by a patriarchal Romanticism which some feminist critics have tried to impose upon it. In a manner analogous to some of Blake's poems, 'Stars' reads the reader, laying bare and questioning the assumptions about gender and its relationship with power which we bring to it.

These forms of postmodern Romanticism may be related, in turn, to two tendencies which Patricia Waugh in her recent exploration of the relationship between Postmodernism and feminism, has termed 'strong' and 'weak' Postmodernism.[38] Waugh argues that 'strong' Postmodernism, which she identifies with the work of Jean-François Lyotard, Judith Butler and Donna Haraway, is characterised by an 'axiomatic assumption of the exhaustion of Enlightenment metanarratives and of the so-called emancipatory project of modernity'.[39] In this account there is no form of enquiry or set of criteria which can be used to ground knowledge, no 'reality' or 'truth' which words and concepts describe, there are simply discourses and language games, which *construct* our sense of reality. Tied up with this position is the thesis that the narrative of inexorable human emancipation and progress embedded in liberalism, Marxism and other kinds of history, is, precisely, a narrative, not reality. Feminism, Waugh explains, runs into a major problem with this account. Whilst the challenge Postmodernism offers to monolithic accounts of gender and patriarchy, for example, might seem attractive, its insistence that there is no reality behind processes of categorisation means that the constituency of feminism – women – and its political project – the emancipation of this group – also disappears. So for the 'strong' postmodern feminist Judith Butler, 'the term "woman" is merely a signifier with no substance, referring to nothing, simply a token in the particular language game in which it happens to be deployed'.[40] One response to this dilemma has been the development of the second position Waugh outlines, that of 'weak' Postmodernism. This account also rejects the possibility of discovering universal truth, values or human (or female) essence, but responds to this, first, by acknowledging this collapse as a problem at the level of politics, that despite its critique there still remains 'the human need to invest in grand narratives' and second, by paying close attention to the multiplicity of perspectives and experiences and making specificity the basis for political engagement.[41] This concentration on the 'culturally situated and embodied subject' and the belief that 'all knowledge is embedded or situated in particular cultures or cultural traditions'[42] may allow feminism to overcome what has been perceived as its major problem over recent decades – the assumption of Western feminism that the experiences, agendas and demands of white, Western, middle-class and heterosexual women are the experiences, agendas and demands of all women. Attention to and honouring of the profoundly different experiences and knowledges of different women, and the abandonment of the assumption that they can be transcended, 'weak' Postmodernism argues, may permit the development of consensus and the conditions for collective action.

I gesture towards this political debate in order to indicate that the discussion of the relation of women and femininity to the category of Postmodernism is never purely about aesthetics, is always political and is always problematic. I have suggested that a certain important strand of feminist criticism, which has taken Emily Brontë as one of its emblems, which has sought to bring the work of women writers (back) into dialogue with the category of Romanticism has, paradoxically (?) had the effect not of fracturing or deconstructing the relationship between gender and power in Romanticism, but of reinscribing it as monolithic. I have further sought to show that Brontë's poetry militates against and re-reads this reading in a way which we might characterise as postmodern. But in no way do I want to argue that the poetry envisages a celebratory escape from power, gender and their coercions; on the contrary, it insists upon and protests against them at the same time as it refuses their philosophical and political bases. I think that feminist criticism does need to continue to claim and interrogate Brontë. As Patricia Waugh points out, the question posed by the relationship of Postmodernism with feminism is 'whether it is possible to preserve the emancipatory ideals of modernity which seem absolutely necessary to the very endeavour of feminism, whilst dispensing with the absolutist epistemological foundations which have been so thoroughly and variously challenged'.[43] As we elaborate the project of postmodernising female Romanticism, we should be alert to what there is to be lost, as well as what there is to be gained.

CHAPTER 5

A sense of endings: some romantic and postmodern comparisons

J. Drummond Bone[1]

At the close of Richard Strauss and Clement Krauss's opera *Capriccio*, the Countess, unable to reach a decision over which lover to take – the poet or the musician – looks at herself in the mirror and asks 'Kannst du mir helfen den Schluss zu finden für ihre Oper? Gibt es einen, der nicht trivial ist?'[2] 'Can you help me find an ending for our opera? Can you give me one which is not trivial?' At which point the major-domo enters and announces that supper is served – and that is the end of the opera, so far as words are concerned, seemingly an answer to her question, triviality itself. But this trivial verbal conclusion is presented in the music as an affirmation. Something has been understood. What?

The opera has been asking whether music or words are more important to an opera, and to that question there is no answer which does not trivialise the question. The question is not trivial, but any answer to it *is*. It is not a matter of the triviality of existence, but of the triviality of endings. There is no *end* which is not trivial – the major-domo, and death, are only walk-on parts. This is what has been understood.

The Countess Madeleine's delightful (musical) smile when she discovers this to herself via the mirror is a twentieth-century aesthetic moment par excellence. No Reality is revealed – the countess's awareness is born out of self-reflection (with a little contingent help from the supper), it is not god-given. Moreover, it is the very opposite of conclusive, it is a downplaying of the importance of conclusions – her two questions are answered by an irrelevance, which tells her, or rather the audience, that answers to questions will never be conclusive, or if they are conclusive, they will be trivial. Reality, with a small 'r', is open-ended.

As soon as that perception formalises itself, it has however a disconcerting tendency to invert. It becomes a revelation of a 'truth', that is, a concept which is anything but 'open-ended', and the moment of its revelation marks a transformation which bears all the hallmarks of an 'end'. At a tangent to my train of thought lies the problem of whether a 'catastrophe' in the mathematical sense can be considered an end (appropriately enough for a paper first given in Zeeman's University), and whether indeed from a religious perspective death should be seen as a catastrophe rather than an end. Paradoxically, ends have qualities which render them more or *less* 'end'-like, and their presumed absoluteness might be described rather as positional *vis-à-vis* more straightforward *continuities*. Ends conceived of as summations, far from being absolute as ends, can actually project themselves beyond their text, and are thus more 'open' in one sense than ends which are accidental – since these tend to accept the termination of their own text as a finality – there being nothing significant beyond the text in their world-view. The metaphysical underpinnings of absolute structures of thought tend to inscribe endings as the beginning of that which lies beyond the text. Open endings, so-called, while downplaying the significance of endings, tend to accept them as final. But this is part of a Looking-Glass strangeness, which infects the duality I have already hinted at when I described the *words* of the major-domo as trivial, but the effect of the music as significant. Can any significant formulation – let's change the word and say more provocatively any significant expression – of contingent openness *where a text stops* escape the inversion which turns it into a significant *end?* Even if we have taught ourselves to think of life as process, of the work of art as texture and not text, endings remain difficult. They may speak of their triviality compared to the richness of change, but their music, even when there is no literal music, reverberates with an absolute fundamental. They sound of god.

Or at least, most do. I am going to examine some of the most apparently postmodern endings in the Romantic period, from poems of Byron's late period, and a few in the period or genre of postmodernism – I am no surer than anyone else which it is. Are these endings open? Do they suggest a radical shift along the spectrum from revelation to relativity? In what ways do the ideologies of form subvert the subversions of the ideologies of content (and for that heuristic distinction let me rely a little on my musical example – perhaps it would be better if I said ideologies of non-lexical and lexical elements)? What happens, in short, in the end? Can we expect an answer to that question which is not trivial?

L–d! said my mother, what is all this story about? –
A COCK and a BULL, said Yorick – And one of the best of its kind, I ever heard.[3]

So stops *Shandy*. If 1767 seems a little early for Romanticism, it is certainly not too early for Postmodernism. *Shandy* has it all. The Romantic lineage into which *Shandy* feeds is of course a Continental one, rather than a British. It is the world of progressive universal poesy, and of the idealisation of the fragment.[4] And it is this strand which lies beneath the modern critics' connection of Romanticism with Postmodernism, a critical connection, as Marilyn Butler has suggested, which possibly owes a significant amount to the Continental roots of its makers.[5] But in so far as Romanticism in Britain is an adoption of the autobiographical imperative, and in so far as it can be seen as an iconoclastic historical moment (leaving the adoption of secular irony aside which is almost wholly irrelevant for British Romanticism), it might be reasonable to see *Shandy* as a proto-Romantic text for English authors as well as a proto-postmodernist text for literature more generally. At any rate, *Shandy*'s end, if end it be, asks a question, and receives a reply which suggests that the matter is trivial, fictional, and a good thing. The fact that we are at an end hints that we should read 'all this story' as the whole book, Shandy's story, and not simply the story of his father's bull. The whole story is a story, but a good one. It is also a story which could go on beyond where it does stop (the cow you remember we are told will calve next week, in that bewildering way that Sterne has with tenses), and in exactly the same manner – indeed Tristram's mother's question is almost an interruption (which may remind us of her initial 'interruption'). Do we realise that this end is the end? To answer that question we would need to embark on a major analysis of the whole novel, but perhaps I might say 'perhaps'. Meantime let *us* go on.

If to break the pentameter was the first heave of Modernist poetry, as Pound would have it, and if to break the cadence was the first heave of atonal Modernist music, as Schoenberg would have it, to break the plot, and thus the cadence and the power of the ending, might be seen as if not the first at least a big heave in the Modernist novel. Sterne is not Fielding. But the endings of Joyce, to take an

obvious example, are anything but open. *Ulysses* as its end approaches behaves as if it had had a plot, even though for most of the
time it has been a very diffused one. It is climactic, and if its actual
end is introverted, not to say masturbatory, the effect of Molly's
rhetoric is the very opposite of introversion – the yes accepts the
blank page beyond the text as the fulfilment of itself – it is a yes to
everything that follows after the end. We have, like Odysseus
precisely, come home. Far from deconstructing the value of the end,
Ulysses reinforces it. And the *Wake*? The only difference here would
be the more strict introversion of the last sentence into the first. The
end is not an end, but a beginning: 'Far calls. Coming, far! End here.
Us then. Finn, again! Take. Bossoftlhee, mememormee! Till thousandthee. Lps. The keys to. Given! A way a lone a last a loved a long
the' – which returns us to the opening: 'riverrun, past Eve and
Adam's, from swerve of shore to bend of bay'.[6] If certain notions of
ending are here under revision (end with a full stop, end with
everything in place), others are being reinforced (endings are
apotheoses, transformations, beginnings). To feel the end of *Finnegans Wake* as arbitrary, trivial, is clearly ridiculous. The end is vital to
our reading of the beginning, and is soaked in a sense of transformation. Though we are certainly now after the end aware that
that beginning and that end are somehow language-stuff, and that
that is 'somehow' different from 'old-fashioned physical' stuff.

   If we look at a more properly postmodern example in Nabokov's
Ada (or should it be *out of* Nabokov's *Ada*?) we find a more complex
case, but still not one which supports the *idée reçue* of Modernist
irresolvability. The last chapter of *Ada* begins: 'Nirvana, Nevada,
Vaniada.'[7] These musing variations on the hero's name – Van –
introduce in the form they take the question of what lies beyond the
approaching end, at one and the same time signalling that end. The
narrator speculates that if Ada and Van had ever intended to die
'they would die, as it were, into the finished book, into Eden or
Hades, into the prose of the book or the poetry of its blurb'. He then
proceeds to write what actually appears as the cover-chat for the
book. This blurb is at once reductive – 'in spite of the many
intricacies of plot and psychology, the story proceeds at a spanking
pace' – and liberating: 'Not the least adornment of the chronicle is
the delicacy of pictorial detail: a latticed gallery ... butterflies and
butterfly orchids in the margin of the romance; a misty view descried
from marble steps; a doe at gaze in the ancestral park; and much,

much more.' Liberating in the sense that we are freed from the interpretative and returned to the particular, freed to consider marginal beauties. The 'much, much more' teases us at the moment of death – the hero and the heroine are dying into the blurb as predicted, because here the novel ends (or if you're reading the blurb first, begins!) – with the opening of a vista. Yet at the same time this last paragraph is rather more elegiac than the end of *Wake* – the 'pretty plaything' stranded among 'forget-me-nots', the very word 'margins', the difficulty of picking out the view in the mist, the *ancestral* gardens, all suggest either time past or a life difficult to make present, to focus sharply. Moreover, and perhaps crucially, this last paragraph is a list which as it grows gradually detaches itself from its explanatory grammar. This is what I meant by talking of a liberation from the interpretative. Its elements begin to hang unabsorbed by a context. They pass with their enunciation. They are almost accidental, and they are already of the past moment as they come into being. But then of course they are gathered up into the futurity and the significance of 'and much, much more'. This last phrase is close in effect to Molly's 'yes' – it accepts the singing silence of the blank page beyond the text. The turn from the open and elegiac to the apotheosis of 'much more', paradoxically an open comparative and yet also a completing, absolutely transforming termination is really quite astonishing, and you can savour the difference by imagining the last phrase deleted. The texture then is multi-stranded – a suggestion that the story is *mere* story, cock and bull, the stuff of pulp fiction; a suggestion that the elements of the story are really free to be and to disappear in artistic ('pictorial') but arbitrary and trivial ways; and an affirmation that to everything there is more. But what we do not have is a simple non-ending any more than we have a simple ending.

What of self-styled postmodernist novels then? Take John Barth as an example. In *Chimera* from 1972 there is ample warning of the approaching end, and indeed it becomes a kind of mock fetish – Bellerus is offered 'last words to the world at large' (before being turned into his narrator who is turning himself into Bellerus's story), and then finally five *last* last words. Protesting that this is not how he had imagined his story he stumbles: 'It's no *Bellerophoniad*. It's a',[8] and we are left with any number of possible completions from 'Chimera' to load of horse manure. Here the end as apotheosis – as transformation of life into myth – is set up and then reduced to the chimerical absurdity of an ancient Greek life retold in modern American prose, read by a limited number of people 'not all of whom will finish or enjoy' it. The moment of apotheosis is ducked by the incomplete sentence, and the reincorporation of that sentence into the tale itself is left implicit only, in the logical assumption that we are reading the tale into which Bellerus has been transformed. Arguably then we do have here a fairly straightforward example of a deconstructed ending, in which the ending as summation and transformation is reduced to utter triviality, and in which the arbitrary ('five more') undercuts any pretensions to a conclusion. But perhaps like the *Wake*, though certainly unlike *Shandy* or *Ada*, there is no attempt at all to mediate between the world-as-language, and what I have called the 'old fashioned physical' world. There is traffic between the two, one might say, but it is all one way – it flows from common-sense expectation to a world-as-language reality (small 'r'). It is almost as if self-reflexiveness negates itself in a world in which only self-reflexiveness is possible. This is an abstract book with an a priori cohesiveness akin to the composition of abstract painting. In the day-to-day physical world, to say that endings are less important to the texture of existence than theology would have it, is not to say that the texture of existence is abstract. Or at least it is not necessarily to say that. The protean nature of life, Socrates' reality like a man with a running-at-the-nose in the Cratylan dialogue, is not only *not* rendered trivial because its ending is trivial, but it reasserts its particular intransigence in not being trivialised by an ending. But *Chimera* on the other hand rather escapes the triviality of an ending by escaping from the shimmering trivialities – the 'sunny trifles' as Nabokov calls them in his first lecture on the European novel at Cornell – the shimmering trivialities of secular existence. Its avoidance of an ending does not feed back into the texture of the text, because in its abstract design there is never any danger that the text could be felt to lack the shape that an ending would supply. It is, from the viewpoint of the non-ending hunter, a victory over an absent enemy (appropriately enough – given the title).

Barth's more recent fiction, his post post-realism, his post-the-literature-of-exhaustion literature, reintroduces, centre stage, those sunny trifles, the butterfly orchids, or in his case Camel cigarettes, Schlitz beer, Yamaha electric organs, air-conditioned Jaguars, room one-seven-six in Gramercy Park Hotel, and a whole library-full of sailing practicalities. On the face of it *Sabbatical*'s ending has some similarities with the trivial particularities of supper in *Capriccio* – except that the discussion here is about the precedence of life over writing, rather than music over words: 'Which comes first? They both come first! How could either come before the other, except as one twin happens to get delivered earlier? The doing and the telling, our writing and our loving – they're twins.'9 The last paragraphs, in the manner of Ada, stroke the reader in different emotional directions: 'let's begin ... at the end and end at the beginning, so we can go on forever. Begin with our living happily ever after.' Here we have the now familiar manoeuvre which reduces the metaphysical importance of ending, only to substitute the importance of a linguistic transformation of ending which looks remarkably similar to the metaphysical transformations which value endings as apotheosis. But we also find: 'Yet we both know that not even a story is *ever* after. Here comes more storms toward Cacaway, and we've yet to retrieve that dinghy. No matter, there's light left.' Here, on the contrary, we seem to be in the world of accident and change, where the shoulder shrug 'there's light left' tells of a world in the future which has nothing to do with a world beyond an ending, merely with what will happen, or not happen, in a flow stretching after and on from the present fleeting moment. But at the last gasp the mood turns yet again 'to commence as we would conclude', with a reference back to the verses which began the novel (in the *Wake* manner), turning the novel into a hermetically self-redeeming circle, cancelling the particular openness of the future, the possible action in the light that's left, or not left, beyond the text. Except that (an 'of course' is appropriate for those who know Barth's work) the unresolved CIA mystery which forms what we could call the anti-plot of *Sabbatical*, provides a counterpoint to the quasi-resolution of the love theme. One plot has a cadence, but another does not (which is even more disturbing than no plot and no cadence). And moreover the end of *Sabbatical* is not the end of *Sabbatical*, because the novel effectively (if not exactly) continues in *Tidewater Tales*.

What then of the ending of *Tidewater Tales*? It almost looks as if it might end with the birth of the twins (the 'twins' who remind us of the twinning of doing and telling in *Sabbatical*): 'Sturdy little D! Bright-eyed V! Welcome to your garden!'10 This I suppose would be a classical ending, a moment of renewal as the moment of closure, the summation of the text in the life beyond it. It might admit only of a short cadential coda by way of aesthetic completion. But Barth drives us on beyond this climax into a chapter self-reflexively entitled 'The Ending'. Here we at last find the 'really', as the narrator puts it, of the CIA plot which has run through both novels, and various loose ends or 'smouldering chestnuts' are accounted for. They are accounted for in the context of an avowedly literary frame – Barth's favourite of Scheherazade as story-teller archetypical – and they lead us into an ending which eats its own tail – 'Its Once upon a time the Ever After of' – which provides us yet again with this seeming inconclusiveness in fact functioning as a hermetic seal to the text. It is certainly a literary seal rather than a real or metaphysical one, but it is a seal nonetheless. What then appears to be entitled 'The Ending' to deconstruct the ending, functions as another real ending. Yet again we are shunted out of the flow of accidental time and into aesthetic shape. My feeling, moreover, is that we tend to read aesthetic shape as metaphysical shape, whatever our good postmodernist, or post-Nietzschean, reader-as-author intentions. The actual ending of the novel may then displace the potential 'classical' ending from the metaphysical renewal of birth to the literary renewal of story-telling, but it does not genuinely subvert the crucial importance of the ending as a moment of transcendence.

Shandy was a direct influence on Barth, as has been noted by Richard Bradbury amongst others, including Barth himself.[11] Whether Byron also influenced Barth I am not sure, though perhaps even that odd ambiguity of verse and prose carries a memory of *Beppo* – 'I've half a mind to tumble down to prose / But verse is more in fashion – so here goes!'[12] And Byron's narrative self-reflexiveness avowedly owes a lot to *Shandy.* But direct influence aside, we can certainly find proto-postmodernist endings in Byron.

All of the examples we have looked at, with the exceptions only of the Joyce, are explicitly concerned with the business of writing. Perhaps the first stone heaved at the metaphysical ending converts it into the 'merely' literary ending, the unimportant triviality of the ending of a tale. But from much earlier than *The Tempest*,[13] that idea too could be read upside down: the first stone heaved at secular materialism converts it into the true world of imaginative faith. The postmodernist has a problem – fiction cannot be 'mere' fiction, since all significance is fiction, but equally it cannot be the fiction of faith, fiction beyond fiction. Non-endings cannot be merely trivial if they are to be significantly trivial, but equally they cannot be transformations in disguise.

At the end of *Vision of Judgment*, concerned once more with the business of writing, the narrator misses the moment of George's entry into heaven:

> As for the rest, to come to the conclusion
> Of this true dream, the telescope is gone
> Which kept my optics free from all delusion,
> And show'd me what I in turn have shown:
> All I saw farther in the last confusion,
> Was, that King George slipp'd into heaven for one;
> And when the tumult dwindled to a calm,
> I left him practising the hundredth psalm.[14]

Here are the traditional story-teller's optics, which feature also in the last chapter of *Tidewater Tales*, wielded there by Scheherazade,[15] but they fail at the crucial last moment. The last line is full of incompletion, if that is possible to say – the present participle, the idea of practice. The narrator of course is deliberately avoiding making the judgement which Southey has so arrogantly portrayed in his *Judgment*. Even the judgement on Southey – whom Byron turns into a prototype of the captain of the Vogon ship in Douglas Adams's *The Hitch Hiker's Guide to the Galaxy* to hear whose poetry is worse than being cast into empty outer space – is postponed indefinitely, to when 'Reform shall happen either here or there'.

The poem's ending has a certain delicacy, however, which does suggest something which is 'over'. The tumult has dwindled to a calm – something has passed – and we curiously take leave of George rather intimately – the first (optic-less) person here is very different from the omniscient voice of the opening of the poem 'Saint Peter sat by the celestial Gate'. It is as if although the characters of the tale continue beyond it, and cannot be summed up, judged, by it, nevertheless a time has passed, irretrievably. Of course the fact that George has to practise the 100th psalm is ridiculous, but there is also a feeling of the elegiac, a whisper that although this ending is trivial it is also not trivial, because the passage of time (not the ending of time) is the only story. We wave him goodbye.

In *Beppo* that feeling, if still low-voiced, is much more than a whisper. The accidental ending ('My pen is at the bottom of a page / Which being finished, here the story ends') is trivial certainly, as is the story itself ('''Tis to be wished it had been sooner done, / But stories somehow lengthen when begun' – the last line of the poem). Laura's comic outburst which diverts the story from any possibility of an 'untrivial' ending also explodes the possibility of any ending. As I have argued, before the poem in the deluge of Laura's trivialities races into time at the point where the plot might in another story have demanded a dead stop in eternity.[16] And yet at the same time it is those same trivial stories which have made *Beppo* popular, this trivial story which has whiled away our own time as readers, and Laura's tirade itself which functions clearly as the climax of the poem, rhythmically speaking everything that follows after only coda. There *is* a signalling of both an approaching end and of the end as meaningful. Is then the gentle farewell gesture at the foot of Byron's page, rather like Nabokov's in *Ada*, a surreptitious reintroduction of what we might now be wanting to call the aesthetics, or by way of aesthetics the metaphysics, of endings? The poem does after all end with the word 'begun', and goodness knows we have seen that device often enough in our extracts from Barth. Does this last line 'lengthen' into the blank page beyond? And is there a sense of redemption, albeit very low-key, in Beppo's happy old age and his friendship ('always') with the count? Even this poem, so firmly rooted in the particular and in the idea of the world as art – so secular that is, and with such a modern conception of the world as word – even this poem's deconstruction of an ending seems to have traces of a transformative possibility.

But surely that is a very different thing from an actual transformative, redemptive, ending? No one, not even the Countess Madeleine, can deny the desire for such endings. The danger, or is it a difficulty or even an interest, comes when the desire is mistaken for the fact. Perhaps what we should be saying here in *Beppo*, and in some of our other complex examples, is that the memory of 'significant ending' is the envaluing colour enriching the texture where the story stops, whereas an actually significant ending would bleach the story with the triviality of transcendence (and a 'trivial stopping' would be merely trivial). Without this memory of what endings were, story-telling is all too easy. And endings, we all know, are not easy.

I have only in passing discussed what earlier I have called the non-lexical elements. For a start there is the very big distinction between verse and prose. In a general way one could note that both *Sabbatical* and *Tidewater Tales* appeal to verse at their openings/endings, both appeals functioning by foregrounding the fictionality of the enterprise, not however to randomise their enterprise, one would hazard, but indeed rather to effect a fairy-tale transformation of the sublunar world. Byron's verse, in its highly organised ottava rima, constantly plays with the arbitrariness of its structure, and here one might argue that the movement does tend towards the deconstructive, since one hears the 'random' constantly rustling in the leaves of the 'merely' conventional.

But it would be much more interesting in fact to analyse, say, the specific rhythmic structures of both verse and prose which often contribute so much to the feeling of finality or otherwise. The end of *Ada*, for example, clarifies an initially elusive sonic and rhythmic pattern as it ends, sharpening the gradually more noticeable 'm' recurrence (margin/romance; misty/marble; much, much more), and presenting the reader with two decasyllabic phrases in classic four plus six formations to make the point of the unspoken continuation of the four syllable last phrase ('a misty view / descried from marble steps; a doe at gaze / in the ancestral park; and much, much more / ...'). The two effects force together the conclusive – and redemptive – beyond the text (the full-close tonic of the revealed alliteration) and the elegiac departure (the 'real' ending which cannot be conclusive). Part of the creative difficulty of the last line of *Beppo* lies with the energy of the middle phrase, 'stories somehow lengthen', which spreads ('lengthens') over the expected break after six syllables, and sets up the upward swing of the concluding three syllables, in marked contrast to the apologetic monosyllable, almost hanging from the previous line, with which the line opens. The manner of the last line therefore can be argued to reinforce the transformative sense of the ending, rather than the elegiacally open one. These endings are not mono-vocal. There is indeed 'much, much more'. Another day.

Endings, we all know, are not easy. Let me try again. Post 1980s Romanticism should have returned Byron to centre stage, but instead, as McGann has noted, it tended to do the opposite. Why? I wonder if it is because Postmodernism is *not* fundamentally a secular hypothesis, but rather an ideology verging on a theology. We need to remember that the same phenomena scientifically studied can be indeterminate at one energy level (at absolute zero so to speak), statistically predictable at another, and absolutely predictable at a third (at our own, say, where Newton's laws function as laws). No descriptive system, whether at the first or meta-level, mathematical or otherwise, can absolutely avoid the inversion involved in the expression of indeterminability. It is a matter of degrees on a scale (and one of the problems of literary discourse is that it rarely marks a scale). But we are spectrum-shifted, as it were, towards the Newtonian end of the explanatory scale. Explanations have a teleological view of existence built in, even explanations in denial of teleology. The more sure they are of themselves (the more certain of their uncertainties) the more spectrum-shifted they become.

One consequence of this shift is that one's starting point on this spectrum almost inevitably determines the meaning one attaches to certain key words, and one group's 'theology' may be another group's model for 'freedom'. The Romantic tradition which unites Shelley and Wordsworth, but which excludes Byron, a tradition which was strengthened in the deconstructionist *and* new historicist phases of critical discourse which parallel (or trail in the wake of) postmodernist fiction, is a tradition, I shall nevertheless venture, which far from eschewing transcendence, redeems it (resurrects it would be appropriate) in a new guise. Bloom, de Man, Hillis Miller, and Hartman are all in their different ways more interested in Shelley and in Wordsworth than in Byron. It is as if Byron, dealing indeed with existence as a plane, does not attract those who wish to *explain* that existence is indeed isomorphically planar. Levinson and Liu likewise expend most of their energies elsewhere. There are of course 'new' interpreters of Byron – McGann (though often by implication, which is indeed arguably Byronic in spirit), Watkins, Christensen, Manning – but one could still sustain an argument that the impact of Byron on a critical period for which he seems on the face of it such an obvious match has been relatively small. Maybe it is Byron's conversational, random, physical materiality which has excluded him from the postmodernist critical pantheon, where it might have been thought to have given him an exalted position. His movement opposes the 'natural' explanatory spectrum-shift. Late Byron is as much post his own Romanticism as Postmodernism is and is not postmodern. Byron's endings look postmodernist, his attitude to experience as art looks post-modern, and in contrast postmodernist endings substituting aesthetic for metaphysical transcendence can look remarkably Romantic. On closer inspection, late Byron therefore might usefully be thought of as less protopostmodernist than some of his Romantic colleagues. It is not likely to be accidental that Shelley has loomed so large in postmodernist critical discourse. Maybe I am escaping an ending of my own in suggesting that the tensions of Romantic and postmodernist endings dramatise

– no, not dramatise, *are* – the tensions between the particular and the sublime present in Kantian and typically European aesthetics – it feels like an escape because it is such a massive generalisation, and yet, of course, that is to take sides and say that large summations are not good endings. Well. Supper should be served shortly.

CHAPTER 6

A being all alike? Teleotropic syntax in Ashbery and Wordsworth

Geoff Ward

I

To read Romanticism and Postmodernism in the light of each other is clearly an aid to understanding the historical origins of Postmodernism, albeit within a larger map of territories, ambitions, dilemmas and curses that the twentieth century inherited from the nineteenth. It is also an aid to understanding Romanticism, or perhaps more precisely a tool facilitating the division of Romanticism into two zones for enquiry, the first and more approachable of which will be a Romanticism recognisable from its affinities with recent writing and its prefiguring of modern habits of thought. The other, more complex area will be that where a phantom or conjectural Romanticism beckons only to turn us away, a door but a closed one; textually, a point where it becomes difficult to read on with confidence because the tropes and turns of argument in play appear to issue from too distant a history, or from a sensibility whose emphases and meanings we are so unsure we have reconstructed correctly that reading dwindles to an opportunity to project whatever we want onto what is effectively a *tabula rasa*. I am thinking not so much of the notorious opacities in Blake, or Shelley's more hectic detonations (though they would certainly be included) as of any moment in reading Romantic texts where meaning recedes sharply and the occluding weight of the past falls like the shadow of a guillotine-blade across the page. Of course a scholar might well argue that this moment of alterity where the past declares itself as such, is exactly the point where editorial and other patient labours of clarification begin. Moreover, a depressive scholar (or a happy deconstructionist, for they are hard to distinguish at this shadow line) would argue that there is nothing special about Romanticism in that the pastness of the past is just as likely to declare itself as

86

simultaneous barrier-and-lure in texts from the Middle Ages or the 1980s to the reader who is reading carefully. Ultimately, existentially, it is not in any case history that severs the lines of communication but rather the lack of connection that is endemic to our every deluded attempt to establish coherence in the world, including the fantasy of accessing the past, and the reading of poetry. Poetry is just one more consolatory strategy with which we seek to cover our existential nakedness, albeit the most sybilline of all our sheltering leaves, in that it discloses the inscription of the endurance by consciousness of a life of self-division and disconnection just as its rustlings charm and soothe with verbal magic. Such at least would be the demystified implication of the more claustral readings of Romantic texts by the darker deconstructionists, preeminently Paul de Man.

And yet one doubt has to be raised sooner rather than later as regards any analysis that lays stress on occlusion and disconnection, including the 'otherness' of the past, as a recurrent feature in the phenomenology of perception, including reading. What is termed 'other' cannot be completely so, otherwise it would not presumably be detectable as an operative factor at all. What is being signalled in the context of reading as 'otherness' announces itself as alterity with a paradoxical and ambiguous familiarity. Not only do we experience this in reading Romantic texts from our present-day coigns of vantage, but we come across episodes *in those texts* where speakers or meditating minds have this experience, where otherness and recognition appear to bud inside each other.[1] Indeed, such episodes would become even more prominent in Symbolist poetry, with Baudelaire's 'Correspondances' only the most obvious example: man passes through a 'Nature' experienced as 'des forêts de symboles / Qui l'observent avec des regards familiers.'[2] It may be that Romantic and contemporary poetry seem newly close because, given the waning influence of Eliot and Pound, and the rising importance of Ashbery, it is now Symbolism rather than High Modernism which works as a bridge between the early nineteenth century and today. Symbolist art is (to risk a crude generalisation) fascinated by icons but wary of massive ambition; ironic by instinct, suspicious of the prescriptive: charmed by fashion, by music and by the aesthetic aspects of religion. The funerals of Gianni Versace or the Princess of Wales are only among the most recent spectacles in our modern Symbolism, so distant from the politics and practice of 'the men of

1914'. In certain respects Symbolism is Romanticism, scaled-down and for sale.

The juxtaposition of Romanticism and Postmodernism urged by this volume is therefore far from arbitrary. The thesis of this essay resides not simply in the idea that the Romantic–Postmodernist link is an interesting two-way thoroughfare for readings to traverse, but that versions of the conjunction of experience and alterity, as sketched above, recur in the significant poetic texts of both periods. Likewise, in both periods the cruces of this alterity are bound in important ways to ambiguities in the power of consciousness to access the past. These lines come from Book Seven of the 1805 edition of *The Prelude*:

> How often, in the overflowing Streets
> Have I gone forwards with the Crowd, and said
> Unto myself, the face of every one
> That passes by me is a mystery!
> Thus have I look'd, nor ceas'd to look, oppress'd
> By thoughts of what, and whither, when and how,
> Until the shapes before my eyes became
> A second-sight procession, such as glides
> Over still mountains, or appears in dreams;
> And all the ballast of familiar life,
> The present, and the past; hope, fear; all stays,
> All laws of acting, thinking, speaking man
> Went from me, neither knowing me nor known.
> And once, far-travell'd in such mood, beyond
> The reach of common indications, lost
> Amid the moving pageant, 'twas my chance
> Abruptly to be smitten with the view
> Of a blind Beggar, who, with upright face,
> Stood propp'd against a Wall; upon his Chest
> Wearing a written paper, to explain
> The Story of the Man and who he was;
> My mind did at this spectacle turn round
> As with the might of waters, and it seem'd
> To me that in this Label was a type,
> Or emblem, of the utmost that we know,
> Both of ourselves and of the universe;
> And on the shape of this unmoving Man,
> His fixed face and sightless eyes, I look'd,
> As if admonish'd from another world.   (lines 595–623)[3]

The projects of Romanticism are forever restated to be undone in its poetry. Coleridge's sunlit dome and caves of ice are built only in imagination, Shelley's wished-for Oneness comes only in death. Wordsworth's aim to reintegrate the self into Nature either is achieved, but in an uncertain way that litters the scene with question-marks as in the story of the boy from Winander, or was achieved, in an Eden of phenomenological equilibrium now faded into the past, or is more typically undone, as the vision of cosmic harmony in 'A slumber did my spirit seal' fragments on re-reading into ironies of muteness, guilt and a very un-sublime egotism. In this passage from *The Prelude* can be seen a mirror rather than a true reversal of this recurrent irony. Rather than beginning with an articulation of integrated selfhood that is then disjoined by the very agent that seemed to promise accretion, reinforcement, ramification, orchestration – that is to say, syntax – Wordsworth presents a picture which spells, *ab initio*, shock, but which syntax goes on to make so resonantly typical that the isolation it depicts is revealed as a common condition. Disconnectedness – of the Beggar from the crowd, of the speaker from 'All laws' and from 'the ballast of familiar life', of written legend from silent figure, of mind from itself – does not become a sign of otherness, because syntactical extension and reiteration have made otherness familiar. In the last line quoted it is 'another world' that signals admonition, paradoxically as intimate and powerful a communicant as can be imagined, by virtue of its distance. What is here and what is of another world, that which brings recognition and that which causes vertigo, are somehow at work inside each other.

The operations of syntax in the passage are multiple and even contradictory, though brilliantly so. In a brief commentary on this passage, Paul de Man invokes Baudelaire's *Les Fleurs du Mal* (thinking, presumably, of such poems of encounter as 'Les Sept Vieillards') when he notes that in the post-Romantic poet 'such moments appear only by instants, as isolated shocks that can never be incorporated in a larger temporal dimension. Unlike Wordsworth, he was never able to re-establish contact, through the figural dimensions of his language, with his real poetic antecedents.'[4] Consciously or not, de Man's emphasis on poetic precursors recalls his one-time colleague Harold Bloom's theorisation of the anxiety of influence, where de Man's more usual insistence is on the unpicking of symbol by allegory and irony so as to *disclose* the 'isolated shocks' against which writers and others insulate themselves by appeal to order and

antecedent. As a rule he looks as it were for the Baudelaire in
Wordsworth. (And indeed this is a 'man of the crowd' episode of a
kind that is developed by Poe and Baudelaire, and theorised in time
by Walter Benjamin.) But if it is syntax that allows Wordsworth to in
some sort re-establish contact with Milton (never a difficult task for
him), it is likewise syntax that allows the poet to modify a phrase in
order to be more precise. The shapes are not, he writes, so much like
those seen on the mountains, as those glimpsed in dreams; the sheet
is not so much a type, as an emblem; and so on. At the same time,
such reformulations do not cancel out their predecessors but seek a
verbal balance – 'The present, and the past', 'Both of ourselves and
of the universe' – which would restore the harmonious and characteristic phenomenology of Wordsworth's more serene articulations, shattered by the bleak spectacle of the 'unmoving man'.
Furthermore, these incessant reformulations add to each other, pile
up words, more or less repeating themselves in an accurate recreation of the ways in which, after a shocking incident, we babble our
way back and forth over the same ground, using slightly altered
terms. There is an interesting relationship at work here between
syntax and panic, as there is in the poems by John Ashbery to which
I am about to turn. Perhaps any prominent or prolonged use of any
style or type of rhetoric is, among other things, an effort to suture
over trauma. The final horror of the encounter which leaves Wordsworth so *bouleversé* is not the plight of the blind beggar in his singular
misery, but such loneliness as an emblem of a universal estrangement. Truthfully speaking it is a concept, allowing recognition and
vertigo to interfuse, that lies at the roots of the trauma.

II

Recently I examined a PhD thesis by a candidate writing on John
Ashbery. The candidate noted in his Preface with an absolutely
heroic evenness of tone that Ashbery had published more new
poetry in the four years it took to write the thesis than Philip Larkin
had published during his entire lifetime. It is true (and some would
say, fortunate) that Larkin was relatively costive in output. Nevertheless the prolificity of the now septuagenarian Ashbery is remarkable,
almost Victorian. Equally nineteenth-century are the quotations
from Walter Pater, Thomas Lovell Beddoes et al. with which the
verse is increasingly peppered, most of all towards the end of the

200-page poem *Flow Chart* (1991) with its double sestina on the death of the poet's mother, as far as I know the first use of the form since Swinburne's 'The Complaint of Lisa' in 1872, and related quite consciously to that poem by its replication of Swinburne's rebus-words. It is easy for those writing about his work to risk losing their paddle in Ashbery's spate. Like one of Ashbery's own speakers about to commit himself when a squall hit, I was just getting ready to review the 100-page *And the Stars were Shining* (1994) when the even longer *Can You Hear, Bird* (1995) – which might have been more appropriately titled, *Can You Keep Up, Reader* – appeared. He must wonder if people now read, or merely dip into, or now feel that they have already read, each successive book. Perhaps this is the reason why the poem called 'Like a Sentence' appears in *And the Stars were Shining*, only to turn up again word-for-word in *Can You Hear, Bird*. How many people noticed? Does it really matter? Is Ashbery's canonisation now so achieved a phenomenon that were he to publish chunks of the telephone directory as his next book (which he virtually did anyway in parts of *The Tennis Court Oath*) it would not alter one line in a profile that is now set in stone, albeit *Symboliste-*marmoreal rather than Mount Rushmore-craggy in design? It could of course be argued, to return to the repeated poem 'Like a Sentence', that to print the same poem in two different collections is not truly to print the same poem. If that sounds too much like the kind of filigrane from which essays on postmodernist poetry are spun, it is nevertheless a kind of no-man-steps-into-the-same-river-twice questioning of the passing moment to which the poetry frequently turns: 'No two employees know it' as one of the voices in *Flow Chart* opines. So what this section intends to ask about the prolific but endlessly valedictory Ashbery of the 1990s is, is it more of the same, a – to draw a phrase from *Can You Hear, Bird* – 'being all alike'; and, is there a larger being-all-alike, an expanded interpret-ation of Romanticism that could include this contemporary poetry? I will draw for support on a theoretical work, *The Secular Grail: Paradigms of Perception* (1993) by Christopher Dewdney, a writer influential in his own country but less well known elsewhere.

Especially by comparison with his fellow-members of the New York School – Kenneth Koch, James Schuyler, Frank O'Hara – John Ashbery appears to have been born middle-aged. Russet tones and a certain Strether-like or Prufrockian ruefulness and reluctance have shadowed his writing from a surprisingly early point. An observer not a participant (with of course a concomitant exploitation, à la early Eliot, à la late James, of all the observer's privileged access to melancholy overview), not so much a Bohemian *flâneur* as simply one who hangs back, riddled with and riddling through self-doubt, Ashbery's dominant tone is of patient doubting striated by moments of near-derailment, near-resolution: 'A look of glass stops you, and you walk on, shaken: was I the perceived?', 'As One Put Drunk into the Packet-Boat' (1975): 'O I have to keep fighting back to find you, and then when you're still there, what is it I know?' and 'Did I order that?', *Flow Chart* (1991). Although Frank O'Hara's accidental death at the age of forty has stamped for all time a kind of Keatsian, *carpe diem*-style glamour on his work, his poetry was in any case nothing if not vivacious. Of course O'Hara was used to darkness, too, but not so as to swamp the conversational ebullience of his poetry. He even ends his lines, often, on an upward lilt, a balletic lift, as the dancers he moved among could do, but going against the tendency of the sentence in English to end on a falling cadence. Likewise though less interestingly, Kenneth Koch's poetry is nothing if not lively in its cartoon colours. James Schuyler's poetry, though more tremulous – *hurt* into linebreaks of the kind theorised by the generation of Donald Allen and Robert Creeley, rather than showing a vanguardist commitment – is not condemned always to stand outside of the expression of happiness, sociability, achieved communication. By contrast Ashbery has always been the first to rain on his own parade, thereby of course protracting its soggy but indomitable progress towards internment in 'the canon', a university cubicle in which a dead writer appears to continue to meditate, rather like the corpse of Jeremy Bentham, embalmed in the University of London, though without Bentham's happy-go-lucky expression.

So death was always there in Ashbery's parade, and not just at the end of it, but spiking the drinks, whispering on the breeze, insinuated. 'As you find you had never left off laughing at death, / The background, dark vine at the edge of the porch' ('Forties Flick' (1975)). 'One died, and the soul was wrenched out of the other ... ' ('Street Musicians' from *Houseboat Days* (1977)), and so on. While writing the poems that were collected as *A Wave* (1984), Ashbery nearly died, like Byron at the hands of his doctors, and though that crisis is alluded to only once, in the opening lines of the title poem, 'To pass through pain and not know it, / A car door slamming in the night. / To emerge on an invisible terrain', *A Wave* is filled as never before with autumnal rumination and *memento mori* admonitions. 'Therefore why weep we, mourners, around / A common block of space?' ('One of the Most Extraordinary Things in Life'); 'It all wears out. I keep telling myself this, but / I never believe me, though others do' ('Down by the Station, Early in the Morning'); '. . . we may live / With some curiosity and hope / like pools / that soon become part of the tide' ('A Fly'). In sum, Ashbery has always written with a sharp sense of mortality, and as the years pass, it is hardly surprising if the poems begin to converge on certain themes. There is, however, an important linguistic shift between the poetry of the 1990s and the work of earlier decades. However melancholy the cadences in the examples quoted, the poems illustrate that melancholy with brilliant images. In the case of a poem such as 'Forties Flick', the deathliness exists in a balance, is a ground against which the vivid figures can be played. The poem of the image dominated the first half of the twentieth century, in poetries as otherwise inimical as Surrealism, Imagism and the work of Yeats or Rilke, and it finds an attenuated shelf-life in the crossword puzzlers of today, Craig Raine or Paul Muldoon. One reason for the popularity of 'Self-Portrait in a Convex Mirror' over other works by Ashbery stems from the fact that it is ingeniously but also quite literally a poem of the image. Ashbery's poetry in the 1990s is primarily one of syntax, rather than images.

It is not unprecedented for syntax to elaborate itself, even to the point of virtual take-over of an older writer's productions. The dictation of the later James, the revised versions of *The Prelude* or *Confessions of an English Opium-Eater*, are among the obvious examples. The equally obvious explanation that, as the brilliance of life fades, there arises the urge to hold on to it, to map it, to seize it and fill all its space, securing the comfort that ongoing syntax provides against silence, is doubtless valid as far as it goes. And yet from a fairly early date, minimalism in (say) Samuel Beckett was offset against a stoicism of syntactical accretion, the Unnamable's 'in the silence you don't know, you must go on, I can't go on, I'll go on'.[5] And in the case of Ashbery there is not only the periodic affinity with Beckett (most of all in *Three Poems* (1972)) but the examples, which were also important to Frank O'Hara, of Gertrude Stein and above all John Cage, whose compositional innovations in music alternate formal restriction and openness to chance. A similar alternation has recurred throughout Ashbery's work, as the artificiality of form in his long-time use of the sestina or the recent, rhymed 'Tuesday Evening' has alternated with the drift towards the aleatory in loose epics like 'Europe' (in *The Tennis Court Oath* (1962)) or 'Litany' (in *As We Know* (1979)). In an attempt to clarify the evolving importance of syntax in his recent work, I set a passage from *Flow Chart* against some observations on syntax by Christopher Dewdney:

> I think it was at that moment he
> knowingly and in my own interests took back from me
> the slow-flowing idea of flight, now
> too firmly channeled, its omnipresent reminders etched
> too deeply into my forehead, its crass grievances and greetings
> a class apart from the wonders every man feels,
> whether alone in bed, or with a lover, or beached
> with the shells on some atoll (and if solitude
> swallow us up betimes, it is only later that
> the idea of its permanence sifts into view, yea
> later and perhaps only occasionally, and only much later
> stands from dawn to dusk, just as the plaintive sound
> of the harp of the waves is always there as a backdrop
> to conversation and conversion, even when
> most forgotten) and cannot make sense of them, but he knows
> the familiar, unmistakable thing, and that gives him courage
> as day expires and evening marshals its hosts, in preparation
> for the long night to come.[6]

Language is always movement forward, streamlined into the anticipation of an ultimate meaning. Meaning is where we are going, it is our intention. Like a plant growing towards light, a sentence grows towards its final meaning, it is teleotropic. This ultimate meaning is the orientation of a sentence at any given point in time. It is a magnetic field in which syntax is the compass needle pointing to the true north of intention.
Both speech and writing are anticipatory motions, propelled by the expectation of sense. The burden of teleotropism, of intention, creates a performance anxiety deep at the root of our apparent linguistic facility. The continual flight of the point of concentration, tracking within the superstructure of intention as a nomadic moment of attention, makes for a restless, anxious lack of stasis.
Like music, discursive language creates self-relational structures whose meaning depends on particular successions of elements. This is both the impatience and the sensuality of the text. ('Synonymic Redundancy and Teleotropism in Sentences')[7]

When any two unrelated gobbets are set together, apparent convergences and discussible differences will always emerge, expressed via syntax and generating more. Dewdney's highly mobile argument is not a gloss on Ashbery's flowing lines. Both are characteristically postmodern, from within their different genres, in characterising ultimate meaning as a performative orientation rather than as an epistemological (or other) achievement. Both, though this is also typical of Romanticism and of the Romanticism within Postmodernism, view self-relational yet discursive flight as intrinsic to productive expression. My quoted excerpt from *The Prelude* and the short section from *Flow Chart* certainly resemble each other in this respect. In fact both texts trust syntax above all else.

Flow Chart offers *tour* after *tour de force*, syntactically, not for the most part in a spirit of showiness but with a chilly hunkering down into the only stratum that can be relied on. This poem, in important respects *the* poem of the 1990s, the most willing of epics since Mallarmé's *Igitur* to risk all on the long syntactical reach, comes the closest of Ashbery's poems to encrypting Barbara Johnson's suspicion that knowledge is an effect of syntax. For both Ashbery and Dewdney, meaning is where we are going, and yet there is the concession that syntax characterises the travel more than it makes real the arrival. Elsewhere in *The Secular Grail* Dewdney argues that syntax is the stylistic equivalent of individuality, the thread of alignment along which meaning condenses, rather than the pathway to final meaning. Just so, the long sentence I quoted from *Flow Chart* contains condensed meanings *en route*, with Ashbery content to subdue the brilliant imagery of his younger phases to the point virtually of cliché – 'the plaintive sound of the harp of the waves' – but refuses or is unable to use syntax, however correct and athletic, to summarise. Everything in the first two thirds of the sentence builds like a wave only to crash on loss of significance when the unnamed he 'cannot make sense of them'. All that can be trusted is that 'he knows / the familiar, unmistakable thing, and that gives him courage', but as the thing is not named it is not graspable, is not there, is at last only the syntax that conjured its possibility only to refuse it, and the sentence concludes with a characteristically Ashberyan foreboding over 'the long night to come'. And this of course is death, at which point the line is appropriately broken.

Such fabulous elongation of syntax to form a labyrinth whose heart turns out to be all thread and no minotaur might seem to offer the questing reader little in the way of ultimate purpose. It is more the case that *Flow Chart* offers pleasures *en route* to a centre that is not reached, because that is not what poetic syntax can do. This will only be frustrating if the reader wants a poem to be soluble, like a crossword puzzle with an answer, in which case Craig Raine or Paul Muldoon will be happy to oblige, though Mallarmé or Wordsworth – or Rilke, who is everywhere in *Flow Chart*, particularly in the first section – wouldn't have been.

And the Stars were Shining, Ashbery's 1994 collection, is certainly a rebuttal to the alleged sameness of his work in the 1990s. The symphonic language-swirl of the 1991 epic is replaced by curt and acidic provocation. Witticisms, so nearly ubiquitous in Ashbery, are not so much absent as begun and then stalled on purpose. In a poem of the early 1980s, 'The Songs We Know Best', Ashbery had the couplet: 'Too often when you thought you'd be showered with confetti / What they flung at you was a plate of hot spaghetti', an appealing McGonagallism. In 'A Hundred Albums' from the 1990s collection, 'we'd' just stopped by for a mug of hot wine 'but it is soup that is being dashed in your face'. No joke. Elsewhere there is a malevolence quite unanticipated in Ashbery's work, as in 'The Ridiculous Translator's Hopes': '. . . vulnerable / as a bride left waiting at the church, inching backward / to the cliff's edge as the photographer gets ready to smile.' Words recur across poems, giving them a curious resonance and urgency, but they are odd words used oddly: like 'stinger' – 'Hold my stinger as a stranger and I will be presently.' One old stinger quoted in the book is Samuel Johnson, and we might return to the use of 'stranger' as a verb, a usage given in Johnson's Dictionary but one that withered over the Romantic period, to speak of Ashbery's strangering the reader.

The vertigo-within-recognition that recurs in Ashbery's Romantic Postmodernism is vividly present in the poem 'Coventry', a place to which – at least in English usage – one is sent malevolently by those who know but now wish to stranger him. The poem begins with a mixture of words that recall Victoriana and children's literature, shot through with something more abrupt and oneiric; one scalds his hand; marmoreal floors are described as 'sweating'. It is a cliché to declare a poem ominous as a dream is ominous, though if that is true anywhere, it is so here. The syntax is truncated, agitated. Where *Flow Chart* banked everything on advancing, 'Coventry' swerves and breaks down, feinting but also passing out: 'I fainted, honey.' There is recognition: 'You'd have to stay in Coventry. / But I'm already there, I protested.', with vertigo inside the recognition.

Or vice versa. 'Honey' has in any case always been a strangely loaded term in Ashbery's lexicon, right from its early use in the first line of 'Leaving the Atocha Station', and in the more famous ' "This honey is delicious / *Though it burns the throat*" ' from ' "They Dream Only of America" ': (both in *The Tennis Court Oath*.) 'I fainted, honey' conjoins intimacy with abandon, recognition with vertigo, uses syntax to account for its loss. Somewhere perhaps in these silences and feintings the trauma may be glimpsed that the longer lines in longer poems suture over.

Fainting is a very late-Romantic, very dark-Romantic thing to do, and also a very female, a powerless display of activity within the Victorian repertoire. Consider the languid, fainting, sleeping, drifting Ophelias of the pre-Raphaelite painters, of Frederick Leighton, the floating sleepers of 'The Punishment of Luxury', the miniature girls of Alma-Tadema. As it happens, Christopher Dewdney's book includes a short biography of Sigmund Freud, structured by the handful of occasions in Freud's life on which he is known to have fainted. Two at least of these vertiginous lapses occurred following an argument with C. G. Jung as when, following a speculative and heated conversation regarding Amenophis IV, a candidate for architect of the first monotheistic religion, the architect of psychoanalysis slid off his chair and into unconsciousness. Jung carried him to a sofa in an adjacent room where on recovering, Freud remarked 'How sweet it must be to die.'[8] What does Dewdney's saturnine cartoon have in common with Ashbery's poem or for that matter with *The Prelude*? *Pas un chat*, except that everything here; the hysteria of fainting, the science cum black art cum Symbolist oneirism of the talking cure, Christopher Dewdney's organicism and his cultural eclecticism, Ashbery's echoes of faded Victoriana in 'Coventry', Wordsworth's self-immersion and self-estrangement which is bequeathed to later writers as a style, and perhaps the whole issue, now, of poetry and our curious faith in it, a form of spilt religion however vestigial, are all Romantic, darkly Romantic. Perhaps Romanticism is the only single concept which can include syntax, and not the other way about. A giddy conclusion: yet as the poet Charles Bernstein remarked in another context, poetry may be a swoon that brings you to your senses.

CHAPTER 7

Virtual Romanticism

Fred Botting

The subject of Romanticism, in at least two senses, is in a state of crisis. It is, moreover, a crisis repeating a crisis at the heart of Romanticism. As an academic subject, 'current scepticism about the distinctiveness and value of literature, the canon, criticism and its theory reworks that original Romantic crisis.'[1] On a broader scale, argues Jerome Christensen, the crisis involves questions of commercial hegemony and ideological contestation, an echo of the social, political and poetic issues reverberating from Romanticism's revolutionary moment.[2] For Edmund Burke, shocked by the 'great crisis, not of the affairs of France, but of all Europe, perhaps, of more than Europe', the romantic reverberations of the French Revolution wonderfully and absurdly disclose a disturbing monster of unimaginable change:

everything seems out of nature in this strange chaos of levity and ferocity, and of all sorts of crimes jumbled together with all sorts of follies. In viewing this monstrous tragicomic scene, the most opposite passions necessarily succeed and sometimes mix with each other in the mind: alternate contempt and indignation, alternate laughter and tears, alternate scorn and horror.[3]

As oppositions collapse and revolve, tearing the social and political fabric of Burke's late eighteenth-century present, an epochal shift ambivalently, monstrously, glowers on the horizon. Such a crisis, moreover, sublime and yet strangely integral to Romanticism, seems to determine the modernity of the last two hundred years in a manner that accords with Jean-François Lyotard's diagnosis of 'the postmodern condition': 'Postmodernism thus understood is not Modernism at its end but in the nascent state, and this state is constant', thereby posing a real question of presentation, the sublime, the imagination and the subject's nostalgia for presence.[4]

In the terms of Jean-Luc Nancy and Philippe Lacoue-Labarthe's discussion of the 'literary absolute' the crisis integral to Romanticism recurs in modernity:

a veritable romantic *unconscious* is discernable today in most of the central motifs of our 'modernity'. Not the least result of romanticism's indefinable character is the way it has allowed this so-called modernity to use romanticism as a foil, without ever recognizing – or in order not to recognize – that it has done little more than rehash romanticism's discoveries.[5]

Analysing the recurrence of the subject of Romanticism involves more than a simple recognition of (post)modernity's present in a Romantic past characterised as a simple revolt against reason and the state: the 'literary Absolute' that Romanticism evokes 'aggravates and radicalizes the thinking of totality and the Subject. It *infinitizes* this thinking, and therein, precisely, rests its ambiguity.'[6] This ambiguity is related to modernity's sense of crisis:

we are all, still and always, aware of the *Crisis*, convinced that 'interventions' are necessary and that the least of texts is immediately 'effective' ['*opératoire*']; we all think, as if it went without saying, that politics passes through the literary (or the theoretical). Romanticism is our *naiveté*.[7]

The naiveté of a persistent Romantic subjectivity confronts crises in literary, theoretical, political formations in the present as an uncanny repetition of structures of anxiety and modernity. In literary terms, Gothic writing, recalling a romance tradition, returns upon Romanticism proper as the latter's disavowed condition of possibility: Gothic's intimacy and proximity become uncanny, residual marks of the repressed romance forms that never cease to make their ghostly reappearances. In political, economic and technological terms national, capitalist and electronic revolutions promise massive global transformations which repeat revolutionary and romantic gestures while at the same time threatening the human subject and the modernity sustaining it with as epochal and inhuman a spectre as Burke imagined at the end of the eighteenth century

Not only is Romanticism (as a particular literary-historical encounter) increasingly recognised in its contemporary recurrence, it also provides a way of thinking that informs discussions of contemporary cultural change. That Romanticism structures the way that subjects in the present present the present to themselves is evinced in both Utopian and dystopian representations of that digital revolution called cyberculture: on the one hand, what might

be called Luddite humanism recoils in horror from the encroach-
ment of the machine on what is seen as human and natural; on the
other, scientific humanism celebrates new technologies as the materi-
alisation of powers previously only imagined Romantically. The
Luddite or technophobic form of reaction to contemporary innovations, moreover, preserving as it does a certain Romantic idea of the
human subject, manifests itself in a variety of ways – in appeals to
rights, selfhood and community, to newly aged nature, holistic
ecology and mysticism. As forms of self-preservation, they owe much
to the sublime in their representations of the riotously anarchic
freedoms of late liberal capitalism, of voracious consumerism, of
global destruction and of technological bewilderment. Informational
and post-industrial revolutions are presented in monstrously apocalyptic tones to exhume spectral memories of fuller times and evoke
residual resistances on the part of human ghosts. Both forms of
Romantic recurrence participate in an experience of the sublime.[8]
The difference is that the experience is negative for the techno-
phobes and positive for those Frankensteinian scientists attempting
to realise their all-too human dreams. (Frankenstein, of course,
endlessly reappears in accounts of new computer and biotechnologies.[9]) They are not simply mirror images: despite the similarities of
structure and the predominance of the sublime, different shapes
emerge. In reviewing the way Romanticism informs current speculations on technological futures (cyberomanticism) and the manner in
which current global crises are recognised in Romantic terms, this
essay traces the way sublime and uncanny figures recall the ghosts of
romance that haunted Romanticism's own self-definition. Recalling
a structure that entwines Romantic and Gothic writing in the
articulation of cultural crisis (how the imagination has always been
virtual), the implications of neuromanticisms for notions of the
human are assessed as both a repetition and a departure from the
structures of modernity.

   The point of convergence – in broad and brief terms – between
Romanticism and cyberculture occurs in the 1960s with the conjunction of social and cultural rebellion against state rationality, calls for
sexual, creative and mental liberation (the latter particularly associated with psychotropic drugs) and the conceptual innovations of the
new science, particularly in mathematics. It could be described as a
latter-day version of the stone and the shell. Two decades later,
contemporary technologies enable the presentation of an imagin-

ative plenitude and synthesis. Romantic projections become digitally realisable, in virtual terms at least. Indeed, the claims made for new electronic and biotechnologies restate Romantic aspirations: while psychedelic drugs render the accepted reality arbitrary, cyberspace allows the total manifestation of one's thoughts 'and reality itself conforms to the wave patterns'.[10] Communication between subjects is direct and immediate, or, as Terence McKenna observes of virtual reality, it occurs in an 'environment of language that is beheld rather than heard'.[11] Specular projection enables the direct and visual presentation of meaning: pure intersubjective communication. Community, too, is virtually restored on the internet.

McKenna also makes larger philosophical claims about the implications of biotechnology for the relationship of mind and body:

> this is the real thing. We're going to find out what 'being' is. It's a philosophical journey and the vehicles are not simply cultural but biology itself. We're closing the distance with the most profound event that a planetary ecology can encounter, which is the freeing of life from the chrysalis of matter.[12]

Being, it seems, is discoverable on the condition that life is detached from the 'material matrix'. In comparison, William Godwin's claims (while discussing the benefits of technological innovation) for the power of mind over matter seem utterly understated.[13]

The idealism of the claims of technophiliacs is nonetheless shadowed by less extravagant observations. John Barlow, co-founder of the Electronic Frontier Foundation, acknowledges the speed of technological innovation and comments that 'the only people who are going to be comfortable with that are people who don't mind confusions and ambiguity'.[14] Such contemporary negative capability, however, might frustrate subjects who want certainty and stability. Indeed, the cyberspatial progression towards the 'construction of the next delusional home for consciousness' may well involve an entirely different, more writerly, subject, suggested by Barlow's account of the 'cyber-village hall': 'in this silent world, all conversation is typed. To enter it one forsakes both body and place and becomes a thing of words alone.'[15] Though many of the Romantic versions of cyberculture have yet to be realised, the digital revolution is driven by the momentum of a curiously eroticised and poetic imagination, cyberspace construed as a 'habitat of the imagination'.[16]

Cyberculture, to update Jameson's (1984) map for the networks of transglobal capitalism, offers a figure of pervasive cultural and political changes.[17] These permeate the expanding study of Romanticism. New academic markets have emerged from the critical and theoretical revolutions of the last twenty years: in Romanticism, the study of romance and Gothic writing, like Mellor's feminist project, have shattered traditional periodised values and certainties to consume different textual products.[18] And, as Steven Goldsmith observes in a recent book on apocalypse and representation (understood in both a political and an aesthetic sense), the crisis is also one of liberal democracy.[19] For John Whale the instance of Ronald Reagan's citation of Thomas Paine in a presidential address is indicative of an ambivalence of late eighteenth-century radicalism: the liberalism it advocates, due to what Whale terms Paine's 'radical literalism' and universalising tendencies, remains appropriable by left or right.[20] Liberalism absorbs conventional oppositions between left and right, so much so that Paine can be declared 'patron saint of the Net' by *Wired* magazine as it advocates a technoradicalism of uninhibited individual and commercial freedoms for the new networked élite.[21] The collapse or collusion of the left–right opposition signals not only a political redundancy, but also a general absorption of politics and agency into the networks of an uncontrollable web of transnational capitalism. To bring Burke's comments on liberal democracy (specifically, the monstrous French constitution) into the present underlines the reversibility of conventional political opposition within a global networked state

wholly governed by the agitators in corporations, by societies in the towns formed of directors of assignats, and trustees for the sale of church lands, attornies, agents, money-jobbers, speculators, and adventurers, composing an ignoble oligarchy founded on the destruction of the crown, the church, the nobility, and the people. Here end all the deceitful dreams and visions of the equality and rights of men.[22]

Despite the inclination towards certain class interests, the image of rampant capitalism folds back on a Thatcherite present in its glimpse of a monetarist and libertarian excess that liberal democracy cannot contain.

Burke offers a vivid image of what Francis Fukuyama has called the 'end of history'.[23] Apocalytic tones resonate. Jerome Christensen has proposed a Romantic alternative to the end of history involving a move beyond ideology to a pretextual, practical

consciousness that can offer some form of 'challenge to commercialist hegemony', a Romanticism described as 'the real movement of
feeling that challenges the present state of things, including the
consensus that would bury it in the past, whether by omission or by
labelling it an ideology'.[24] Christensen's position depends on a
moment of recognition: 'the contemporary scene of imperial break-
up, ethnic crack-up, and commercialist mop-up closely, even eerily,
parallels the European aftermath of Waterloo, when commerce first
conquered conquest'.[25] The parallel is uncanny but the exhumation
of Romanticism, the calling up of a ghost already haunting the
present, constitutes another nostalgic appeal to a lost past, a gesture
of mourning that recognises a lack and vainly calls up an autonomous political agent who can resist the present state of things.
Christensen thus rather ironically repeats Burke's response to the
French Revolution, or the London seen by Wordsworth in 1802 and
in *The Prelude*.

For the subject once believing itself at the centre of history, the hero
of a particular Enlightenment narrative of progress and power, the
advent of the end of history, configuring an unthinkable assemblage of
economic and technological terrors, constitutes a sublime moment,
an awful glimpse of its own dissolution. The eeriness and uncanniness
of historical recurrence binds two ends of modernity over abyssal
crisis points. Sublime distintegration, the encounter with an unthinkable otherness, seems to govern both ends of modernity. In Lyotard's
celebrated report on knowledge, the postmodern does not succeed the
narratives of modernity but shadows them with the heterogeneity
associated with the sublime. Like the postmodern within modernity, it
'puts forward the unpresentable in presentation itself'.[26] In the same
vein, Patricia Waugh describes the way Romantic aesthetic impulses
have 'spilled over' into scientific and political domains leading to 'a
shared crisis mentality connected to a sense of the fragmentariness of
the commercialised world with which Enlightenment reason is seen to
be complicit: in both the aesthetic becomes the only possible means of
redemption'.[27] The sublimity of the crisis and extent of commerci-
alism, however, may well have exceeded the possibility of cognitive
mapping or aesthetic redemption.

The relation of the sublime to Romantic criticism is discussed in
Neil Hertz's account of the notion of blockage. The essay begins
with Thomas McFarland's commentary on the state of Romantic
criticism in 1976. The reading of McFarland examines comments

about the proliferating 'flood of publication' being a threat to the integrity of the Romantic scholar's mind.[28] McFarland's fear of computers writing for computers intensifies concerns about the way the informational sublime disturbs the equanimity and integrity of the reading subject. For Hertz (citing Thomas Weiskel), however, the excess of the sublime discloses an identification with the father, a point at which a paternal injunction inhibits and reduces – blocks – the bewildering movement of sublimity. Hertz argues that blockage is wanted:

the scholar's *wish* is for the moment of blockage, when an indefinite and disarrayed sequence is resolved (at whatever sacrifice) into a one-to-one confrontation, when numerical excess can be converted into that super-erogatory identification with the blocking agent that is the self's own guarantor of the self's own integrity as agent.[29]

The blockage renders dizzying, incomprehensible multiplicity singular, providing an object that remains constitutive of the subject or a site for terrific subjective recuperation. It is, indeed, the sublime terror that, for Burke, evokes instincts of self-preservation. While McFarland's object of anxiety is the computer, Wordsworth's fear, according to Hertz, is presented in the form of the city in Book VII of *The Prelude*. The city is thus Wordsworth's computer: Bartholomew Fair becomes 'a city within the City, a scale model of urban mechanisms, designed to focus his fear'. The 'rapid appositional sequence' of sights, sounds and signs confuses seeing and reading as it moves in a dream-like procession.[30]

In Mary Jacobus's account of Wordsworth's 'dream of language' (which focuses primarily on the dream of the Arab from Book V of *The Prelude*) it is unreadability which comes to the fore 'in the condensations and displacements of the dream-text' as well as in the figure of the blind beggar and the city which supplants the Alps with 'urban illegibility, a system of signs where differences ... have no law, no meaning, and no end'.[31] But where Hertz sees the encounter with the blind beggar as opening up a 'more radical flux and dispersion of the subject',[32] Jacobus looks at the constitutive, as well as the fragmenting, effects of the sublime:

vital or life giving anxiousness in Wordsworth's poetry characteristically gives rise to both motion and speciality: to intimations of a ghostly life beyond the image which at once blocks it out and conjures it into being (a process described by Coleridge as 'the substitution of a sublime feeling of the unimaginable for a mere image').[33]

The substitutions enabled by poetry – substitutions of a sublime feeling for an image – appear later in Book V with the 'mystery of words' passage. Language, there, exhibits an uncanny doubleness, its mystery veiling and revealing a ghostly life in the 'turnings intricate of verse'.

This doubleness is also important in considerations of the way the sublime drives the possibility of the imagination and distinguishes it from mere image. The anxiousness associated with the object of fear – the sublime feeling reduced to the blockage of a single thing – enables the poetic subject to reach a point of imaginative transcendence. For Jacobus, 'in London, Wordsworth, the imaginative showman, confronts us with the misbegotten forms of a materialized imagination in order to dissociate his own creative vision from its fallen counterpart'.[34] The materialised, mechanised imagination seen in London provides one image (the condensed chaos of images) that establishes the differential conditions, the object, against which the imagination rediscovers itself as subject or prime agent.

Transcendence remains, however, only an imaginary, specular and spectral moment of recovery: the ghostly life intimated beyond mere images remains dependent on the movements of the dream-text, on the dreams, phantasms and visions which allow for the disclosure of something beyond. But beyond or behind every sequence of images and signs lies something else. It is something, however, which may only be another text, another linguistic system, a 'ghostly language of the ancient earth', to quote Wordsworth. As Jacobus also notes, the occasion of Wordsworth's Arab dream lies in his reading of a biographical account of a dream by Descartes. Dreams, it seems, regularly announce the dark and ghostly machinations of texts that are recombined according to the unconscious logic of signification. The best example is perhaps De Quincey's opium dreams, where opium becomes an allegory, if not the cause, of the Romantic imagination. Opium takes the dreamer beyond temporal and spatial limits so that, for De Quincey, 'space swelled, and was amplified to an extent of unutterable infinity. This, however, did not disturb me as much as the vast expansion of time.'[35] Opium allows the 'fantastic imagery of the brain' to conjure up vast cities and temples and ' "from the anarchy of dreaming sleep", callest into sunny light the faces of long-buried beauties, and the blessed household countenances, cleansed from the "dishonours of the grave" '.[36] But the imaginative ascents and descents are literary effects, not the literal falls into 'chasms and sunless abysses' that De Quincey claims they are: the opium-eater says they recall the poetry of Coleridge, the drawings of Piranesi and Wordsworth's *Excursion*, which 'might have been copied from my architectural dreams'.[37] Dreams succeed rather than precede the poetry. The heights and depths of the dreams, moreover, disclose the shadowy power of the imagination as it loosens the connections between dreamer and human identity and reality, unwinding 'almost to its final links, the accursed chain which bound him' and darkly reformulating the imaginative aspirations of the first Romantic generation.[38]

Dreams – themselves an effect of reading according to De Quincey – deliver the imagination up to the movements of literary language, to the point that the imagination becomes the effect, not the cause of literature. Indeed, the imagination can be said to be virtual. For in its attempt to realise thoughts, to fully represent perception and thus close the gap between thought and thing, the imagination discloses the difference of words. For words, even as they articulate thoughts and things, approximate, shape and also diverge from the objects they present. Poetic language both presents and displaces the possibility of representational stability. As Robert Young argues in his Lacanian reading of *The Prelude*, the *objets a*, the objects of fear – the beggar, the city, the Arab – only redouble and displace the imagination, rather than providing it with stability:

imagination, the represencer of a lost totality and healer of wounds is the phantasmatic goal of Wordsworth's quest, haunting him with its lure of an I-magus power of mind over itself and its own evanescence. It becomes the idealised image that presents itself in the face of the mind's own division, image of the esemplastic faculty of undivided power. As imago, artifical representation of an object, the 'waxen image' which he himself has made, it is a suitable term for the desired stability of the *objet a*. But can't the imago as representation also be the imago as phantasm, ghost or apparition? Stability is undermined even by the images of the imagination themselves: wind, mist.[39]

For Young, the metaphor of synthesis claimed by the imagination dissolves in confusion and obscurity, leaving the subject annihilated before the desire of the Other, fading in the chains of signification that are supposed to confer his identity. Identity, like the imagination, becomes a phantasmatic, ghostly effect of language's metonymic movements.

This ghostliness, moreover, is an effect of a romance or Gothic imagination, the version of the imagination that has to be repressed as a materialised or mechanical imagination by Wordsworth, and turned into fancy by Coleridge in order to distinguish it from that which is truly Romantic. The latter is defined against (and also in terms of) the former in the *Biographia Literaria*. Describing the products of circulating libraries as idle wastes of time rather than valued reading, Coleridge goes on to examine the effects they inculcate as 'beggarly day dreaming', recalling the blind beggar of Wordsworth's London:

the whole *material* and imagery of the doze is supplied *ab extra* by a sort of mental *camera obscura* ... who *pro tempore* fixes, reflects and transmits the moving fantasms of one man's delirium, so as to people the barrenness of an hundred other brains afflicted with the same trance of suspension of all common sense and all definite purpose.[40]

It is not just that romances offer material and reflective images – 'moving fantasms' – of delirium, but that these singular reflections and materialisations have effects: they communicate with and contaminate other brains. Coleridge's criticism accords with eighteenth-century attacks on fiction. It echoes the abundant and virulent criticisms of romances and novels as sensational, unnatural and irrational wastes of time. But romances were dangerous too: they proliferated, according to John Cleland in 1751, as a 'flood of novels, tales, romances and other monsters of the imagination' that corrupted the minds and morals of readers; 'out of nature', they were 'monsters of perfection' that 'transport the reader unprofitably into the clouds, where he is sure to find no solid footing, or into those wilds of fancy, which go forever out of the way of human paths'.[41] The contaminations of fiction, the transports of metaphorical identification, subverted the symbolic structures of the conventionally real and proper world and led to disillusion, discontent and insubordination. As a dangerous torrent that threatened imminent social and familial breakdown, romances became sublime, as sublime, indeed, as the 'flood of publication' envisaged by Thomas McFarland in his account of Romantic criticism.

Like eighteenth-century critics, McFarland offers the properly paternal and authoritative solution: 'read less, not more'.[42] The discrimination and cultivated understanding of enlightened criticism meets a Romantic integration of awareness. McFarland echoes Coleridge, duplicating the critical position that Coleridge duplicates.

But the form of imagination deplored by the latter as 'beggarly day dreaming' enables the production of the Romantic imagination later in the *Biographia Literaria*: 'it is the prerogative of poetic genius to distinguish by parental instinct its proper offspring from the change-lings which the gnomes of vanity or the fairies of fashion may have laid in its cradle or called by its names.'[43] What separates the gnomes and fairies of romance imagination from the self-evident light and truth of Romantic imagination is the, undoubtedly pater-nal, power of that parental instinct called poetic genius. It is poetic genius that supplies the final and transcendental signified, the end point and cut of differentiation. Poetic genius arrests the moving fantasms, the material and images of beggarly day dreaming, the corrupting movements of romance delirium, with a paternal no.

A problem remains, however, for the Romantic imagination which is itself bound up with beggars, fantasms and dreams and tied to the necessary negative differentiation from their beggarly incarna-tion. But what is the difference? In 'Kubla Khan', a poem of the imagination if ever there was one, the material and images of beggarly day dreaming appear as Coleridge falls into his opium reverie 'in which all the images rose up before me as *things*'. Waking with a 'distinct recollection of the whole', the vision fragments after the interrupted attempt at dream transcription causes the whole to pass 'away like the images on the surface of a stream into which a stone has been cast'. The idea and wholeness of imaginative vision, fragmentarily present in the poem, is sustained only by the poet's assertion of his glimpse of totality, untranscribable though it was. All that affirms imagination is a poet's assertion of the kind advanced in *Biographia Literaria*: 'I am because I affirm myself to be.'[44] The poetic voice brings itself and its imaginative totality into existence. But it is an existence that remains virtual, an effect of poetic enunciation alone as it insists on a difference between the delirium of romance imagination and the truth of the Romantic one.

Metaphor not only substitutes images, it also arrests, anchors, their movement so that the subject can find some stability in the identification and affirmation of meaning. Between the delusional movements of romance imagining and the authoritative identifica-tion of Romantic imaginative assertion lies the minimal difference of an inaugural metaphor, the 'I' that symbolically substitutes itself and its identity for the real being of an inarticulate body in the act of enunciation enabled by self-affirming imaginary (mis)recognition.

The difference, and the effects, moreover, are articulated in Lacan's distinction between mourning and psychosis, the former associated with the paternal metaphor, the latter described as delusional.[45] But both states, for Lacan, appear as effects of loss, when the symbolic fabric (the Other) articulating conventional reality and subjectivity, has been rent (by death) to disclose a hole in the real. This hole appears sublime to the subject who experiences the loss. The experience of the hole in the real is similar in mourning and psychosis: swarms of images, signifiers torn from signifieds, cascading without a point to arrest their momentum or stabilise their meaning. In mourning, however, the loss is dealt with by identifying the object of anxiety (*objet a*) and reintegrating it by means of symbolic ritual into an order regulated by the paternal metaphor, the phallus. In psychosis, however, the direction is different: the law of the father, the Other is disavowed, and any metaphor takes its place in delusional form.

These states, then, as they describe an encounter with a crisis that is difficult for the subject to comprehend, seem to describe the condition of Romanticism as it confronts the multiple significance of an age rent by revolutions. In the age of electronic, capital and liberal revolutions, responses to the multiple effects of epochal crises are structured in a similar manner. In a contemporary context, Slavoj Žižek identifies a rift between nation and contemporary capitalism. As the permanent production of excess, capitalism cannot be regulated by a master discourse or paternal metaphor: 'with capitalism, however, this function of the Master [to provide just measure and prevent excess] becomes suspended, and the vicious circle of the superego spins freely'.[46] This is the state, for Burke, of the post-revolutionary French social, political and economic order and also the state of meanings and literature, encountered not only by Romantic poets, but by conservative Burkean critics like T. J. Matthias (1805).[47] It is also the state of contemporary hyperreality: as Baudrillard observes in *The Transparency of Evil*, the age of the transpolitical, transeconomic and transaesthetic means that there is no regulating totality or metaphor, no global paternal function.[48] Instead, everything is viral, connected in metonymic chains whose sliding cannot be arrested, delusional effects of signification as simulation.

But the crisis defining the state of Romanticism and the state of the present, though structured, re-presented or ghosted similarly is not the same. In an essay on cybernetic culture Bill Nicholls examines the shifting definitions of the human within different forms of capitalism: in early capitalism the human is defined in opposition to the animal or natural world; in monopoly capitalism it is the world of machines that becomes the object of differentiation and identity; while in post-industrial capitalism, cybernetic systems present the difference. The relation between the human and its other, however, remains ambivalent: 'human identity remains at stake, subject to change, vulnerable to challenge and modification as the very metaphors prompted by the imaginary Other that give it form change. The metaphor that's meant (that's taken as real) becomes the simulation.'[49] The ambivalence Nicholls identifies, moreover, disturbs the historical periodisation he proffers. Indeed, with Romanticism the ambivalence appears intense in respect of differentiations between the human, the natural, the machine and, in the shape of creations like scientific monsters, cybernetic systems as well. In regard to the present, moreover, Nicholls' narrative seems rather optimistic in imagining a transcendence (a negation, conservation and sublation of past forms): 'the cybernetic metaphor contains the germ of an enhanced future inside a prevailing model that substitutes part for whole, simulation for real, cyborg for human, conscious purpose for the decentred seeking of the totality'.[50] The organic metaphor, the germ of the future, remains unequivocally Romantic.

Other visions of the future are less Utopian in their transcendent prospects. Cyberpunk fiction, most notably. Which is not to say that novels like William Gibson's cyberpunk 'classic' *Neuromancer* are not Romantic, far from it. But its ways of envisaging a future within the terms of past figures stress important differences. *Neuromancer* reformats the matrix of romance and Romanticism. It relates a quest romance involving the penetration of a Gothic stronghold and the mystery of its labyrinth and the subversion of the power of a cloned and cryogenically frozen industrial dynasty. In a world of digitally organised corporate control, commercial and criminal exchanges of drugs, software and biotechnology go hand in hand. It is a near future in which immediate communication is a daily activity, where information is transmitted and received in an unmediated neural space, where memories are revived as ghostly holographic images, simulations undistinguishable from the lost origin. Humans have the capacity of 'dreaming real' and death is surpassed biologically and digitally: personality can be stored in data banks, overcoming the boundaries of life and death.[51] Cyberspace, moreover, offers other great Romantic syntheses. Humans are no longer restricted by time and space, 'jacking in' to the matrix (plugging one's brain directly into the datascape) allows mind to transcend matter in the 'bodiless exultation of cyberspace'.[52] For the subject consciousness 'divided like beads of mercury... his vision was spherical, as though a single retina lined the inner surface of a globe that contained all things, if all things could be counted'.[53] The matrix presents the specular subject with complete imaginative plenitude.

The matrix is sublime: in its play of light and dark, imaginative possibility and shadowy powers, the infinity of data takes the form of a cityscape with its awesome towers of ICE and immense spires of gleaming data. This awesome and aestheticised realm overcomes the Romantic antithesis of country and city in a virtual dimension which allows the subject – the console cowboy – to wander as freely as any poet. The sublime space of the matrix also takes the subject beyond consciousness – to encounter the braindeath of the flatline: 'beyond ego, beyond personality, beyond awareness he moved... grace of the mind-body interface granted, in that second by the clarity and singleness of his wish to die'.[54] The synthesis of mind and body, self and Other, obliterates all separation in a singularly fatal fusion. The locus of this fusion, the Other, is the matrix itself:

Cyberspace. A consensual hallucination experienced daily by billions of legitimate operators, in every nation ... a graphic representation of data abstracted from the banks of every computer in the human system. Unthinkable complexity. Lines of light ranged in the nonspace of the mind, clusters and constellations of data. Like city lights, receding...[55]

This graphic abstraction realised neurally in the brain also represents the dreamspace of the Romantic imagination, mind and totality united like a digital aeolian harp. But, like dreams, they fade, too absolute for the human subject. In the novel, the actual subjects are not human at all, but two AIs, Wintermute and Neuromancer, artificial intelligences engaged in a struggle to become a new entity. Wintermute is 'live mind', machinic, chill rationality fused with the desire for new synthesis, a process Neuromancer resists.[56] The latter is personality, creation, immortality, a necromancer of the nerves calling up dead and perfectly simulated beings. Indeed, in this neural romance of personality, the living dead of the matrix's data banks combine to form a new being, a higher consciousness transcending that of humans. There is, however, the spectacle of ultimate fusion, a perfect Hegelian synthesis, an absolute transcendence resulting from the union of Wintermute and Neuromancer. In a discussion at the end of the novel between Case, the human protagonist, and the new entity, the totality of the transcendence is made plain: 'I'm the matrix', it says, 'Nowhere. Everywhere. I'm the sum total of the works, the whole show.'[57] God, indeed, but not the naturalised or humanised image of absolute being. Humans are left behind: transcendence or synthesis is not theirs, the final signified is, as always, somewhere else.

This inhuman conclusion might well conspire in the negatively sublime and dystopic renderings of the near future, as happens in the novel itself. The computer police arrest Case for what is no less than species treason: 'You have no care for your species. For thousands of years men dreamed of pacts with demons. Only now are such things possible.'[58] Recognising the inhuman implications of artificial life, they present the future as a Gothic romance in which realisable monsters of the imagination transport one forever out of the way of human paths. The flight of metaphor, the excesses of romance imagination continue to threaten and, ultimately, dispel illusions of human security and transcendence.

Left behind, the human figure becomes empty and utterly unbound. Another repetition of Romanticism, of a romanticised dissolution, sees the subject teetering on the sublime brink of ultimate horror. As Nick Land observes, 'the high road to thinking no longer passes through a deepening of human cognition, but rather through a becoming inhuman of cognition, a migration of cognition out into the emerging technosentience reservoir, into "dehumanized landscapes . . . emptied spaces" where human culture will be dissolved'.[59] The arrival of cyberculture, then, leaves the human figure, romantically, like Wordsworth in the dream of the Arab (or Percy Shelley glimpsing the awesome Power of 'Mont Blanc', or Manfred proposing self-oblivion or John Clare envisioning eternity or Baudrillard in the deserts of America) anxiously confronting the desolate and awful zones of a symbolic and real vacuity.[60] But, in *Neuromancer*, the meat – the accursed share of technological redundancy and thus a residually human organic part – continues to talk: 'it'll change something'.

CHAPTER 8

The sins of the fathers: the persistence of Gothic

John Fletcher

This essay is an attempt to describe the literary idea of the Gothic, and to relate its organising thematic as an imaginary version of history to the experience of secular modernity and Enlightenment and to its capacity as a hardy literary perennial to re-seed itself in new circumstances. In particular it will make use of Freud's analysis of the Uncanny as a psychic and aesthetic phenomenon and will consider two widely separated works, E. T. A. Hoffman's *The Sandman* (1816), discussed at length by Freud and roughly coeval with the end of the first flourishing period of Gothic writing in English, together with a contemporary mass cultural text, the Hammer Horror film *Hands of the Ripper* (1971), an instance of the current revival of Gothic themes and narratives in popular forms. The British Hammer Gothics like the US 'Poe cycle' directed by Roger Corman might be compared to the early nineteenth century Gothic chapbooks and Bluebooks that re-cycled for a larger mass audience the expensive three-volume productions of the 'Terrorists' destined for the middle-class lending libraries.[1]

THE MOBILITY OF GOTHIC

Technically, the Enlightenment dispensed with the patriarchy: it gave up the cult of the ancestor ... Ferdinand Tonnies defined the modern as one who feels free to forget the dead.[2]

In 1697, at the turn of the seventeenth century, John Evelyn in his *Account of Architects and Architecture*, wrote:

It is the ancient Greek and Roman Architecture which is here intended, as most entirely answering all those Perfections required in a faultless and accomplished Building; such as for so many Ages were so renowned and reputed by the universal Suffrages of the civilized World, and would doubtless have still subsisted, and made good their Claim, and what is recorded of them, had not the Goths, Vandals and other barbarous Nations subverted and demolished them, together with that glorious Empire, where those stately and pompous Monuments stood, introducing in their stead, a certain fantastical and licentious Manner of Building, which we have since called Modern (or Gothic rather), Congestions of heavy, dark, melancholy and Monkish Piles, without any just Proportion, Use or Beauty, compared with the truly Ancient.[3]

We have here a contrast between a lost civilised Perfection, the classical heritage of Greece and Rome, embodied in an Empire, and the intervening Dark Ages whose agents are the barbarous Goths and Vandals; it involves a temporal contrast of 'the modern (or Gothic rather)' as against 'the truly Ancient'. Twenty-eight years later in 1725, Alexander Pope, in the preface to his edition of the plays of Shakespeare, wrote:

I will conclude by saying of Shakespeare, that with all his faults, and with all the irregularity of his drama, one may look upon his works, in comparison with those that are more finished and regular, as upon an ancient majestic piece of Gothic architecture compared with a neat modern building: the latter is more elegant and glaring, but the former is more strong and more solemn. It must be allowed, that in one of these there are materials enough to make many of the other. It has much the greater variety, and much the nobler apartments, though we are often conducted to them by dark, odd, and uncouth passages. Nor does the whole fail to strike us with greater reverence, though many of the parts are childish, ill-placed, and unequal to its grandeur.[4]

Here the Gothic has been re-aligned. It now contrasts with the modern and has come to signify ancientness. It involves an imaginary reference back to a repudiated but newly fascinating past that is now felt to possess majesty, strength and solemnity. No Goth, however, as Chris Baldick has remarked, ever wrote a Gothic novel or even built a Gothic cathedral.[5] What these opposed usages of the term 'Gothic' make evident is that it functions, through all the bewildering range of objects to which it has been applied, in some way analogous to a shifter in linguistics. It positions its object of reference, either by alignment or contrast with the present moment of enunciation, in the temporal schema of an imaginary history. In this we can glimpse something of its original ideological function as a denunciatory term designating the recent medieval and Catholic past and its cultural residues, as barbarous, superstitious, monkish – the Dark Ages.

Evelyn still participates in that humanist polemic in which, as long as the Gothic designates those aspects of the dominant cultural formations that are to be displaced, it is wholly negative. For Pope, writing with the self-consciously Augustan confidence of the 1720s, the modern is regular and correct, and Shakespeare's dramaturgy, with its mixing of theatrical genres and its hyperbolic and conceited rhetoric considered 'irregular' by much Augustan taste, is designated Gothic, albeit a Gothic that is now felt to be 'ancient and majestic' even if in parts 'dark, odd, and uncouth'. This shift by which the Gothic is no longer a synonym for the modern as against 'the truly Ancient' as for Evelyn, but comes to designate that which has been lost, from which we the moderns are separated, the other in antithesis to modernity, is a movement that reconstitutes the Gothic, through a process of cultural mourning, as a lost object of nostalgia and admiration, alongside the negative connotations of the uncouth and the irregular that still operate in Pope's passage. Even in Evelyn's denunciation of the Gothic disorder and irregularity faced with which 'a judicious Spectator is rather distracted and quite confounded',[6] one may detect retrospectively the emergent features of a proto-Sublime; for these features will be revalued by Burke, as the pleasurably agitating and terrifyingly vertiginous state of mind, produced by the Sublime as an ungraspable and non-totalisable form.[7] With this reversal and transvaluation the Gothic becomes the discourse of modernity about its own pre-history, about the archaic that has been surpassed for modernity to be put in place. It is in that very movement, however, that the Gothic has potentially become the repository of whatever is felt to have been lost in the advance of civilisation and Enlightenment. These connotations and positionings are relatively independent of content, however, as we can see in the historical irony of Pope's designating Shakespeare's plays, of all things, as Gothic; for Shakespeare's plays are the products of that Renaissance humanism embodied and transmitted in the classical syllabus of the Tudor grammar school and university that formulated the denunciation of Gothic in the first place.

Forty years after Pope's Preface, Horace Walpole published in 1765 *The Castle of Otranto: a Gothic Story*, the first self-consciously Gothic novel in English. The title-page of the first edition describes it as translated by 'William Marshall Gent.' from the original Italian of Onuphrio Muralto, Canon of the Church of St Nicholas at Otranto. The preface speculates that it was possibly written in

Italian sometime between 1095 and 1243, first printed in Naples in 1529 in the Gothic black letter, and recently rediscovered by the translator 'in the library of an ancient catholic family in the north of England'.[8] Walpole's Preface is a fascinating mixture of recommendation and disavowal. The story is commended for the purity of its Italian style, its lessons of virtue and 'the rigid purity of its sentiments'. The element of the miraculous, however, is apologised for and deprecated – all the supernatural romance machinery of miracles, visions, necromancy and dreams – and its author, 'the artful priest', writing as a defender of the empire of superstition, is attributed with the intention to 'confirm the populace in its ancient errors and superstitions ... his work can only be laid before the public at present as a matter of entertainment'. After the great and unanticipated success of the first edition, Walpole came modestly before the public as the real author in the Preface to the second edition some four months later, confessing that his ambition was 'to blend the two kinds of romance, the ancient and the modern', to combine the supernatural machinery of the marvellous from the ancient romance with the psychological and behavioural verisimilitude of the so called modern romance, the novel, arguing that in the modern romance 'the great resources of fancy have been dammed up, by a strict adherence to common life'.[9] Significantly he justifies this hybridisation of verisimilitude and the marvellous by appeal to a Shakespeare who is 'Gothic' in Pope's sense, and whose generic crossing Walpole defends from Voltaire's notorious denunciation of Shakespeare's barbarism in the name of the neoclassical unities.

Walpole's literary model is not, however, ancient or medieval romance at all but Shakespeare and the Jacobean drama. He takes over the drama's five act structure, and the narrative material of ducal or princely usurpation, ghostly visitation, incest and beseiged virtue, the sententious utterances of the noble characters as against the garrulousness of the low-life characters, even the labyrinthine interiors of court and castle come straight out of *Hamlet* or the tragedies of Webster or Beaumont and Fletcher. This might lead one to ask why *Hamlet*, *The Revenger's Tragedy*, *The Duchess of Malfi* or *The Maid's Tragedy* are not Gothic texts given the similarities of their material to much later Gothic narrative, and I think the answer must lie in the relation of the drama's crimes and marvels to the question of modernity. For the tyrannous Italian or Spanish dukes and usurpers of the Jacobean stage are felt to be excitingly modern, and the courts of southern Catholic Europe presented as the site of a *realpolitik* embodied in the new and scandalous figure of the machiavel. Italy, in particular, for the sixteenth- and early seventeenth-century English, even for a virtuously Protestant figure like Milton, is still in the cultural vanguard of Classical and Humanist learning. Where the ghosts and crimes of *Hamlet* have a northern European and so potentially 'Gothic' ambience, Shakespeare has notably 'modernised' the ancient Scandinavian setting of his sources. The student-prince of Denmark has lately come from Luther's Wittenberg, one of the intellectual centres of international Protestantism as a militant movement of renovation and reform, and the play is strikingly filled with the latest gossip about the boy-actors and theatres of contemporary London. Nothing could be less 'Gothic' in Walpole's sense of the word. For the bourgeois and even aristocratic practitioners of the late eighteenth-century English Gothic novel, southern Catholic Europe with its Inquisition and still feudal *ancien régime* could represent the unreformed, unenlightened and unreconstructed past. The North/South polarity in the imaginary mapping of cultural progress had been reversed. Modernity and its cultural avant-garde were firmly Northern European and British. The Gothic works at the interface between these different temporalities, between modernity and its pre-history. Gothic narrative as a generic hybrid from its first instance has that characteristic apparatus of documentation, meta-commentary and scholarly verification that seeks to ground its construction of the marvellous by locating it in the remote and barbarous past. The Gothic fabrication of the ancient and the marvellous from the beginning works through a mimicry of the procedures of scholarly and critical truth-telling, through an appeal to a reader located in a present moment of non-marvellous and incredulous modernity.

For a general theory of the Gothic the most significant element is the following disavowal from Walpole's Preface to the first edition:

Yet I am not blind to my author's defects. I could wish he had grounded his plan on a more useful moral than this, that *the sins of the fathers are visited on their children to the third and fourth generation*.[10]

My major proposition will be that this 'unuseful' – i.e. Gothic and superstitious – moral, with its burdened legacy of ancestral and patriarchal guilt, 'the sins of the fathers', is encrypted at the heart of all Gothic fiction and might be said to constitute its problematic as a genre: its concern with lineage, heritage, patrimony and the transmission of dark secrets, history as nightmare.

A further differentiation is necessary, however, to specify the
Gothic as a generic tradition, and that is a differentiation between
the Gothic as a literary idea and the Gothic as it operates in the
discourses of architectural and art history. I will dramatise this
differentiation as a distinction between the Gothic House and the
Gothic Cathedral as different kinds of retrospective cultural construction. As well as writing the first Gothic novel in English, Horace
Walpole also built the first Gothic Revival house, Strawberry Hill,
outside London. In 1747 Walpole bought, in Pope's phrase 'a neat
modern building', and gradually Gothicised it in the course of the
1750s, a process by which Gothic motifs such as arched doors and
windows, niches, fan-vaulting, tracery and finials were reduced to a
system of ornamentation and applied to an essentially eighteenth-
century structure. Strawberry Hill has no relation to the constructional principles of medieval architecture and Walpole made no
attempt to reproduce medieval domestic space. His antiquarian
interest in the Gothic is a form of pastiche, lovingly modelling his
fireplaces on the tombs of Westminster Abbey that were denounced
seventy years before by John Evelyn ('let any Man of Judgement look
awhile upon King Henry the Seventh's Chappel at Westminster ...
on its sharp jetties, narrow Lights, lame Statues, lace, and other
cutwork and crinkle-crankle'[11]). Walpole's Gothic house is essentially
a literary fantasy in plaster, papier-mâché and imitation stonework.
All 'cutwork and crinkle-crankle', it was dismissed contemptuously
as 'a Gothic mouse-trap'[12] by William Beckford, author of *Vathek*
(1782) and builder of Fonthill Abbey whose octagonal tower more
than 276 feet high came crashing down in 1825 some twenty odd
years after it was built.

Neither Walpole's filigree 'Gothick' nor Beckford's gargantuan
sublime were based on the reconstruction of medieval built forms,
but were concerned with the production of an imaginary *mise en
scène*. Like the term Gothic itself, the Gothic house is a culturally
mobile form that even in its earliest manifestations had but an
allusive and imaginary reference to medieval realities. The Dark
House on the Hill in Hitchcock's *Psycho* (1960) that looms menacingly
behind the 1950s motel is an exemplary instance of this mobility of
the literary Gothic. Architecturally it is a late nineteenth-century
suburban mansion with a mansard roof and nothing of the medieval

about it. It is however the Gothic Dark House, which materialises in Baldick's succinct and suggestive formula 'a fearful sense of inheritance in time with a claustrophobic sense of enclosure in space'.[13] In the course of the narrative the motel, which is part of the film's American 1950s world of cheap hotels, estate agents' offices and secondhand car lots, is gradually gothicised and rendered sinister as the site of Norman Bates's entrapment in the past and its compulsive repetition in the present. The motel parlour with its Victorian interior and stuffed owls signals the migration of the Gothic from the Dark House on the hill into the contemporary world of the motel, and its usurpation of modernity is confirmed when we learn that the new highway has by-passed the motel which has now become a backwater.

Kate Ferguson Ellis in her study of early Gothic fiction, *The Contested Castle*,[14] has suggested a gendered typology of Gothic narratives with respect to the Gothic House and its domestic world. She distinguishes a female Gothic or 'insider' narrative of entrapment and claustration in the Gothic House that is pertinent to the social confinement of women in the late eighteenth and early nineteenth centuries within the family and the ideology of the domestic sphere, and their disempowerment as independent economic and political agents. The lineaments of this tradition are clear from Anne Radcliffe's *The Mysteries of Udolpho* (1794) to Charlotte Brontë's *Jane Eyre* (1847) to Charlotte Perkins Gilman's *The Yellow Wallpaper* (1892) to Daphne Du Maurier's *Rebecca* (1938) and Shirley Jackson's *The Haunting of Hill House* (1959) and beyond.[15] By contrast she distinguishes a male Gothic or 'outsider' paradigm which helps to bring into focus a group of narratives, Lewis's *The Monk* (1796), Godwin's *Caleb Williams* (1794), Hoffman's *The Sandman* (1816), Maturin's *Melmoth the Wanderer* (1820), Hogg's *Confessions of a Justified Sinner* (1824) which one can extend to include Dickens's *The Mystery of Edwin Drood* (1870), Stevenson's *The Strange Case of Dr Jekyll and Mr Hyde* (1886), James's *The Jolly Corner* (1908) and perhaps Bram Stoker's *Dracula* (1897) among others, that turn on a mirroring or doubling of the male protagonist and a story of persecution, exile or wandering. She correlates this typology with the different positions of men and women in relation to the domestic world within an ideology of 'separate spheres'.

This typology has a suggestive pertinence as long as a simple correlation of author and narrative is not assumed, and a certain

GOTHIC IS A GENRE OF OUTSIDERS + EVEN PRISONERS

cross-gendering is allowed. For from Walpole's *Otranto* (1765) to Poe's *The Fall of the House of Usher* (1839) to Wilkie Collins's *The Woman in White* (1860) and Dickens's *Great Expectations* (1860) to Henry James's *The Turn of the Screw* (1898) it is clear that the 'female' Gothic paradigm of the-woman-in-the-house has been a central preoccupation of male authors and characterises many male-authored Gothic texts. The reverse relation is less common, but the possibility of a female-authored 'male' Gothic narrative of doubling, persecution and exile from the domestic exactly characterises the enigmas of Mary Shelley's *Frankenstein* (1818) in relation to gender that have led feminist critics to pose the question, 'Is there a woman in this text?'[16] The logic of the Uncanny as articulated by Freud is, I will argue, relevant to both male and female paradigms.

By contrast with the Gothic House from Walpole's Otranto to Hitchcock's motel, the Gothic Cathedral comes to signify a tradition of architectural scholarship, reconstruction and innovation that distinguishes rather than confuses the Romanesque from the Norman, from the various gradations of early English and high Gothic – the tradition of Pugin, Ruskin and Morris. In 1853 John Ruskin published *The Stones of Venice* containing his famous chapter, 'The nature of Gothic', and which William Morris was to republish forty years later as a separate book from the Kelmscott Press. It elaborated a Utopian critique of the intellectual and manual divisions of labour as developed within the work processes of industrial capitalism, in particular of the de-skilled, repetitive and alienated nature of production-line factory work. By contrast it celebrated a division of labour in which, Ruskin argued, the anonymous collectivity of craftsmen who built the great cathedrals allowed for the expression of a labourer's unalienated pleasure in his labour. This ethical and political criticism produced an aesthetic where, in Morris's formulations, 'art is the expression of man's pleasure in his labour' and 'beauty is once again the natural and necessary accompaniment of productive labour'.[17] Associated with a critique of an industrialised, market-driven society, the return to an idealised pre-capitalist collective past is the springboard for a Utopian vision of a future society, as in Morris's *Dream of John Ball* (1886), where the defeated fourteenth-century peasant leader, John Ball, has a vision of a future socialist society on the other side of a capitalism that was itself yet to come. The Gothic as a vehicle of social critique and Utopian hope here rejoins modernity and even Modernism.

The emblem of this is Lyonel Feininger's neo-cubist woodcut, 'The Cathedral of Socialism', published in the Bauhaus Manifesto of 1919.[18] This referred to the conception of its author, Walter Gropius, of an integral or total work of art that would bring together all the arts and crafts. This 'crystal symbol of a new and coming faith', he called the 'Cathedral of Socialism'.[19] The literary Gothic, by contrast, centred on the Gothic or Dark House, is governed by a different dynamic, which is one of repetition and return – the sins of the fathers – in an introverted and familial space of private fantasy, rather than a collective vision of social transformation. The theorist of this tradition, I will suggest, is Sigmund Freud.

PSYCHOANALYSIS AS A GOTHIC SCIENCE

When Freud's father died, he dreamed of a plaque bearing the injunction: 'You are requested to close the eyes'.[20] In John Huston's biopic of the young Freud – *Freud: the Secret Passion* (1960) – loosely based on Sartre's rejected script, Freud is represented as free associating round this mysterious command, trying to understand his inability to enter the cemetery and stand by his father's grave and its puzzling representation in his dream. The association that comes to him is the biblical injunction: 'The sons shall close their eyes to the sins of the fathers.' Freud thinks he has recovered a repressed memory of having witnessed a scene of seduction between his father and his sister, and it is this refusal to close his eyes that is keeping him from discharging his filial and ritual duty. It turns out that his sister had not been born at the time the memory claims to date from; Freud exonerates his father, accuses himself of a rivalrous jealousy that sought to dishonour him, and goes on to postulate infantile eroticism and the Oedipus Complex and to invent psychoanalysis. Huston's film closes with the young Freud heroically proclaiming his scandalous theses in the teeth of an enraged Viennese medical establishment and finally being able to stand in filial acknowledgement by his father's grave. The question as to whether he has obeyed the injunction and closed his eyes, and what relation psychoanalysis might have to 'the sins of the fathers' remains unanswered.

Freud represents himself as moving from an appeal to the real event of actual seduction as the cause of the special case of hysteria to the centrality of unconscious fantasy in the formation of sexuality in general. This emphasis is always in uneasy alliance with a recourse to biology on the one hand, and a neo-Lamarckian conception of an acquired heritage of memory traces of pre-historic events on the other. Freud postulates a universally transmitted set of fantasies that he calls the primal fantasies, which give a distinctive structuration to psychic life and especially sexuality. These take the form of three scenes that centre on the symbolic father or *Urvater* – the father's seduction of the daughter, the father's threatened castration of the son, both of which form attendant scenes of a triptych, on either side of what comes to be designated in the singular as the primal scene: the father's prior and violent possession or rape of the mother. Laplanche and Pontalis in their classic essay, 'Fantasy and the Origins of Sexuality',[21] stress the connection with Freud's 1908 paper 'On the Sexual Theories of Children' which first described these fantasies systematically as childish speculations driven by the questions, 'Where do babies come from?' and 'What is the difference between the sexes?'. They interpret them as subjective myths of origins.

Walpole's Gothic theme of 'the sins of the fathers' remains a never satisfactorily formulated irritant at the heart of Freud's work. He returns again and again to the problem of cultural and psychic transmission across the generations. There is the dubious Lamarckian hypothesis of a genetically transmitted heritage of scenes and memories that are said to be the expression in myth and legend, personal fantasy and neurosis, of the unconscious memory traces of patriarchal pre-history, the savage dramas of the *Urvater*, or primal father, despot of the primal horde and possessor of its women, against, whom the sons band together and perpetrate the primal crime of patricide. It is these scenes that reappear in the form of the primal fantasies, Freud speculates, as infantile myths of origins through which the child elaborates imaginary solutions to the enigmas of his existence. There are also the anthropological concepts of totem and taboo with their account of cultural tradition as a compulsive transmission of non-negotiable and absolute injunctions and prohibitions from one generation to another. There are the extraordinary speculations of *Moses and Monotheism* (1939) about the transmission of a collective guilt in Jewish history for the murder of Moses the primal lawgiver. Freud compared this store of phylogenetic schemas and inherited fantasies to the Kantian transcendental categories of space, time, causality etc. that organise the influx of sense-data derived from actual experience. They are, he claimed, 'precipitates from the history of human civilization'.[22] Laplanche and Pontalis suggest a way of reading this encapsulation of the structuring role of primal fantasies within the framework of phylogenesis 'as a prefiguration of the "symbolic order" defined by Lévi-Strauss and Lacan in the ethnological and psychoanalytic fields respectively'.[23] Pre-history and its phylogenetic heritage, they suggest, are the theoretical symptom of an impasse in Freud's thought, trapped in a binary opposition of inner and outer, subjective fantasy and the real event. They are the substitute for a missing concept of structure, an order of signifiers that pre-exist the subject, a premature structuralism *avant la lettre*.

The French tradition of psychoanalysis in various ways can be seen to address this Gothic problematic at the heart of psychoanalysis, Lacan's neo-structuralist account of the Symbolic order of signifiers, rooted in Lévi-Strauss's theory of kinship structures, Laplanche's own more recent theories of the enigmatic signifier and the psychotic enclave that give a fundamental role to parental inscriptions and implantations in psychic life. However, it is in the work of Nicholas Abraham and Maria Torok that an explicitly Gothic imagery and terminology enters into psychoanalytic theory. Abraham and Torok are concerned with the formation of a psychic crypt for the burial of a forbidden and determining word, the trace of a secret drama, that cannot be uttered as such but only finds expression through allosemes and synonyms, that function as cryptonyms (words that hide). Incorporated into the psychic structure of the child, these undead parental secrets give rise to what Abraham calls the phantom-effect, that is not identifiable with the traditional conception of the dynamic unconscious. In his essay, 'Notes on the Phantom: a Complement to Freud's Metapsychology' (1975), Abraham argues that 'the phantom is meant to objectify... the gap that the concealment of some part of a loved one's life produced in us ... Consequently, what haunts us are not the dead, but the gaps left within us by the secrets of others.'[24] What is at issue here is a particular form of cross-generational transmission of trauma that cannot be verbalised or acknowledged in the earlier generation, yet remains active but unspeakable. 'It is the children's or descendants' lot to objectify these buried tombs through diverse species of ghosts. What comes back to haunt are the tombs of others ... the burial of an unspeakable fact within the loved one' (p. 288). The phantom, then, is not the expression of the living subject's own wishes, forbidden or otherwise, as in the classical model of repression followed by the return of the repressed. The phantom 'passes from the parent's unconscious to the child's ... it works like a ventriloquist, like a stranger within the subject's own mental topography' (pp. 289–90). 'The phantom which returns to haunt bears witness to the existence of the dead buried within the other' (p. 291). It is sustained by secreted words that can dominate the subject's entire life in the form of phobias, obsessions, that can be libidinally invested and set the terms for hobbies, leisure or indeed intellectual activities. Abraham comments, 'These are often the words that rule an entire family's history and function as the tokens of its pitiable articulations' (p. 292).[25] With the work of Abraham and Torok, psychoanalysis begins to acknowledge its vocation as a Gothic science of family transmissions and secrets, and to accord a properly metapsychological status to the sins of the fathers and the Gothic logic of return and repetition by which they rise and walk down the generations.

FREUD AND THE UNCANNY

Freud's work in general and his 1919 essay on 'The Uncanny' (*Das Unheimliche*)[26] in particular provide us with some fruitful elements for theoretical reflection on the Gothic. The 1919 essay covering the field of the ghostly and the spectral, of doubles and reflections, locates the Uncanny in three ways:

(1) socially, as the apparent and disturbing confirmation of previously surmounted animistic and supernatural beliefs and superstitions within a modern, secular culture: the social uncanny;

(2) psychically, as the return of what was once familiar and known but has been submitted to repression – the return of the repressed: the personal uncanny; he gives as analogies the repetition of what was once desired or loved in the form of phobic objects and the persecutory figures of paranoia;

(3) aesthetically, as the generic mixing of verisimilitude and the marvellous but with a different effect from Walpole's hybrid. Freud remarks that the events that would be uncanny in one literary convention lose their uncanniness in a different one, e.g. the marvellous events of fairy tales, the New Testament miracles,

the ghosts in *Julius Caesar* or *Macbeth* are not uncanny because they testify to the laws of a supernatural or magical universe as generically specified. They only become uncanny when they are in conflict with the generic world of the text, the postulates of the 'common reality' of secular modernity and its literary regimes of realism and naturalism.

Freud's insistence on the Uncanny as an event that disrupts the rules of verisimilitude anticipates Tzvetan Todorov's structural account of the Fantastic and its relations to the Uncanny and the Marvellous.[27] Todorov argues that the Fantastic is constituted as a genre by a continually maintained hesitation as to whether apparently supernatural events are susceptible to a rational explanation and so are shown to be in conformity with the secular universe of modernity, or whether they are indeed as they appear and so testify to a supernatural or magical world. For Todorov the Fantastic is not an autonomous genre, but is constituted as a hesitation on the borderline between two adjacent genres, the Uncanny and the Marvellous – what Todorov calls the Uncanny being the realm of the supernatural explained, and the Marvellous the supernatural sustained. The literary Gothic, he adds, can fall into either of these two genres while the Fantastic is the very hesitation between them, an evanescent genre that disappears retrospectively if the hesitation is resolved one way or the other.

Freud's account of the Uncanny appears to share with Todorov the insistence on the necessary contradiction between the supernatural and the reader's expectation of the rationally explicable. However, Freud can be said to reject in advance, so to speak, Todorov's version of a hesitation between alternatives, an either/or logic that can be resolved or not one way or the other. He does this in his discussion of E. T. A. Hoffman's novella *The Sandman* as an example of the literary Uncanny. Freud begins by rejecting the argument of the German psychologist Jentsch (1906)[28] that the Uncanny in Hoffman's tale is caused by the reader's uncertainty as to whether the figure of Olympia is a living person or a doll. Freud rejects the Jentsch/Todorov argument that the hesitation and uncertainty are the basis for the uncanny effect in the story. Freud locates the Uncanny instead in the figure of the Sandman from whom the tale takes its title. The Sandman with his repeated threat to the protagonist Nathaniel's eyes, Freud argues, is a castrating paternal imago returning from Nathaniel's infantile past and the reader's. This locates the Uncanny firmly in the field of Walpole's Gothic moral that the sins of the fathers return to the third and fourth generations.

Freud's conception of the relations between the Uncanny and its opposite, the known and familiar, is subtler than Todorov's account of a hesitation followed by an either/or decision. Working through the entries in various German dictionaries Freud traces a signifying drift that throws into crisis the clear-cut binary opposition that appears to hold between the pair of German terms, *heimlich* and *unheimlich*, canny and uncanny. This is an opposition between, on the one hand, the known and familiar, the domestic and intimate 'security as in the four walls of one's own house'[29] – and its opposite, the strange, the unknown or disturbing, on the other. While the *Unheimliche/*Uncanny begins as the negation of the *Heimliche*, by a process of semantic slippage, or drift, from the first signification of *Heimlich* as the familiar and the domestic there evolves a second signification – what is hidden, concealed from sight, withheld from others, secretive, sinister, even taboo, as in the *heimlich* chamber or toilet, the *heimlich* chair, the *heimlich* or private parts; magic as the *heimlich* art. Freud cites from Sanders's *Wörterbuch der Deutschen Sprache* (1860) an example of this slippage at work:

'The Zecks [a family name] are all "heimlich".' in sense II. ' "Heimlich"? ... What do you mean by "heimlich"?' 'Well, ... they are like a buried spring or a dried-up pond. One cannot walk over it without always having the feeling that water might come up there again.' 'Oh, we call it "unheimlich", you call it "heimlich". Well, what makes you think that there is something secret and untrustworthy about this family?' [30]

The archaic root meaning is relevant here: *Heim* signifies the home, household or family. As Freud remarks, 'From the idea of homelike, belonging to the house, the further idea is developed of something withdrawn from the eyes of strangers, secretive' and he summarises its paradoxical logic: 'Thus *heimlich* is a word the meaning of which develops in the direction of ambivalence, until it finally coincides with its opposite *unheimlich* [uncanny]. *Unheimlich* is in some way or other a sub-species of *heimlich*' (p. 226). The deconstructive implications of Freud's argument are clear, as Derrida and others have seen: the *Unheimliche/*Uncanny does not lie outside the *Heimliche*, in a relation of inside/outside, governed by the law of mutual exclusion and non-contradiction. Rather the *Unheim-*

liche is that species of strangeness, of the alien that breaks out from within. As Freud notes, the Uncanny appears as a sub-species of the term it negates. It is the concealed or shadowed side of the *Heimliche* that improperly emerges. In Schelling's definition cited by Freud, 'everything is *unheimlich* that ought to have remained secret and hidden but which has come to light' (p. 225). The *Unheimliche/* Uncanny is a doubling or return of the *Heimliche*, a disturbing repetition. To rephrase Freud, the *Heimliche* through its signifying drift coincides with its opposite so as to include or intern it.

One can draw two conclusions from this:

(1) Todorov's structural account of a hesitation followed by a choice between clear cut alternatives is undermined by the way in which in Freud's account the Uncanny inhabits its opposite and breaks out from within. One tendency in Freud's essay is indeed to account for the Uncanny as 'that class of the frightening which leads back to what is known of old and long familiar' (p. 220). This runs the risk of domesticating the Uncanny, merely reducing the alien to the familiar while leaving the latter reassuringly untouched. This coincides with Todorov's account of the Uncanny as the reduction of the Fantastic to the known and familiar. However Freud's tracing of that movement internal to the *Heimliche* that renders it unlike or other than itself sets up a different dynamic. As Schelling's definition suggests, the *Unheimliche/*Uncanny is the very manifestation of that shift, the moment when the *Heimlichkeiten* or secrets (sense II) of the *Heimliche* (sense I) are revealed and the familiar is found to have been strange or alien, inhabited by the other, after all.

(2) The Freudian Uncanny is not just another example of the general law of the return of the repressed. What gives it a further specification is the return of that archaic but still active root connection between the familiar and the alien, the private and the sinister that passes through the home, the household, the family. In his meditation on the paradoxes of the Uncanny, Freud has articulated the logic of the Gothic as a genre and of its organising matrix, the Gothic house: the continual re-finding or reactivation of the *Heim* within the *Unheimliche*, of the family and the familial within the Gothic and its familiars, revealing the strangeness of that familiarity.

The Gothic House or *Heim* is the site of that imaginary reference back to the dark past with its inherited burden of crimes and secrets, inhabited by the dead that won't lie down but rise and walk, that legion of ghosts, vampires, zombies whose generic designations, the undead, the living dead, indicate their paradoxical status athwart the categories and choices – alive or dead, inside or outside – of commonsense rational expectation. Despite the moments of retro-spective explanation, of secondary revision, installed at the end of many Gothic narratives, a moment overprivileged by Todorov as determinant of genre, what the logic of many Gothic texts entails is not Todorov's either/or, or even the uncertainty and hesitation between them, but a deconstructive both/and. As the phrase 'living dead' suggests, neither alive nor dead but both, neither subjective fantasy nor objective event but both. This paradoxical logic of the Uncanny repeats the logic that Laplanche and Pontalis see as characterising the concept of the primal fantasies. These are Freud's attempt to refuse the either/or alternatives of subjective fantasy and real event, insisting on something *unheimlich* and alien, something experienced as demonic and from the other, the internal foreign body that organises psychic life from within. Lacan's neologism *extimité*, not the intimate but the extimate and Laplanche's coinage not *étrangété*, strangeness, but *étrangereté*, strangerness, in their at-tempts to translate Freud's *Unheimlich* into French point to this disturbing repetition of someone else and something else as the traumatic kernel, the phantom that haunts the space of interiority.[31]

THE SANDMAN AS AN UNCANNY TEXT

In his essay on 'The Uncanny' Freud elaborates a partial though powerful reading of Hoffman's novella that turns, not on the ambiguity of Olympia as either doll or woman (the motif which Jentsch had located as the site of the uncanny effect in the narrative), but on the figure of the Sandman, from whom the story takes its title. Freud sees him as the bearer of the trauma of castration through his repeated threats to either Nathaniel's eyes or the eyes of Nathaniel's fiancée, Clara, or of the beloved doll, Olympia. I am concerned, however, not with the details of Freud's reading and the growing secondary literature it has generated, but with tracing the structure of equivocation within the tale.

The narrative begins as a citation of documents in the manner of much Gothic writing, an exchange of letters between the under-graduate Nathaniel, his fiancée Clara and her brother Lothario, in which the status of the Sandman is debated between them. Nathaniel is prompted to write by the visit of an Italian eye-glass seller, Giuseppe Coppola, which had plunged him into a state of melancholy and despair. In order to explain these intense, apparently irrational and disproportionate emotions, Nathaniel identifies the Italian Coppola with the old German lawyer Coppelius from his childhood, and both with the symbolic figure of the Sandman. This leads him to relate his childhood traumas associated with the Sandman, so as to explain how 'some quite private association rooted quite deep in my life could bestow such significance on this event that the mere person of that unfortunate tradesman could produce an inimical effect'.[32] Nathaniel writes this narrative to Lothario but unwittingly addresses the letter to Clara who, to Nathaniel's chagrin, replies with an extended discussion of his obsession with the figure of the Sandman.

Nathaniel's narrative is in part an account of the genesis of his childhood conception of the Sandman which can be grasped in terms of the three dimensions of the social, the personal and the aesthetic Uncanny as outlined by Freud. The Sandman who sprinkles sand in children's eyes is a legendary figure belonging to popular superstition and folklore. He is a fanciful personification of the red, sore eyes of the child reluctant to go to bed, first invoked by his middle-class mother who doesn't believe in his actual existence but explains him as a figure of speech. It is Nathaniel's old nurse who next elaborates the Sandman as the cruel and punitive figure of peasant folklore, who steals naughty childrens' eyes and carries them in a sack up to the moon to feed his own children. So Nathaniel acquires the fantasy of the Sandman from the older generation and the cultural traditions they transmit. Nathaniel does not just associate the Sandman with the cultural legacy of legend and story, however, but with two traumatic incidents from his childhood. In the first he is threatened with the loss of his own eyes after he has been caught spying on the uncanny night-time activities of his father and the old lawyer, Coppelius; in the second he discovers his dead father lying on the floor beside his unconscious mother after a terrible nocturnal explosion. In both these incidents Nathaniel identifies the legendary figure of the Sandman with the Coppelius whom he knows and fears from his visits to the family home. It is this composite figure, Coppelius-as-the-Sandman who threatens Nathaniel with the loss of his eyes and whom he holds responsible for the death of his beloved father. Coppelius survives the explosion but disappears, until years later Nathaniel identifies him with the figure of Coppola, the Italian eye-glass seller. For Nathaniel the Sandman is both a personal trauma and a cultural legacy.

The third dimension of the aesthetic Uncanny, the conflicting interpretations provoked by the irruption of the Uncanny event or figure within the world of secular modernity, emerges explicitly with Clara's analysis of Nathaniel's childhood narrative. Nathaniel had argued that Coppelius has reappeared in altered form – from Coppelius to Coppola – in order to persecute him and ruin his chances of happiness. Clara (her name in German, *Klara*, has associations with *Aufklärung*, Enlightenment) by contrast with the uncanny doll-woman Olympia, is canny or *heimlich*. She represents the maternal and domestic. Her letter is also the embodiment of the Enlightenment assumptions of rational explanation and she affirms her belief that 'all the ghastly and terrible things you spoke of took place only within you, and the real outer world had little part in them' (p. 95). She warns Nathaniel, in terms that are themselves uncannily proleptic of Freud and psychoanalysis, that though even cheerful hearts may have a 'presentiment of a dark power which strives to ruin us within ourselves' (p. 96), this has an internal subjective reference only. This 'uncanny power' has 'assumed within us the form of ourself, indeed ... become ourself', it is 'a mirror-image of ourself' (pp. 96–7). This 'dark, psychic power', she quotes Lothario as saying, animates forms in the outer world that are 'enkindled by ourselves' and have power over us because they are 'phantoms of our own ego' (p. 97).

Throughout the narrative Nathaniel wavers between Clara's perspective that the Sandman is a subjective image that only has power over him if he allows it, and a discourse of the supernatural that speaks of the objective existence of demonic forces. Nathaniel insists that while each of us thinks himself free, we are 'the tortured plaything of mysterious powers', and that as regards art and science 'the inspiration that alone made creation possible did not proceed from within us but was effectuated from some higher force from outside' (p. 103).

The terms of the debate, then, seem clear-cut. Rationality in the form of Clara tells Nathaniel: the Sandman's power is only your belief in him. Nathaniel insists that an evil force had taken possession of him while he was hiding and listening from behind the curtain to his father's nocturnal activities with Coppelius. Nathaniel is the portrait, partly ironic and partly compassionate, of a gloomy, self-preoccupied narcissist whose obsessive fantasy is repeatedly manifested in his drawing 'the strangest and most hideous pictures of him [the Sandman] on tables, cupboards and walls everywhere in the house' (p. 88) in childhood, and in the torrent of poems, canzoni, sonnets, stories, novels and 'an entire mystical theory of devils and cruel powers' (p. 104) that he pours forth to Clara and Olympia in adulthood. The level of the narration does, however, as Freud pointed out, appear to validate Nathaniel's claims. It presents the figures of both Coppola and Spalanzani, the makers of the doll Olympia with whom Nathaniel falls in love, in conspiracy against him, as well as the final return of Coppelius the lawyer, who reappears in the closing scene in the market place, as the crazed Nathaniel runs amok on the church-tower. Coppelius predicts to the crowd Nathaniel's suicidal leap to his death at their feet, which is precipitated by Nathaniel's recognition of him. The final scene concludes, 'As Nathaniel was lying on the pavement with his head shattered, Coppelius disappeared into the crowd' (p. 124). The story presents us explicitly with two clear-cut, alternative explanatory systems – the psychological versus the demonic – while validating both of them in different ways. The result is an uncanny text that disables the competition between systems of explanation, and by insisting on both the psychic and the demonic, the subjective and the objective together, is characterised by the logic of both/and rather than the logic of either/or. Instead of a simple opposition of the real and the imaginary, the external and objective as against the internal and subjective, we have a third dimension that cuts across and involves both. Following Lacan we might tentatively call this dimension the Symbolic.

Not just an idea of the unfortunate Nathaniel, the multiform figure of the Sandman manifests himself in the proliferating series of father-figures described by Freud. In Freud's account the function of the father is split or doubled into opposing imagoes of the good and bad father: Nathaniel's benevolent actual father and the persecutory Coppelius. This pairing is then reproduced with Coppola doubling Coppelius while Professor Spalanzani, Olympia's apparent father, so welcoming to Nathaniel's attentions and desires, repeats his own father. Over and above this series of actual characters is the folkloric figure of the Sandman, a haunting and uncanny fantasm who isn't reducible to any one character but binds the series together. Just as the artificial *unheimlich* doll Olympia replaces the real woman Clara in Nathaniel's affections (in his final murderous assault on Clara he seems to have confused or identified both of them), and Coppola's telescope replaces Nathaniel's own eyes which he forfeits as the price of its delusory vision of Olympia, so the Sandman as a symbolic figure or fantasm shadows and replaces his actual father. In the narrative's oedipal configuration of the father, the fiancée and the eyes as organs of desire, their violent substitution by the Sandman, the doll and the magical telescope can be read as a representation of the castrating predominance of the Symbolic, and its capacity to mediate the real so as to determine what it means and can be made to signify. This capacity gives it both an objective, a social and signifying force, and a subjective consistency, a capacity to activate and give form to the subject's psychic drives and forces from within, to bind them within an imaginary scene and in relation to a dominant figure, that may well be experienced as a form of demonic possession.

As Nathaniel spies on his beloved father and Coppelius, he is distressed to see his father's 'gentle honest features' distorted 'into a repulsive devil-mask. He looked like Coppelius' (p. 91). After his father's death, Nathaniel is relieved to note that 'his features had again grown mild and gentle, as they had been in life' and he comes to feel that 'his bond with the diabolical Coppelius had in any event not plunged him into eternal damnation' (p. 94). Nevertheless the mystery of the relation between them – 'what it could be that he had to do with my father' (p. 88) – remains enigmatic. It drives him to spy on them, which is the formative moment from which, as if from the traumatic power of that scene, he dates his own possession by Coppelius. It is as if he inherits this relation to Coppelius from his father. The Sandman does seem to be, in Lacan's words, 'that obscene, ferocious figure in which we must see the true signification of the superego'[33] and that presides over the paranoid transactions between the oedipal male subject and a patriarchal culture. He can be seen as the emanation of the symbolic order of a whole culture and its system of formative myths and fantasies, the patriarchal unconscious and its collective symbolic reality. Lacan's concept of the 'Symbolic', derived from the structural anthropology of Lévi-Strauss and the linguistics of Saussure, is a synchronic abstraction that is, however, perhaps not best suited for trying to grasp the temporal even historical dimensions of the Gothic Uncanny. Laplanche's conception of the psychotic enclave that bears the parental inscription of a non-negotiable demand or categorical imperative, and Nicholas Abraham's conception of the phantom that arises from the incorporation of unspoken parental secrets, both point more fruitfully to trans-generational dynamics at work in the Gothic Uncanny. For while Coppelius is no aristocrat, and the narrative is located in a distinctively bourgeois milieu, he is presented as both an advocate and representative of the law and as an aged and curiously outdated figure, dressed in oldfashioned court dress with black stockings, shoes with jewelled buckles, a wig, hairbag and cravat. He seems a figure of the *ancien régime*, who marks the historically archaic quality of the punitive legacy he represents.

POSTMODERN GOTHIC?

Todorov has claimed that 'psychoanalysis has replaced and thereby made useless the literature of the fantastic' (p. 160), by making explicit the fantasies and processes of the Unconscious it has rendered the Fantastic redundant. The fascination of Peter Sasdy's *Hands of the Ripper*,[34] which begins in a Gothic house and ends in a cathedral, is that it incorporates psychoanalysis the better to outflank it. It shares the logic of the Uncanny, for against the either/or explanations of a hubristic and triumphant modernity – either known and familiar or alien and external, either subjective fantasy or objective demonic force – it outflanks modernity, and like *The Sandman* it insinuates both. It rewrites the figure of the Gothic predator and his legacy by fabricating a narrative, not so much about Jack the Ripper as his daughter Anna (Angharad Rees), and her encounter with Dr John Pritchard (Eric Porter), the first English psychoanalyst, we are given to understand, and his failure to cure her. Like *The Sandman, Hands of the Ripper* sets up a clash of rival interpretative systems, between the discourse of spiritualism with its séances and mediums for contacting the spirit world, and the discourse of psychoanalysis that seeks to render disturbing and uncanny phenomena intelligible by tracing their genesis to the experiences and events of everyday family life.

The film is the story of Jack the Ripper's daughter, Anna, an orphan who works for a crooked medium Mrs Golding (Dora Bryan) who employs Anna to act the part of the voices of the dead from the spirit world, from behind a curtain. The medium is also a part-time brothel keeper who sells Anna as a virgin to one of her gentleman clients, an MP called Dysart (Derek Godfrey). Anna kills brutally and bloodily a number of times through the film and her victims, with the final exception of the psychoanalyst, are all women. The killings occur when Anna is in an hypnotic trance induced by light dazzling her from a bright surface – jewels, mirrors, highly polished metal – and are triggered off by an embrace followed by a kiss. In the four main killings the woman who gives the kiss is killed. These acts of violence are presented as the uncanny after-effects of the primal scene from Anna's infancy which we see as the credits roll, but which neither the amnesiac Anna nor anyone else in the film has evidence of.

The film doesn't save its moment of trauma for the end as a climactic conclusion, as the flash-back melodrama conventionally does, as in Hitchcock's *Spellbound* or *Marnie*. Instead of gradually working its way round to implicating the familial and the *Heimliche* in the monstrous / *Unheimlich*, *Hands of the Ripper* detonates the opposition between the two in its opening moments by showing the Ripper coming home from his night's work on the streets, and bringing his violence home with him to act it out on the family hearth. Here the scene of homecoming leads to the mother's discovery of blood on the hands of her child's father, and her horrified recognition – 'It's you! You're the Ripper!' – provokes the re-enactment of the Ripper's psychotic violence, directed not at the prostitute on the street but at the figure of the mother (whatever her supposed marital status her significance is secured by the iconographic implications of the white dress and the glowing fire).[35] Where traditional melodramas would end with the final recall of the buried trauma, *Hands of the Ripper* begins with it in the title sequence, as the tranquillising musical score and freeze-frame credits give the stillness of a tableau to the scene of violence – a tableau that is addressed to the girl-child watching through the bars of her cot, by a grotesquely tender even seductive father. Both the music and the kiss of the Ripper-Father still the child's distress, leaving her with this enigmatic scene as his legacy.

The psychoanalyst who discovers the scene of Anna's first killing (of Mrs Golding), keeps concealed her identity as the killer, retrieves Anna from a jail cell full of prostitutes by adopting her: 'all you have to learn, Anna, is to become one of the family'. He wants to study and cure Anna, we are told, by using the methods of 'this new man

Freud in Vienna'. In a long argument with Dysart the MP (to whom Mrs Golding has sold Anna as a virgin), he stands for enlightened rationality and compassion – instead of just punishing the killer, we should attempt to understand and cure whatever drives him to kill. Dysart insists that a length of stout rope around the neck is the appropriate solution to Anna's problem. The film presents an opposition between the punitive, superstitous and hypocritical morality of the traditional lawmaker, with its insistence on the objective existence of Evil as an external force, as against the enlightened modernity of the psychoanalyst.

He makes little progress, however, in getting Anna to remember or regress – he uses hypnotism with only partial success – and by a twist of the plot he is forced by Dysart to take Anna to visit Madam Bullard the Royal Medium (Margaret Rawlings). Very different from the first medium, Madam Bullard detects the violence in Anna and gradually 'sees' the primal scene of paternal violence that we have witnessed and recognises Anna's father, not only as Jack the Ripper but as a highly placed – it is hinted a royal – personage, whose name she won't reveal. In the course of the interview, Madam Bullard embraces and kisses Anna who promptly stabs her. The analyst's plans unravel rapidly. Dysart, when he hears what the Royal Medium has said, exits threatening to go to the police, and Dr Pritchard still refusing to believe the medium persists in his attempts to hypnotise Anna, unwisely kisses her and thus brings on the return of her murderous violence against the good Dr John, as she calls him.

The film ends with the psychoanalyst confessing his mistake and belatedly acknowledging the truth of what the Royal Medium saw, that Anna's father is indeed Jack the Ripper. Having been impaled with a sword by Anna, he drags himself, wounded and dying, into a hansom cab to a spectacular rendezvous with Anna on the floor and under the dome of St Paul's Cathedral. Here he attempts to rescue his prospective daughter-in-law, the blind Laura (Jane Merrow) who has taken Anna to the Whispering Gallery. Laura, blind and always requiring a chaperone, is the very figure of a disabled and dependent femininity. To comfort Anna disturbed by the whispering voice of her murderous father, Laura kisses her and provokes the violent return of the Ripper acting through the person of his daughter. The confidence of Enlightenment rationality is shown to be hubristic and misplaced and the discourse of spiritualism as that which tells the truth about the existence of the demonic is apparently affirmed. This defeat of the psychoanalyst is translated into an extraordinary narrative climax, a delirious moment of melodramatic excess where, as in Freud's reading of *The Sandman*, the paternal function is split into two opposite imagoes and a struggle ensues between the benevolent, loved father and the monstrous persecutory father.

Psychoanalytically, the film's ending substitutes one primal fantasy for another. From the violent drama of parental intercourse in the opening sequence, we conclude with that other scenario, summarised by Laplanche and Pontalis as 'a father seduces a daughter'. Anna is rescued fron her dark paternal legacy by a further permutation of the very terms of that oedipal symbolic order encoded in the system of primal fantasies. In the final shot, Anna and Dr John lie side by side on the floor of St Paul's like tragic lovers, just as Anna's final leap from the Whispering Gallery into Dr John's arms is a kind of *Liebestod*. Iconographically Anna's hands are now clean, whereas after the other killings she was shown standing in a trance, her hands covered in blood. She appears as the pale virgin and it is the analyst's hands that are blood-stained. It is in fact his own blood from the death-wound inflicted by Anna – in narrative terms he is innocent – but visually the iconography of the opening scene is reproduced: the pale-faced woman-in-white and the dark-suited man with blood on his hands.

The film systematically ironises and discredits the psychoanalyst's aims and pretensions. Psychoanalysis as a theory is absent from the film's dialogue, it is not spoken as such – at most Pritchard talks about conditioning like an early behaviourist. Where psychoanalysis is present is visually, in the *mise-en-scène* and cinematic composition of the film, as in the classical scenarios of the primal fantasies in the opening and closing sequences. Anna literally 'falls' for Dr John the analyst, like a delirious, indeed the ultimate form of transference. She turns out to be the too perfect analysand, mounting the railings in response to his call – 'Anna, come to me! Come to me!' – and hurling herself in a deathleap into the astonished analyst's arms. Seen in a point of view shot from the analyst's appalled gaze, Anna's figure, cloak flying, is then profiled against the sun-burst marble floor pattern of St Paul's invoking the traditional motif of the celestial apotheosis, a *trompe-l'oeil* traditional in Baroque cathedral art. Rather than ascending, however, she descends on him in a negative or inverted apotheosis. Fleeing from the psychotic violence of the monstrous Gothic father, she enacts the unspoken erotic connection between her and Dr John, the good father, obvious throughout the film. In doing so she also returns to and repeats her relation to the originary scene of trauma, as the visual rhyme between the railings of the Whispering Gallery from which she leaps and the brass railings of her cot through which as an infant she witnessed the primal scene, makes clear. Anna,[36] the small infant witness, has now escaped from behind those bars, like the child in Blake's 'Infant Sorrow': 'into the dangerous world I leapt'. Her response to the enigmatic message contained in that scene – the knife and the kiss – is an embrace that obliterates the paternal object.

The film appears to affirm the discourse of spiritualism with its account of a spirit world that is, in Anna's words, 'so mad, so full of hate and so unhappy', against the analyst's claim that they are just dreams. However the film's enactment of Walpole's Gothic and unuseful moral – the return of the sins of the fathers – through the daughter's possession by her murderous paternal legacy, and the good analyst-father's attempt to free her from that legacy, are both mapped along the classic lines of the Freudian primal fantasies.

This account raises two questions. The film's relation to the question of modernity, and to the related question of feminism.

Paradoxically, it is the psychoanalyst for all his enlightened compassionate values who is presented as 'Victorian' in his dogmatic commitment to secular rationality, his refusal of the possibility of demonic possession. From the film's point of view he is blinkered, old-fashioned, 'period' i.e. 'Gothic'. Where or how is the moment of enunciation inscribed in a film that enacts the defeat or obsolescence of secular modernity? If we take the discourse of spiritualism as the trace of that late 1960s and early 1970s counter-cultural 'wisdom', with its validation of astrology, eastern mysticism, culturally un-orthodox discourses of the supernatural, then the film can be read as a proto-New Age, syncretic, postmodern or at least anti-modern reversal of the relations between modernity and the Gothic. Modernity itself now seems Gothic, the psychoanalyst a figure of a blind and redundant past, mocked from a point in time beyond him.

The film also shows the trace of a late 1960s, early 1970s feminism. There is the wall graffito, 'Votes for Women', across which the camera pans slowly in the opening sequence in Whitechapel; more significantly there is the embodiment of the demonic paternal legacy in a daughter and not a son, and the ironic presentation of the psychoanalyst as a self-deceived patriarch: 'All you have to learn, Anna, is to become one of the family'. Within the film's spiritualist discourse, however, Anna as an autonomous narrative agent is completely effaced. She is understood simply as the passive and unwitting vehicle of the father's psychotic violence. By contrast the Freudian iconography of Anna's murders suggests that the violence is as much Anna's as her father's. Her murders are elaborately contextualised responses to a kiss and an embrace that position her as feminine, and so place her in the mother's postion in the primal scene. The medium Mrs Golding, rescuing her at the last moment from Dysart to whom she has sold her as a virgin, murmurs, 'There, there dear – it has to happen to all of us, sooner or later', kisses her and is run through with a poker; the maid Dolly dresses Anna in Dr Pritchard's dead wife's clothes as a 'lady', calls her a little doll, kisses her and has her throat cut. Long Liz the prostitute fondles Anna in a predatory way, kisses her and is stabbed in the eye with a needle. Anna's violence is readable each time as her repeated response to sexual aggression, solicitation, positioning as the feminine object of desire. Offered a choice of the two positions played out in the opening scene, Anna violently repudiates the seductive kiss that interpellates her as feminine and in so doing re-enacts and directs outwards the paternal violence inscribed in that scene. The conservative pessimism of the Gothic resides in the film's contradictory suggestion that the violence is both Anna's and her father's and inescapable – the violence of his imposition and the violence of her repudiation that coincide in the same murderous gesture.

CONCLUSION

Hoffman's text validates Nathaniel's arguments for the objective existence of demonic forces and the reality of the Sandman, as against Clara's 'enlightened' explanation of him as a phantom of Nathaniel's ego, a subjective delusion. Similarly, *Hands of the Ripper*, as in its titular motif of the substitution in the very act of violence of the scarred and hairy male hands of the Ripper for the slender hands of the young girl, insists on the possession of Anna by the demonic reality of the Ripper-Father. As with Clara, the analyst's attempt at an explanation in terms of Anna's subjectivity is apparently exposed as a rationalist denial of the reality of the demonic. The demonic reading of both narratives, however, denies any agency to the protagonists, reducing their implication in the uncanny or supernatural phenomena to a certain mechanism, represented by Hoffman's motif of the puppet or doll, 'the tortured plaything of mysterious forces'. This 'official' demonic explanation of both texts denies the way the protagonist's subjective implication in the mechanism and 'objectivity' of the demonic is elaborately contextualised and situated by each narrative: Nathaniel's narcissistic rapport with the passive mirroring and echoing of the doll Olympia, Anna's murderous refusal of the kiss that interpellates her as the doll-woman. If each protagonist is engaged in a longing for or repudiation of the feminine as object of desire, this subjective implication is structured and mediated by a paternal function that is split into the benevolent, rational father of modernity and the demonic, archaic father of pre-modern superstition and its Gothic rescension.

The equivocation which characterises the body of the Gothic text as a whole, and not just the retrospective simplification of its final moment of closure (privileged by Todorov as a determinant of genre), insinuates a both/and that posits an unsurpassed archaic residue at the heart of modernity. The persistence and return of the paternal imago that characterises both the time of the text, as well as the time of the genre itself, seems more salient than its splitting into the polarities of good and bad. The descent of the giant body-in-pieces that is the dream-kernel of Walpole's founding text[37] is ascribed to the figure of Alonzo the Good in a nostalgic narrative of restoration. However his uncanny repetition gives him more in common with Hoffman's *ancien régime* Coppelius-as-Sandman or indeed with the postmodern archaisms of the Hammer Ripper or the persecutory Freddy of Wesley Craven's *A Nightmare on Elm Street* (1984) who is slain only to return again in a dozen subsequent sequels. This 'undead' trauma of ancestral desires and secrets, the tenacity of their return, accounts in part for the mobility and persistence of Gothic as a form that is cognate with the epoch of modernity as a whole and has shown such surprising ability to rise and walk again from the apparent grave of its own obsolescence as a dated tradition, from the 1790s to the 1890s to the 1990s. Preoccupied always with the question of limits, of residues and archaisms, with what resists the modern and remains both active and unsurpassable within it, perhaps it is only with the proposed obsolescence of modernity itself, that the traditional vocation of Gothic will converge with the dystopian fantasies of a science fiction concerned with the unsurpassability of a Dark Future rather than a Dark Past. Marx's spectre haunting Europe from the future will come, not from the threat of the now historically surpassed 'communism' of the Stalinist command-economy, but instead from the very postmodern dissolution of historical meta-narratives of emancipation and enlightened modernity, materialised so vividly in the urban Gothic spaces of *Bladerunner* (1982), with its Udolpho-esque, crumbling skyscrapers, off-world colonies and ubiquitous surveillance. If modernity and its unfinished project of Enlightenment were indeed to become obsolescent, and the Dark Past's Gothic House become the Dark Future's Gotham City, then the 'postmodern' future will appear either belated or demonic or both.

CHAPTER 9

Romantic irony and the postmodern sublime: Geoffrey Hill and 'Sebastian Arrurruz'

Andrew Michael Roberts

In this article I want to consider some of the relations between Romantic irony, as that attitude was formulated and practised by F. W. Schlegel and other members of the German Romantic movement and certain forms of postmodernist irony, which will here be understood primarily with reference to Lyotard's concept of the figural and his account of Postmodernism in terms of the sublime.[1] These relations will be brought into focus by a reading of Geoffrey Hill's 'The Songbook of Sebastian Arrurruz'; at the same time I shall propose that Hill has affinities with Postmodernism which have not been adequately recognised.

'The Songbook of Sebastian Arrurruz' is a sequence of eleven (or twelve) poems and prose poems by Geoffrey Hill, attributed by him to the imaginary Spanish poet whose name appears in the title. The indeterminacy here is of some importance. Between 1965 and 1968 Hill published in journals six poems (two alone and a group of four) under the title 'From the Songbook of Sebastian Arrurruz'. These were included (with some revision) in the eleven-poem 'Songbook' included in Hill's 1968 volume, *King Log*. However, a further 'Copla by Sebastian Arrurruz' appeared in 1972; this was not added to 'The Songbook' when this was reprinted in Hill's *Collected Poems* of 1985.[2] The effect was to imply an absent coherence located in a fictional ur-text from which Hill made selections. Not only selections, either; Hill commented that 'Arrurruz is a shy sensualist with a humour that could be said to balance the sensuality except that the finer nuances have been lost in the translation.'[3]

These manoeuvres around the borders of fictionality and textuality may recall those found in the metafiction of such novelists as Borges, Barth and Calvino – a genre that has acquired the status of a postmodernist canon. Nevertheless, Hill is not generally a poet who would spring to mind as an instance of postmodernist style or practice. More likely candidates would be John Ashbery, the L=A=N=G=U=A=G=E poets, John Cage, or others who engage in radical experimentation with form and referentiality. The common perception of where Hill 'stands', a perception based partly on his poetry but also on his criticism, the attitudes of his most frequent interpreters, his manner in interviews and his intellectual and institutional affiliations, would place him in a conservative tradition politically and stylistically, epitomised by the influence of T. S. Eliot.[4] He would seem to belong to an intellectual milieu that would regard the very conception of 'Postmodernism' with suspicion or outright contempt. Even confining attention to the poetry, there is much evidence against any idea of Hill as postmodernist. A widely held conception of Postmodernism would regard it as secular and iconoclastic, whereas Hill's poetry frequently works with Christian paradigms and icons; as aleatory and playful, whereas Hill's poetry is highly wrought and mannered; as celebrating the contemporary, whereas Hill's poetry might seem to disdain it; as recklessly relativist, whereas Hill's poetry is marked by moral seriousness; as assimilating art to consumer culture and breaking down the barrier between 'high' and 'popular' culture, whereas Hill's poetry, in its tone, allusions and mode of self-presentation, lays claim to a high 'literary' status.

However, while the use of the term 'Postmodernism' to denote a coherent stylistic category has a certain local value in literary studies, the philosophical theories of postmodernity would call into question any idea of a canonical or exemplary postmodernist text, if this depended on an historical essentialism that allowed such a text to stand as pure exemplum of a movement or period. A more flexible way of relating literary movements to a wider cultural theory of Postmodernism is that proposed by Peter Nicholls, who suggests the use of Lyotard's conception of the postmodern as a mode, not an epoch, in order to 'think continuities between early and late parts of the century and at the same time to recognise divergences within the otherwise abstractly epochal "moments" of Modernism and Postmodernism'.[5] This approach recognises the possibility of Modernist and postmodernist modes co-existing within the same oeuvre and even the same work or text. Lyotard writes: 'The nuance which distinguishes these two modes may be infinitesimal; they often coexist in the same piece, are almost indistinguishable; and yet they testify to a difference (*un différend*) on which the fate of thought depends and will depend for a long time, between regret and assay'

(*PMC*, 80). My aim, then, is not to place Hill within a unified postmodernist canon but to identify the postmodernist sublime (a particular relation to the idea of the unpresentable) as an element in a rhetorical and philosophical dynamic which structures his work.

The most persistent impulse of Hill's poetry has been the elegiac, and many of his poems reflect on the relationship of the living to the dead, on emotions of loss, and, with gestures of anxious reflexivity, on the problematics of elegy: the distance between poet and subject and the attendant risks of exploitation, appropriation, aestheticisation.[6] 'September Song', an elegy for a child victim of the Nazis, has a central parenthesis which emphasises the ambivalence of the elegiac: '(I have made / an elegy for myself it / is true)' (*CP*, 67). This is at once an assertion of the truth of the elegy (it is a true elegy), and an admission of the egotism which is its motivation (it is true that I created it for my own purposes, for my own pleasure, or to express my own feelings of loss). Should these two meanings be conceptualised in terms congenial to Modernist practice, as an Empsonian 'ambiguity', or in more postmodernist terms, as indeterminacy or 'flicker'?[7] The latter would seem more appropriate since these are not merely alternative readings, but generate a regressive paradox. The 'truth' of the elegy depends upon its honesty about the poet's motives. But this honesty is evinced in the other sense of 'it / is true': an honest admission of the impure motives of elegy and the impossibility of 'true elegy' in an absolute sense. In effect, this parenthesis defines 'true elegy' as a category to which a poem can only belong if it admits that it is *not* true elegy.

This regressive, reflexive paradox is set up through the ironising of an emotion (the *sense* of identification with the suffering of the dead child, producing the conviction of a true elegiac impulse) by a scrupulous self-criticism which questions the moral validity of such an emotion. The paradox may therefore be seen as an instance of Romantic irony, described by Ernst Behler as 'an infinite mental spiral in which the individual mental ego hovers between naive experiences and critical reflections on its experiences while viewing its own passions with disillusioned detachment'.[8] However, the lines could also be read in Lyotard's terms, according to which the paradox would manifest the figural – 'the resistant or irreconcilable trace of a space or time that is radically incommensurable with that of discursive meaning' – thus pointing to the unpresentable event of the child's experience.[9]

F. W. Schlegel identifies elegy as the median form of 'transcendental poetry', which he defines in terms of 'the relation between
ideal and real':

It begins as satire in the absolute difference of ideal and real, hovers in
between as elegy, and ends as idyll with the absolute identity of the two ...
this sort of poetry should unite the transcendental raw materials and
preliminaries of a theory of poetic creativity – often met with in modern
poets – with the artistic reflection and beautiful self-mirroring that is
present in Pindar, in the lyric fragments of the Greeks, in the classical elegy,
and, among the moderns, in Goethe. In all its descriptions, this poetry
should describe itself, and always be simultaneously poetry and the poetry
of poetry.[10]

Reflexivity is crucial to this definition, as is indicated by the terms
'self-mirroring' and 'the poetry of poetry'. Schlegel associates this
reflexivity with irony: his taxonomy of irony in 'On Incomprehensi-
bility' includes, as the final category, the 'irony of irony' (Wheeler,
37). Hill's work moves between the two poles of reflexive satire and
reflexive idyll, without touching either absolute and is aptly
described by Schlegel's phrase, 'simultaneously poetry and the
poetry of poetry'. Hill's poetry simultaneously engages closely with a
range of historical, religious, personal and mythical subjects and
maintains a reflexive awareness of its own processes and limits –
notably the processes of literary construction and the limit imposed
by that which eludes representation.

In the terms of Peter Nicholls's argument, Hill's reflexivity would
exemplify, not Baudrillard's conception of the postmodern as a
world where 'the "real" is conceived of as pervasively "textual" or
semiotic' (Nicholls, 12), but the understanding of the postmodern
supported by Lyotard's account and exemplified by 'a body of recent
American fiction', which has attended to

questions of temporality and narrative, and specifically to what Lyotard has
called the 'event', the singular moment which can be spoken about only
after it is over, and which is composed of 'simultaneous and heterogeneous
temporalities'. The event is, in this sense, a kind of temporal *figure* which
can't be incorporated into a dialectic or reduced to a 'meaning' within a
historical narrative of equivalent other meanings (the time of the history
narrated is not that of the narration itself). Lyotard's most powerful
example is, of course, Auschwitz, an event which can't be remembered (as
a simple historical 'fact') but which can't be forgotten either. (Nicholls, 14)[11]

It is precisely this figural unpresentability (which Lyotard terms the 'immemorial') to which Hill's poetry has repeatedly returned via elegy; his elegies are haunted by a sense of radical estrangement or distance between the discursive time of his own text and the unpresentable, figural historical event. His sequence about Europe in the twentieth century, 'Of Commerce and Society', attempts to consider the problems of recollection and understanding posed by Lyotard's 'most powerful example' of the immemorial:

> Many have died. Auschwitz,
> Its furnace chambers and lime pits
> Half-erased, is half-dead; a fable
> Unbelievable in fatted marble.   (*CP*, 49)

There seems, then, to be a link between Romantic irony and the reflexive, ironical self-questioning of Hill's poetry. Furthermore, the latter can be placed within the form of postmodernist writing that Nicholls identifies: a form which recognises the undecidability of the past but continues the project of ' "working through" or *anamnesis* which Lyotard connects with the postmodern' (Nicholls, 14). However, Nicholls identifies Romantic irony with the discursive, voyeuristic irony of Baudelaire's 'To a Red-haired Beggar Girl' – a matter of the triumph of a master code, of discourse, over the sensible or figural. Hill's poetry, on the other hand, uses reflexive irony for a sustained critique of voyeurism. Whereas Baudelaire's poem disembodies the poet (Nicholls, 8), fixing the girl as bodily self-presence, distanced by the detachment of the observing Romantic ironist, Hill's 'September Song' places the poet firmly at the centre of the poem, through the prominent 'I' of the parenthesis (deictics are cited by Lyotard as a form of the figural) while registering a tragic distance which is precisely his own failure to be an observer, precisely the impossibility of the unpresentable, unknown bodily experience of the dead child being subsumed in the poet's discourse. While Baudelaire abolishes social distance only to replace it with aesthetic distance (Nicholls, 7), Hill maintains a distance by a critique of his own impulse to aestheticisation.

How convincing is it to see Hill as a Romantic ironist, bearing in mind Nicholls's rather contrary understanding of the implications of such irony? Hill has identified a strain of Romanticism in his own work, while showing an appropriately Schlegelian spirit by being ironical about his own inclination to certain Romantic gestures: criticising certain contemporary versions of Romanticism, he acknowledges that 'my thesis is as much symptomatic as diagnostic ... in its account of certain aspects and effects of Romanticism it is itself a part of that which it describes; in some respects its tendency to "swim up against the stream" of much current thinking about the nature and function of poetry is itself a minor Romantic trait'.[12] Kathleen Wheeler, discussing *Illusionstörung*, 'the disturbance or destruction of illusion characteristic of much Romantic writing' describes the aim of self-transcendence, as advocated by Novalis and Schlegel, in terms which associate it with a form of reflexivity: 'the self-criticism that involves a humorous parody or ironizing of the self and leads to transcendence of the self as ego is represented in the work of art when it, too, ironizes itself, and when the author ironizes himself or his audience' (Wheeler, 19). The view of Hill as a Romantic ironist is supported by his comments on the positive role of the self in poetry, which centre on the idea of creation or discovery of the self (involving self-criticism), and the heuristic and constructive role of language. In 1983 he described the writing of poetry as follows:

One is ploughing down into one's own selfhood and into the deep strata of language at one and the same time. This takes effort and may be painful. Selfhood is more vital, recalcitrant, abiding, than self-expression ... The pains to which I refer are those examples of self-discovery and self-rebuke which seem inseparable from the technical process itself.[13]

In discussing poetry and the self some two years earlier Hill alluded to Nietzsche's radically ironical conception:

There's a fine ironic phrase of Nietzsche's about 'this delight in giving a form to oneself as a piece of difficult, refractory and suffering material'. In such a phrase the difficulties, refractoriness and suffering of the personality and the difficult and refractory nature of language itself are seen to cohere. (*VP*, 87)

This account bears comparison with Ernst Behler's description of Romantic irony as a mode in which 'irony and masquerade become the devices for this intellectual attitude which often cloaks a vulnerable personality plagued by melancholy, loneliness and profound suffering' (Behler 1988, 43). However, it also looks forward to postmodernist and poststructuralist conceptions of the self as discursively constructed.

Hill's use of Romantic irony bears closely on his relation with Modernist poets and with his contemporaries, because in each case it is a question of subjectivity in poetry that is at issue. Hill has endorsed Eliot's view of poetry as an 'an escape from personality' but has proposed a reinterpretation that brings Eliot's statement closer to Romantic self-transcendence, arguing that 'the word "escape" was not a particularly happy choice and left Eliot vulnerable to misinterpretation, but if we can accept that he means "transcendence" I see very little to quarrel with in the statement' (*VP*, 86–7). Hill's comments on his contemporaries have focused on his disdain for the confessional and anecdotal. He has echoed Allen Tate's 'beleaguered minority opinion that "self-expression" is a word that "should be tarred and feathered"' (Sermon, 1) and, when asked whether he used the persona of Sebastian Arrurruz as 'an avoidance of a kind of confessional poetry' he replied: 'I don't take the confessional poetry quite seriously enough to think that I have to go to great lengths to try to avoid it – I just don't like it very much and get on with my own work.'[14] This remark may accurately convey Hill's own attitude to a particular genre in post-war poetry, but it does not do justice to the complex ways in which Hill's work raises the whole issue of subjectivity in poetry, an issue overloaded with the pressures of Romantic and Modernist theory and practice. In particular, 'The Songbook of Sebastian Arrurruz' neither avoids nor ignores the rhetorical and philosophical dilemmas posed by subjectivity, but engages with them through a series of accomplished ironic manoeuvres.

The poems of 'The Songbook of Sebastian Arrurruz' are reflections on the loss of love, on sexual nostalgia, on fantasy, on memory and on the writing of poetry. Memory and writing are presented as attempts to recoup or preserve past experience that necessarily reshape it and therefore sacrifice something of its immediacy:

> Already, like a disciplined scholar,
> I piece fragments together, past conjecture
> Establishing true sequences of pain;
>
> For so it is proper to find value
> In a bleak skill, as in the thing restored:
> The long-lost words of choice and valediction.   (*CP*, 92)

Here the piecing together of fragments into a sequence refers to memory but also, reflexively, to the sequence of poems itself, while 'restored' evokes the ambivalent aspect of the restoration of a painting or precious object: such a restoration is an attempt to recover the 'original' state yet by definition involves the creation of a new state. Arrurruz's poems treat his memories like precious, sensuous objects. Working over and renewing the memories he distances the experiences:

> A workable fancy. Old petulant
> Sorrow comes back to us, metamorphosed
> And semi-precious. Fortuitous amber.
> As though this recompensed our deprivation.   (*CP,* 95)

The poems form an aesthetic object which substitutes for and displaces a lost sense of emotional plenitude and sexual satisfaction. The context here is one of melancholy and ironical self-mockery ('like a disciplined scholar') and therefore remote from the extremity of tragedy and suffering suggested in 'September Song'; nevertheless, it is again the 'immemorial', that which can be neither remembered nor forgotten, that is being considered. In Lyotard's terms, Arrurruz's activities of recalling and composing convert the event into signification or discourse, yet despite this repression the figural continues to manifest its presence within the discursive. The various features which Lyotard identifies as the traces of the figural would seem to have in common an incompatibility with a model of language as a synchronic system of differential signification; they include, as summarised by Nicholls, 'the visual and spatial nature of a text', 'a desire which operates within the play of meanings', 'the nondiscursive engagement of the body's experience' and 'the incommensurability of time frames by which an order of narration is disrupted by the present in which the narration takes place' (Nicholls, 6). The last of these is a particular instance of what Bill Readings, characterising the figural, terms 'the resistant or irreconcilable trace of a space or time' (Readings, xxxi) and Arrurruz's thoughts circle around such a trace. He longs for the *presence* of experiences which are now in the past, whereas what he is able to evoke is only their existence as *past* or absent experiences.

In 'The Songbook' the trace of the figural may also be detected in the evocation of desire and the body; or rather through the sense of the impossibility of evoking these things in words (hence a 'nondiscursive engagement'). The sense of impossibility is made vivid by the action of desire within poetic metaphor. In one sense poetry, speaking and writing become metaphors for sexual desire:

It is to him I write, it is to her
I speak in contained silence. Will they be touched
By the unfamiliar passion between them?   (*CP*, 93)

But in the elaboration of this metaphor, what is figured becomes rather a metonymic displacement of desire. Through fantasy, Arrurruz recognises that sexual desire is always already discursive as well as figural; always constituted through structures of difference and signification as well as inhabited by that which eludes such structures:

There would have been things to say, quietness
That could feed on our lust, refreshed
Trivia, the occurrences of the day;
And at night my tongue in your furrow.   (*CP*, 98)

Certain of Arrurruz's metaphors weave together or overlay event and verbal construction, as in poem 5:

Love, oh my love, it will come
Sure enough. A storm
Broods over the dry earth all day.
At night the shutters throb in its downpour.

The metaphor holds; is a snug house.
You are outside, lost somewhere. I find myself
Devouring verses of stranger passion
And exile. The exact words

Are fed into my blank hunger for you.   (*CP*, 96)

Here the 'snug house' is a metaphor for the effect upon Arrurruz of his own previous metaphor – the sense of exclusion generated in him by the metaphor of the storm. Yet the house, despite being a metaphor for the consequences of a prior metaphor, is also a physical reality. In these lines, as in an Escher drawing, one can see two incompatible things going on simultaneously within a seamless work of art, an effect of 'flicker' comparable to that of the parenthesis in 'September Song'.[15] In the poem the failure of metaphor is also its success: the storm/house metaphoric sequence fails because it is unable to recall the living presence of the lost woman but succeeds because it captures the emotional consequences of its own failure. The play of metaphorical inclusion and exclusion represents the way in which Arrurruz feels both excluding and excluded. The ironical and paradoxical self-mirroring of the poem's rhetorical strategy itself mirrors Arrurruz's own attitude of self-mocking irony:

I imagine, as I imagine us
Each time more stylized more lovingly
Detailed, that I am not myself
But someone I might have been: sexless,
Indulgent about art ...   (*CP,* 97)

Behler's 'infinite mental spiral' of 'naive experiences and critical reflections' informs the whole sequence, marked as it is by Arrurruz's intense nostalgia and longing for unmediated physical and emotional relationship, combined with his highly intellectualised awareness of the processes of fictionalisation and stylisation which his nostalgia generates:

Why do I have to relive, even now,
Your mouth, and your hand running over me
Deft as a lizard, like a sinew of water?   (*CP,* 100)

However, if these poems can be read in terms of Romantic irony, they can also be read in terms of the blocking together of incommensurable elements (here event and representation) described by Lyotard, and in terms of his analysis of the processes of the Freudian dream work, an analysis which also extends to reflections on poetry.[16] In each of the last three groups of lines quoted above, there is a notable foregrounding of metaphor, style and figure of speech. In the first two quotations such elements are explicitly thematised in reflexive gestures: 'The metaphor holds'; 'Each time more stylized'. In the third case, the rapid shift from simile to metaphor to simile (lizard, sinew, water) not only functions itself as a metaphor for speed, agility and sexual pleasure but also makes the reader aware of the processes of metaphorical flow. In 'The Dream-Work Does Not Think' Lyotard finds a figurality at the heart of poetic discourse:

The great linguistic figures, of discourse, of style, are the expression, right in the heart of language, of a general disposition of experience ... through their agency... a discourse may enter into communication with the images that are reputed to be external to it, but which in fact depend for their organization on the same signifying matrix.[17]

The poems of 'The Songbook' similarly work with a play of ideas of externality and internality. At moments Arrurruz identifies desire with the unpresentable, with that which lies outside language, with the bodily and non-discursive; this implies an idea of his poetry as ascetic substitute for (or displacement of) sexuality. Yet he continually discovers desire at the heart of poetry/discourse, and discourse at the heart of desire. Lyotard observes:

Even more than the dream, poetry is interesting not for its content, but for its work. This work does not consist in *externalising*, in images, forms in which the poet's desire, or ours, is accomplished once and for all, but in *reversing* the relation of desire to figure, in offering the former, not images in which it will be fulfilled and lost, but forms (here, poetic forms) by which it will be reflected as a game, as unbound energy, as process of condensation and displacement, as primary process. [18]

Such an offering of poetic forms to desire is what Arrurruz indulges in, feeding 'exact words' to his 'blank hunger'. In the first stanza of poem 5, Arrurruz's onanistic fantasy has effaced the woman's otherness by incorporating her into an omnipotent fantasy. In the second stanza, having recognised this effacement ('You are outside') he devours poetic discourse in order to reintroduce the Other that is necessary to maintain desire, a desire which works within the poem but cannot be contained or spoken by it: 'Desire does not speak; it does violence to the order of utterance' (Reader, 19).

To identify the importance of the figural in 'The Songbook' does not of itself define its relationship to Modernism and/or Post-modernism since Lyotard sees language and its other (the discursive and the figural) as necessarily coinherent. When Lyotard comes to distinguish Postmodernism and Modernism, in *The Postmodern Condition*, it is in terms of a small but crucial nuance (a *'différend'*). Modernism and Postmodernism, he argues, are modes within a modernity which 'takes place in the withdrawal of the real and according to the sublime relation between the presentable and the conceivable' (*PMC*, 79). However, the modern places the emphasis 'on the powerlessness of the faculty of presentation, on the nostalgia for presence felt by the human subject, on the obscure and futile will which inhabits him in spite of everything' (*PMC*, 79). The postmodern emphasises 'the power of the faculty to conceive' or 'the increase of being and the jubilation which result from the invention of new rules of the game' (*PMC*, 79–80). Modern and postmodern are both marked by the sublime, with its emphasis on the un-presentable, but while the modern sublime indulges in 'good forms' which provide solace for the 'missing contents' (81) of the unpresen-table, thereby exhibiting a nostalgia for the unattainable, the postmodern sublime creates new forms in order to 'impart a stronger sense of the unpresentable' (81). New, avant-garde work starts in the postmodernist mode but generates rules which then become the basis of new Modernist 'good forms'; hence what is initially post-modernist becomes Modernist. Given the constant modulation in Lyotard's thinking, the 'unpresentable' referred to in *La Condition postmoderne* (1979) cannot be simply equated with the 'figural' evoked in *Discours, figure* (1971); nevertheless they clearly belong to the same strand of thought.

Sebastian Arrurruz's sequence of poems is, on these definitions, clearly in the modern mode. His nostalgia for the unpresentable presence of sexual and emotional experiences which are now in the past recalls that of Proust, whom Lyotard cites as an instance of the modern sublime (*PMC*, 80). But what of Hill's sequence, textually identical with that of Arrurruz except for the title and epigraph, yet radically distinguished from it by the metalevel of irony introduced by our knowledge that Hill is the author? As I have suggested, one way to conceptualise Hill's relation to Arrurruz is in terms of Romantic irony: Arrurruz as ironic mirror for Hill, as a means to self-transcendence and self-mockery. But Hill's sequence might also be conceived in terms of Lyotard's postmodern sublime: Arrurruz's nostalgia being the means by which Hill's sequence 'searches for new presentations, not in order to enjoy them, but in order to impart a stronger sense of the unpresentable' (*PMC*, 81). Romantic irony serves to create the distance between Arrurruz's nostalgia and Hill's search for new forms.[19] It might be objected, of course, that 'The Songbook' does not employ 'new forms'; that its forms are distinc-tively Modernist, which means, in the 1960s, distinctly not new. In various ways it calls to mind such canonical poems of Anglo-American 'high' Modernism as *The Love Song of J. Alfred Prufrock* and *Hugh Selwyn Mauberley.* Arrurruz's role in 'The Songbook' somewhat resembles that of Prufrock in Eliot's poem. Arrurruz clearly has temperamental affinities with Hill, but is portrayed with a mixture of sympathy and irony which resembles Eliot's presentation of Pru-frock. There are other resemblances: both personae write songs (as indicated by the titles of the poems), and write of failure in love. The often noted uncertainty of reference in Eliot's first line, 'Let us go then, you and I', is matched in some of Arrurruz's poems: the 'him' to whom Arrurruz writes (*CP,* 93) might be the reader of his poetry, his own past or unrealized self (his poems invent an unlived life of passion with his lost wife), or a male friend. Both Prufrock and Arrurruz imagine what it would be like to have a different personality: Prufrock fantasises a decisive and impressive self, while Arrurruz, in the appropriately titled 'Postures', imagines 'that I am not myself / But someone I might have been'. Like Hugh Selwyn Mauberley, Sebastian Arrurruz is a poet both identified with and mocked by his creator. At the same time Arrurruz's activities as poet and archaeologist, and the form of his book, suggest self-conscious allusions to Modernism. The phrase 'I piece fragments together' (*CP*, 92) suggests Eliot's 'These fragments I have shored against my ruins' and the critical commonplace of the Modernist era as having been possessed by a sense of fragmentation.

However, rather than seeing Hill as merely borrowing the techniques of an ahistorical Modernism, I would see him as ironically and self-consciously engaging with literary history. He remarked:

I gave Arrurruz the chronology 1868–1922, which enabled him to celebrate the centenary of his birth on the date of publication of my second book (we shared a celebration party), and also enabled him to die on the very threshold of modernity, without having had the advantage of reading *The Waste Land* or *Ulysses*. (*VP*, 95)

Here the much-debated question of whether Postmodernism is an epoch or a mode finds playful embodiment in Arrurruz's fictive combination of transcendence of historicity (sharing a party with Hill) and historicity (dying before *The Waste Land*). 'The Songbook' is in various senses a pre-Modernist, a Modernist, and a postmodernist text. Pre-Modernist in terms of the life of its fictional author and technically Modernist in its use of the persona, it is postmodernist in its oblique, self-conscious, almost jokey allusions to Modernism, combined with a minimalism and a deceptive simplicity of style. It represents the work of a poet (Hill, not Arrurruz) who engages with the Eliotic ideal of impersonality, as well as with associated effects of difficulty, fragmentation and dense allusiveness. Thus the doubling of Hill and Arrurruz is a doubling of two poets, one profoundly influenced by Modernism, the other precluded by his death from reading its archetypal texts. This doubling is a parodic fulfilment of Eliot's doctrine according to which 'the existing monuments form an ideal order among themselves, which is modified by the introduction of the new (the really new) work of art among them'.[20] 'The Songbook' employs the strategic anachronism of postmodern architecture, evoking a form of 'double coding' through its allusions to literary history.[21] It manifests the 'temporal irony' which Bill Readings sees as a feature of Lyotard's conception of the postmodern: 'postmodernism for Lyotard is primarily an understanding of the historical event as composed of simultaneous and heterogeneous temporalities' (Readings, 24). The writing and publication of 'The Songbook' is such an event (or series of events), combining the irreconcilable temporalities of author and persona: 'work and text have the characters of an event' (*PMC*, 81). 'The Songbook' incorporates, predates and postdates Modernism, evoking and playing with both its techniques (the persona) and its poetics (fragmentation, impersonality). If Postmodernism is, according to Lyotard, Modernism 'in the nascent state' then Arrurruz (whose second name means 'arrowroot', suggestive of roots and organic metaphors) presides over a set of poems which are both on the brink of Modernism and at its end.

So 'The Songbook' would seem to represent a working through by Hill of his relationship to Romanticism and Modernism. Lyotard applies the Freudian concept of *Durcharbeitung* or 'working-through' to the work of the avant-garde:

Just as patients try to elaborate their current problems by freely associating apparently inconsequential details with past situations – allowing them to uncover hidden meanings in their lives and their behaviour – so we can think of the work of Cézanne, Picasso, Delaunay, Kandinsky, Klee, Mondrian, Malevich and finally Duchamp as a 'perlaboration' (*durcharbeiten*) performed by modernity on its own meaning.[22]

This brings me back to the question of Hill's position in contemporary poetry. He would not seem to be part of the avant-garde which, in so far as that term is appropriate, might in the 1960s (when 'The Songbook' was published) have included 'the British Poetry Revival' and might now include poetry generated using computer software, video poetry and performance poetry.[23] But nor has Hill ever been part of the more commercially successful mainstream such as Hughes, Heaney, 'Martian' poets, writers of parodic narratives and, more recently, the 'New Generation' poets.[24] 'The Songbook' did not involve the radical innovation of technique and form that generally signals the avant-garde. Nevertheless, the case seems strong for seeing it as a working-through of Modernism and as an instance of the postmodern sublime in its playfulness, self-consciousness, double-coding and strategic anachronism. At the same time it can be seen to use certain of the attitudes and manoeuvres of

Romantic irony as a way of placing itself at a distance from the nostalgic Modernist sublime which is part of the subject of 'The Songbook' rather than its mode.

The appropriateness of the term irony to the postmodern remains a matter of some debate. Ernst Behler suggests that 'at the breaching of the limits of communication ... postmodern thinking and writing begin to operate through circumlocution, indirectness, configuration, and ironic communication'.[25] Alan Wilde bases his account of Postmodernism on the concept of 'suspensive' irony (tolerant of uncertainty and absurdity), distinguished from the 'disjunctive' irony of Modernism which wishes 'simultaneously to be true to incoherence and to transcend it'; this distinction has some resemblance to Lyotard's differentiation of nostalgic and celebratory relations to the unpresentable.[26] On the other hand Candace Lang, who attacks Wilde's view of poststructuralism as simplistic, claims unequivocally (and somewhat moralistically) that 'postmodern literature's and poststructuralist theory's preoccupation with language and subjectivity has nothing in common with the narcissistic, onanistic, and potentially solipsistic discourse commonly termed romantic irony'.[27] A less absolute and more subtly modulated formulation is offered by Peter Nicholls, who distinguishes two versions of Modernism and two versions of Postmodernism and in each case identifies irony with the version in which discourse dominates over figure (Nicholls, 6, 12). In the case of Modernism, this involves the voyeuristic control of Baudelaire, a stance which, as I have argued above, Hill explicitly rejects in his poems about the tragic atrocities of the modern world. In the case of the postmodern, irony, in Nicholls's view, 'becomes a necessary product of that view of the contemporary world which sees it as thoroughly assimilated to a model of discourse ... [in which] the "real" is conceived of as pervasively "textual" or semiotic' (Nicholls, 12). He instances, in addition to the work of Jean Baudrillard, that of Donald Barthelme, and notably a story by the latter which seems to evoke a Schlegelian 'infinite absolute negativity' as a way of subordinating the exterior world to discourse. Hill's poetry, on the other hand, seems to suggest an alternative use of Romantic irony within the mode of the postmodernist sublime. Here it enables a complex form of historical awareness. The historical, extra-textual 'reality' of event is evoked while an ironical stance makes it possible to acknowledge the unpresentable nature of such an event. Hill's work would thus take its place within Nicholls's other form of the postmodern, that which attends to temporality, narrative and event (rather than being purely 'spatial') and which recognises the unpresentable or untellable nature of much of the past (whether personal or collective), but which does not therefore abandon it in favour of a 'textualised sense of postmodern reality, locked in a perpetual present of empty signification' (Nicholls, 15).

The question of the relationship of Romantic irony to the postmodern sublime is clearly part of a larger question about continuities and ruptures between, on the one hand, the tradition of German philosophy within which Romantic irony takes its place, and on the other Postmodernism and poststructuralism. The most obvious rupture lies in the language of transcendence that characterises Romantic irony, as against the explicit rejection of transcendence in postmodernist and poststructuralist thought. Hill, while by no means a 'typical' postmodernist writer, occupies a revealing position in relation to the problematic tension of period and mode in theories of the postmodern. The distinct strain of Romantic irony in his work is combined with a self-consciousness about the possibility of anachronism, resulting at times in an effect of pastiche; one might say that Hill employs Romantic irony in relation to postmodernist elements in his work, and employs postmodernist irony in relation to Romanticism. Each side of this dual irony requires the other, since simply to 'be' a Romantic ironist in the second half of the twentieth century, without a postmodernist irony about that historical relationship and placing, would be self-defeating: it would be unironical and uncritical about one's own historical and ideological position. One implication of this might be a self-ironising conception of Postmodernism, the trajectory of which is indicated by the way in which two sets of criteria – those based on period or temporal location and those involving mode or genre – destabilise each other. In such a conception, the necessity and incompatibility of both conceptions would generate the unfixed quality of Postmodernisms.

CHAPTER 10

'Uprooting the rancid stalk': transformations of Romanticism in Ashbery and Ash

Stephen Clark

I

Airplanes to London,
and then it was hard not to uproot the rancid
stalk of romanticism so I left it there
as an experiment.   ('Eternity sings the Blues' (*HL*, 40))

John Ashbery's exemplary status in the canon of Postmodernism has now been established for over two decades, a position perhaps difficult to reconcile with his own insistence that 'all my stuff is romantic poetry rather than metaphysical or surrealist'.[1] The work of this 'free-lance artist' who remains 'The first and last of the romantics' ('The Art of Speeding' (*HL*, 42)) incorporates diverse elements of this 'majestic lineage' ('Kamarinskaya' (*HL*, 94)): Keatsian sensuality, Wordsworthian reminiscence, Coleridgean synaesthesasia, Tennysonian luxuriance, Whitmanesque inclusiveness, Emersonian self-contradiction. For Harold Bloom, it embodies the expiry of the Romantic tradition; for Helen Vendler, the re-enunciation of 'timeless, representative truths in an American vernacular'; for Marjorie Perloff, a continuation of French *symbolisme*.[2] All these critics, however, agree that Ashbery's poetry may be identified with a private sphere romanticism whose primary concern is to articulate the dramas of consciousness unfolding to itself. For a secular age, it offers both the consolations of the aesthetic and the astringency of negative self-reflexivity; the presence of a muted, even clichéd, late Romantic vocabulary allows sentiment and scepticism to co-exist, and the yearning for transcendence to be exposed in such a way as to enhance its poignancy and appeal: 'the avoidance of all metaphysical temptations becomes itself a kind of religion' (*RS*, 60).[3]

Direct genealogies from Romanticism to Postmodernism are intrinsically problematic: if nothing else, the latter's overt refusal of

157

teleology renders the division of the past into successive periods suspect, 'once we forget about its progress / And actually begin to feel better / For having done so' ('Litany' (*AWK*, 55)).[4] Since the 1980s, however, such holistic models of Romanticism have been forcefully challenged in favour of an emphasis on its ideological functions; and in this essay I wish to contend that Ashbery's poetry, for all its apparently introspective orientation, possesses similar political, even imperial, corollaries.

This dimension may be highlighted through contrast with the aesthetic closely, indeed obsessively, modelled on Ashbery's work by John Ash. The British poet's affiliations to Romanticism are as pervasive as those of his mentor, though generally in the somewhat 'rancid stalk' of an affected decadence. The indebtedness is evident not merely in the reduplicable features of Ashbery's style – disjunctive similes, slithering pronouns, opaque allusions, truncated narratives, elided tenses, ebullient cliché – but also in a more general emulation of the 'central perimeter / Our imaginations orbit' ('Fragment' (*DDS*, 82)). Postmodernism has been defined by Stuart Hall as 'the way the world dreams "America"', but those 'dreams' themselves 'are insatiably expansionist' (*RS*, 12);[5] though much has been made of the a-referentiality of 'They Dream only of America' (*TCO*, 13), there is a literal and immediate sense in which 'the idea' of Ashbery's British acolyte 'was to be at the centre of things' ('Glowing Embers: Paraphrases & Fictions' (*BS*, 56)).[6] The 'anxiety of affluence', I shall argue, extends beyond individual writers onto their respective cultures; as such, it allows insight into what may be termed the postmodern ideology, and may 'show us where the balance-of-power lies in the yet-once-again altered scheme of things' ('The New Realists' (*RS*, 83)).[7]

II

Proponents of Ashbery's radicalism have invested heavily in the residual prestige of techniques of shock, provocation and disruption, despite his own declared scepticism towards the avant-garde: 'when you get a situation where everybody is a subversive, sabotage becomes status quo: art can only be destroyed once' (*RS*, 250)).[8] Keith Cohen argues that 'Ashbery aims consistently at the glibness, deceitfulness, and vapidity of bourgeois discourse and in his poems subjects this discourse to a process of disintegration'. Yet what precisely does 'bourgeois' mean in an American and postmodernist context? Cohen is himself obliged to acknowledge that Ashbery's poetry is at least as much a 'celebration' of the collapse between high and low culture ('I say "celebration" because there is no clear denunciation of the process itself') as an indictment of the mass media's power of assimilation:

[T]he voice of the poems seems at one moment seems to be mouthing the discourse, at the next moment to be mocking it … It is like trying to differentiate between a well-molded graduate from Harvard Business School and a comedian's impression of a business-man. Indeed throughout Ashbery's work there is this problem of determining exactly where the ax falls.[9]

The possibility that the 'comedian' is also from Harvard cannot be entertained.[10] Instead Cohen has somewhat desperate recourse to positing an ironised speaker of a dramatic monologue:

Ashbery always makes us aware that there is a subject speaking, collective or individual, who has been mystified *already* by the naturalisation process … It is not monopoly capitalism, but, rather, as in ventriloquism, a subject using that voice, speaking that ideology, as though it were his own. (139–40)[11]

The terms of the argument do not, however, allow for the possibility of a 'subject' who has not undergone this process: no explanation is offered for the poet's own miraculous exemption from indoctrination, though evidently 'at home within bourgeois discourse and … partially of it.'[12] Ashbery's writing tends to be identified with an interior quest for a lost paradise:[13] a perhaps more tangible destination would be the imperial metropolis of New York, 'a logarithm / Of other cities' ('Self-Portrait in a Convex Mirror' (*SP*, 184)). His 'words, distant now, and mitred, glint' (*FC*, 4), possessing 'Supreme dominion' while 'instantaneously extending [their] hesitation to an // Empire' ('Fragment' (*DD*, 84)). Their 'attractive worldliness' ('Baked Alaska' (*HL*, 56)) exudes inclusiveness, courtesy, and a gracious invitation to overhear, if not participate in, sophisticated conversation: 'What brio in your chat, how / do you keep going' (*FC*, 57). Readers are simultaneously treated with a relaxed intimacy and paid the compliment of having mastered its sophisticated conventions. There is no anxiety as to relations with this audience, certainly no solipsism in this diffuse and amiable poetic voice. It is important both to prize its 'known civic pride, and civil obscurity'

('The one thing that can save America' (*SP*, 44)), and to acknowledge the economic and political privilege upon which its 'kindness / and late imperial emblems' (*FC*, 157) depend.

> This is America calling:
> The mirroring of state to state,
> Of voice to voice on the wires,
> The force of colloquial greetings like golden
> Pollen sinking on the afternoon breeze.
>
> ('Pyrography' (*HBD*, 8))

Douglas Crase celebrates this as 'an attitude at last fitted to the actual country Americans live in now', which, crucially, 'isn't English at all – it's American'. The 'force of colloquial greetings', however, represents precisely the opposite of 'the common sense of belonging to no community, of lacking authentic public experience together': if, as Crase remarks, 'we are talking about a poet who writes with the stereo on', we are also talking about a poet (and a critic) who cannot conceive of being without a stereo.[14] Ashbery defines 'the sum of my hedonistic, my seriously hedonistic philosophy' as 'only movies and love and laughter, sex and fun'; similarly there are constant reassurances that 'America is a fun country' (*VN*, 59)) and 'back in / soulless America, people are having fun / as usual' ('You would have Thought' (*CHB*, 174)).[15] 'The subtle hegemony / Of guilt that loops you together' ('Litany' (*AWK*, 41)) is occasionally invoked; but claims that 'Inside this privileged attitude' lurks 'a revolutionary spark' must be set against the appeal to 'Let the cycle of greed begin again; the sheer poetry of it will win over all but a few / viewers' (*FC*, 161; 64). The 'middle-class apartment ... with a good library and record collection' abruptly interpolated into 'The Skaters' (*RM*, 56) embodies a material affluence that permits textual destabilisation to be regarded with equanimity: 'Not everyone can afford the luxury of / just being not alive, but being at the center, / The perfumed, patterned center' ('Fantasia on "The Nut-Brown Maid"' (*HBD*, 78)).[16]

At times the mood appears almost Panglossian: 'I must / Make do with happiness, and am glad / To do so as long as everyone / Is happy and doesn't mind' ('Litany' (*AWK*, 61)). When 'another, more urgent question imposes itself – that of poverty', the issue is not, notably, how to endure these privations, but 'How to excuse it to oneself? The wetness and the coldness? Dirt and grime?' ('The

Skaters' (*RM*, 48)). One solution offered to contemplating 'original uses / Of famine' is ordering 'brined shrimp' ('Litany' (*AWK*, 48)):

> Sometimes
> I think we are being punished for the over-abundance
> Of things to enjoy and appreciate that we have,
> By being rendered less sensitive to them.   ('Litany' (*AWK*, 32))

Yet at the very least it is culturally contingent that 'most days are well-fed and relaxing': 'Home becomes more than a place, more even than / a concept', but only 'for this élite minority' (*FC*, 35; 23–4). 'Love is after all for the privileged', not a personal but a collective prerogative ('A Wave' (*W*, 83)), and Ashbery's eudaemonic exhortations themselves might be seen as 'ways / Our love assumed to look like a state religion / Like political wisdom' ('Written in the Dark' (*Sh*, 30)).

'Two Scenes' announces 'Destiny guides the water pilot, and it is destiny' (*ST*, 9), 'Clepsydra' talks of 'infant destinies' which had 'suavely matured' (*RM*, 32); and 'Unreleased Movie' ponders 'the busy destiny / Predicted by these teeming lines' (*AG*, 28). The term might be read as residually theological, or, alternatively, as a secular acceptance that the postmodern self has 'turned out to be mass-produced' ('Litany' (*AWK*, 67)). 'Our conception of our destiny' may also, however, be interpreted in nationalistic terms: the 'graver destinies' which 'were being unfurled on the political front' offer further 'proof / Of our slow, millennial, growth ring after ring' ('Litany' (*AWK*, 44, 41); 'The Sun' (*AWK*, 117)). There is at the very least a triumphalist dimension to proclaiming the 'investment years' of the 'post-war boom' ('Korean Soap Opera' (*HL*, 78)) as 'the golden age, our / Golden age' ('April Galleons' (*AG*, 96)).

Ashbery's characteristic techniques of multiple perspectives, temporal coalescence and elided narratives emerged out of his ambition to 'write poems as inexact as mathematics' ('Litany' (*AWK*, 46)). His 'personal pronouns', notoriously, 'very often seem to be like variables in an equation', but their very instability emphasises 'the fact of addressing someone', and indicates 'we are all somehow aspects of the consciousness giving rise to the poem':[17]

> Research has shown that ballads were produced by all of society
> working as a team. They didn't just happen. There was no guesswork.
> The people, then, knew what they wanted and how to get it.
> ('Hotel Lautréamont' (*HL*, 14))

Ashbery repeatedly eschews uniqueness: 'this very poem refutes it, /
springing up out of the collective unconscious / like a weasel
through a grating' ('The Decline of the West' (*SS*, 46)). This is public
sphere poetry: humane, accessible, always with an explicit investment in communication: 'what / Energies they poured into the
mould of their / Collective statement' ('Litany' (*AWK*, 42, 54)).[18] To
offer a mere smattering of possible examples. 'The Pied Piper' refers
to 'notes / Most civil' (*ST*, 69); 'How Much Longer will I be Able to
Inhabit the Divine Sepulcher' envisages 'Shaking hands in front of
the crashing of the waves / That give our words lonesomeness'
(*TCO*, 26); in 'A Wave', the poem is 'Beaming, confounding with the
spell of its good manners' (*W*, 70); 'Litany' assures us that 'always an
old-time mannerliness and courtesy informs / The itinerary' (*AWK*,
26); *Flow Chart* praises our 'deliberate civilization' for having 'invented neighbourliness' and prays 'for some civility from the air
before setting out as my ancestors had done' (*FC*, 164, 186).

'A list of cultural entanglements and his cultured acquaintances'
would, as Crase says, 'be staggering'.[19] Confirmation is offered in
the two pages of celebrity names in *The Vermont Notebook*, itemised
with the same dead-pan precision as an earlier list in the same
volume.

Gulf Oil, Union Carbide, Westinghouse, Xerox, Eastman Kodak, ITT,
Marriott, Sonesta, Credit Mobilier, Sperry Rand, Curtis Publishing,
Colgate, Motorola, Chrysler, General Motors, Anaconda, Credit Lyonnais,
Chase Manhattan, Continental Can, Time-Life, McGraw-Hill, CBS, ABC,
NBC. (*VN*, 13)

This is the contemporary equivalent of a Homeric invocation of
presiding deities.[20] The multinationals represent not the antithesis of
the world projected by Ashbery's poetry but the very condition of its
possibility: 'should anyone question the validity of this process / You
can point to the accessible result' ('A Wave' (*W*, 87)). As hierophant of
this globally ascendent culture, it should cause Ashbery no surprise
that

> In the occupied countries,
> You are raised to the statute of a god, no one
> Questions your work, its validity, all
> Are eager to support it, to give of themselves.
>
> ('Litany' (*AWK*, 46))

I now wish to examine one of the most devoted of those who 'give of themselves': John Ash.

III

One of the few points of consensus about John Ash is that he may be classified as that rare and almost unprecedented specimen: a British postmodernist.[21]

> I regard the world as a TV
> on which I change channels at will,
> never moving from the bed
> ('Croissant Outlets in Seattle' (*D*, 16))

Ash wishes to be anything but English: 'that compromised personality you disowned years ago' ('The Grapefruit Segments: a Book of Preludes' (*G*, 30)). In pursuit of this self-estrangement, he develops a style that eagerly solicits 'the inspiring visit / of the semiologist' ('American Bagatelles' (*G*, 13)): ludic, culturally eclectic, self-referential. It mocks the reader as uncouth if unable to emulate its moments of heightened self-consciousness, but as naive if unable to see through them as rhetorically fabricated illusion. Its exquisite superficiality is explicitly located in a late Romantic tradition of *fin-de-siècle* chic – 'The cleaning fluid is running out. The century is coming to an end' ('Twentieth Century' (*BP*, 79)) – which disparages the quotidian from the perspective of an assiduously cultivated world of fictive stimulants.

Ashbery refuses to oppose these two realms: the aesthetic becomes an everyday and unexceptional activity. Where 'Houseboat Days' directly incorporates Pater ('To flash light / Into the house within ...' (*HBD*, 39)), the highly cadenced doctrine becomes domestic and communal in its new context, and throughout his poetry, no attempt is made to segregate the the poetic from the prolix or demotic, the language of 'the common people, not the *common* people'.[22] In contrast Ash is a conscious, even insufferable, elitist – 'nearly all my friends are either writers or painters, a few are composers' – and his verse feels at all times compelled to flaunt its high cultural credentials: interviewing Ashbery, he feels obliged to lecture his mentor on the niceties of serial composition while the American poet confesses his attraction to 'the gloom and cosiness of Victorian life'.[23]

The relation between the two poets may perhaps be seen as a

parable of our times: the small-town kid from Manchester (if that counts as small) who went in search of the big-time in New York and never returned.

> Fellow was over
> Here recently from the British Isles.
> Wanted to see something of how the life goes
> On. He never made it back.　　　　　　　　('Litany' (*AWK*, 65))

Or as Ash puts it, 'right I'm signing off now because I'm going to New York in two days. One of the great moments in my life. So long suckers.' The experience of a new and liberating culture – 'The band ditches Offenbach for a Gershwin tune' ('American Uncles' (*D*, 14)) – produces breathless euphoria: 'approaching New York' is 'almost like falling in love'. The encounter is dramatised in terms that are beguiling in their stubborn innocence yet perilously close to unctuous parasitism:[24]

> The air was so sweet
> on your arrival it was as if
> the trees in the park blossomed, although the year was ending,
> ending in glory. You had crossed the ocean. Now
> you stepped from the avenue into the rotunda
> and smiled toward the statue of a woman. Wine was poured
> at the top of the curving stairs and the mirrors
> were filled with the faces of those who justified
> all your writing, messengers from another life.
>
> 　　　　　　　　　　　　　　　　　　　　　　　　('In Rainy Country' (*BP*, 3))

Ashbery figures foremost amongst 'those who justified / all your writing'; and it is admittedly tempting to dismiss Ash as a cross between a gratuitous duplication and junior partner. The American poet offers the maxim that 'the more you like a poet, the less you ought to write like him'. Otherwise there is the danger of producing 'only provincial watered-down versions of whatever is currently being explored elsewhere' (*RS*, 88): 'The siblings are standardized but substandard' ('In an Inchoate Place' (*CHB*, 60)).[25] Yet Ash shows no frustration or unease with this dependence, even seizing upon the similarity of their respective names: 'Somebody came up to me after I had been in New York for several months and I'd had several poems in the *New Yorker* and said "you know for months I thought you were a typo". And Peter Porter once described me as the manx version of John Ashbery.'[26] One might have expected at least a degree of resentment, but instead Ash glories in being subsumed:

'what Ashbery does and what I do ...'. The backdrop to this composite figure is revealing:

The interview took place in John Ashbery's apartment in Chelsea. It was repeatedly interrupted by the sound of sirens rising from 9th avenue and a ringing telephone. Chelsea is located north of Greenwich Village on the west side of Manhattan. Ashbery's apartment looks out towards the Hudson river and the heights of New Jersey. To one side of the view is a seminary with a very English-looking belfry, on the other is a massive red brick bulk of London Terrace, a complex of apartments constructed in vaguely Byzantine-Romanesque style, surmounted by strange pavillions concealing water tanks. Shortly before this interview began the entire panorama had been set alight by one of the gaudiest sunsets I have ever seen.[27]

This is making it with a vengeance: at the epicentre of high culture, the 'ringing telephone' (outdated) signifying social status (elsewhere Ash suggests that one must learn to 'commune with one's answering-machine'). The references to 'English-looking' and 'London' are subordinated to the 'Byzantine-Romanesque style', a parallel between empires pursued in several recent poems. The unimpeded imperial gaze surveys an 'entire panorama', illuminated by the 'gaudiest sunsets', a transferral of arousal. (The 'sound of sirens' and 'strange pavillions' also suggest a quasi-oriental eroticism.) The transference of allegiance to a more vigorous and satisfying culture appear unequivocal, permanent and complete. Yet, almost as an afterthought, Ash remarks, 'Yes I love Americans and I love New York, but I am constantly reminded that I am a European by the strange gaps in their knowledge or understanding.'[28] Even a post-modernist aesthetic is altered by its site of enunciation: Ash's work preserves a residual fidelity to a specifically British historical experience and exposes the ideological dimension to Ashbery's poetry in its very attempts to reproduce it.

Ash declares that 'it is absolutely impermissible to praise or blame a writer because he possesses or lacks what the prejudices of the time declare to be national characteristics', and consoles himself that 'well-intentioned critics' who 'have sought to uncover the English-ness' of his writing 'are balanced by those who find me madly French, or a native New Yorker born out of place'.[29] The preoccupation of British post-war poetry with the local, the commonplace, 'the trivial journey with the shopping-bags and the children' ('Epigraphs for Epigones' (*D*, 34)) is sneeringly disparaged. There are obvious exceptions. Ash's excellent, if infrequent, strain of provincial realism (In Manchester, 'I will take my ease amid the clean / Victorian buildings and quiet oils of its canals' ('Nostalgia' (*D*, 52)) is clearly indebted to Larkin and further continuities are evident in their respective treatments of exile, introspection and imaginary unlived biographies.[30] Nevertheless it is difficult to think of a contemporary poet so aggressive in his rejection of 'national characteristics' in favour of those of the *New Yorker*. (The Francophone element is much exaggerated: Ash, unlike Eliot and Ashbery, has never attempted composition in French.) In the next section, I shall contrast Ash's 'The Ungrateful Citizens' with Ashbery's 'The Instruction Manual' and examine the consequences 'When the tall poems of the world, the towering earthbound poetic utterances / Invade the street of our dialect, penetrate the avenue of our patois' ('Finnish Rhapsody' (*AG*, 15)).[31]

IV

'The Instruction Manual' opens leisurely, almost prolixly:

As I sit looking out of a window of the building
I wish I did not have to write the instruction manual on the uses of a
　new metal.
I look down into the street and see people, each walking with an inner
　peace,
And envy them – they are so far away from me!
Not one of them has to worry about getting this manual out on schedule.
And, as my way is, I begin to dream a little, resting my elbows on the
　desk and leaning out of the window a little,
Of dim Guadalajara! City of rose-colored flowers!
City I wanted most to see, and most did not see, in Mexico!
But I fancy I see, under the press of having to write the instruction manual.

(*ST*, 14)

The poem fits so exactly into the tripartite generic pattern of Romantic lyric (location; imaginative excursion; return) that it has often been suspected of parody: Shapiro for example reads the poem in terms of alienated labour producing clichéd fantasies.[32] The 'dream' offers a guided tour of a picturesque, intimately known, wholly invented environment: 'How limited, but how complete withal'. The view from the 'good high place' of the 'church tower' means the 'whole network of the city extends before us'. The benign inclusiveness of tone ('The mind / Is so hospitable, taking in everything / Like boarders' ('Houseboat Days' (*HBD*, 38))) comfortably situates itself within the academic genre of tourist poetry, which, as von Hallberg notes, served as 'outward signs of the cultural heritage America was taking over after the war'.[33]

The best place to establish difference between Ash and Ashbery is where they are most apparently alike, in 'The Ungrateful Citizens':

> It occurs to me that I would like to write a poem about Naples.
> Perhaps I have always wanted to do this, and only realised it just a minute
>   ago,
> but, alas, I have never been to Naples, and yet my desire to write about
>   the place
> becomes more insuperable by the second. I have become convinced that
>   my writing desk
> is on the same latitude as Naples. I have only to lean back in my chair,
> and I incline toward the city of my dreams, and in my dreams my feet
> rest in Manhattan while my hair rustles against the wharves of Naples . . .
>
>   (*BP*, 81)

The poems are so close as to represent formal imitation rather than indirect influence. This is evident not merely in the metre, the ingenuous exclamatory tone, and the idle reverie of the narrator, but also more specific details. In Ashbery the 'young and pretty' wife has a 'shawl' which is 'pink, white, and rose'; the 'young fellow' and the 'young girl' exchange 'shy words of love' behind the bandstand, and there is 'young love, married love and the love of an aged mother for her son'; in Ash, the 'young girls' wear 'pink and white dresses'; 'shy lovers' seek 'corners in which to commune'; and the 'generations' are 'nightly conjoined in perfect amity'.

There are two noteworthy differences. Firstly, the poet is obliged to make a peculiar detour: it is necessary to dream of Manhattan before one can dream of Naples; secondly, there is no comparable economic underpinning in Ash's poem, no equivalent frame involving the 'schedule' for production of the 'manual'.[34] Ashbery's poem may appear to posit antithetical worlds of utility and imagination, toil and leisure, boredom and beauty. Yet the 'dream' represents not a release from but a logical consequence of the 'manual'. It is because of the technological superiority that it represents that 'dim Guadalajara' is so completely at the disposal of the American writer. The holiday mood (the only worker is an absent bank clerk) is achieved at the expense by reducing the Mexican city into 'one of

the other made-up countries / Where we can live forever' ('Hop O'
my Thumb' (*SP*, 33)).

Abolition of location is a characteristic Ashberyian trait: 'The
map is again wiped clean' ('The Whole is Admirably Composed'
(*HL*, 30)); more farcically, 'My wife thinks I'm in Oslo – Oslo,
France, that is' ('Worsening Situation' (*SP*)); and the catalogue of
rivers in 'Into the Dusk-Charged Air' is merely a logical if bizarre
extreme.[35] Yet the 'portable laugh eclipsing another place' ('The
New Realism' (*TCO*, 59)) implies at the very least disregard of, and
arguably contempt for, its independent existence. In 'The Task', the
'fugitive lands crowd under separate names' after a 'new pennant'
has been raised 'up the flagpole' (*DD*, 13); and a similar imperial
mastery is implied in the recurrent completeness of survey:

> It is the erratic path of time that we trace
> On the globe, with moist fingertip, and surely, the globe stops.
>
> ('And you know' (*ST*, 57))

> For I am condemned to drum my fingers
> On the closed lid of this piano, this tedious planet, earth
> As it winks to you through the aspiring, growing distances,
> A last spark before the night.   ('The Skaters' (*RM*, 42–3))

> The whole is stable within
> Instability, a globe like ours, resting
> On a pedestal of vacuum, a ping-pong ball
> Secure on its jet of water.
>
> ('Self-Portrait in a Convex Mirror' (*SP*, 70))

In Ash the 'long flights of stairs' allow no such vantage, but instead
lead to a 'lightless courtyard' in which a 'skinny child is crying under
lines of washing'. Instead of a uniform contentment, 'it seems that
all but the richest and most conservative of citizens cannot wait to
leave my Naples'. The final lines are of rebuke, bitterness and
disenchantment: the dream of being able to dream cannot be
sustained:

> They glare at me and say: 'This is not Naples. This is a place on which the
>   world has turned its back.
> A cloud of lies covers it. The mansions you saw are hovels, the churches tin
>   shacks,
> the parks and gardens vegetable plots and stony fields in which we scratch
>   for a living.
> And this is not even the site of wars and massacres, only a place of ordinary
>   wretchedness.

No, we cannot be the amorous ballet the tourist requires for a backdrop –
O take us away, perhaps to that *island of fragrant grasses* mentioned in a
   fragment of Petronius.'   (*BP*, 84)

The throwaway reference to Petronius, exemplary decadent of an
earlier empire, cannot disguise the association of '*island of fragrant
grasses*' with a more familiar 'green and pleasant land'. One should
not be misled by the 'hovels' and 'tin shacks': the landscape of 'parks
and gardens' is essentially suburban. Ash's residual affiliation is to
his own culture and to that 'place of ordinary wretchedness',
Larkinesque England, 'in which we scratch for a living'. His are 'old
songs of a reduced inheritance' out of which emerges 'a voice,
summoning / slandered histories' ('Soul Music' (*D*, 47–8)).[36]

Yet if Ashbery presents himself as 'a shy appraiser gazing un-
endangered into / the reflecting globe', his poetry cannot wholly
ignore that the fact that 'the horrible clashes / hadn't gone away'
(*FC*, 43): 'Will our pain matter too, and if so, when?' (*FC*, 121). I now
wish to examine Ashbery's dramatisation of these 'clashes' and Ash's
attempted emulation of his composure.

v

'The Instruction Manual' is an early and arguably unrepresentative
text, from *Some Trees* published in 1956.[37] Yet elsewhere in the
volume, there are frequent asides to the Cold War – in 'Glazu-
noviana', 'the bear / Drops dead' (*ST*, 22); in 'Illustration', 'rockets
sighed / Elegantly over the city' (*ST*, 49) – and this political strand
continues throughout: 'That world is a war now' ('The New
Realism' *TCO*, 59); 'We cannot keep the peace / At home, and at the
same time be winning wars abroad' ('Fragment' (*DD*, 80)); 'We have
the technology to tame the edges' ('Point Lookout' (*CHB*, 90)).
Ashbery's work of the 1990s also reflects the precise historical
moment of the dissolution of the eastern bloc: a 'halting yet
prosperous time / when games of strength were put away' (*FC*, 12).
It has now become possible to 'obtain the release of certain
compromised acquaintances' if we are

   ready to reclaim territories surrendered in a moment
of temporary insanity, and others as well that were never in question
until they became bones of contention just seconds ago in the new climate
of sharpened political awareness that hungers always for new victims

(FC, 80)

There are even moments of belligerence towards the 'rival cesspool / of other nations', and outbursts of plaintive nationalism, 'everything you see on television is a fraud, is planted to confuse distraught / patriots like yourself' (*FC*, 22, 39).

The Tennis Court Oath, usually regarded as Ashbery's most politicised work, possesses conspicuous outcrops of patriotic rhetoric:

> You were not elected president, yet won the race
>
> ('The Tennis Court Oath' (*TCO*, 11))

> And I am proud
> of these stars in our flag we don't want
> the flag of film
> waving over the sky
> toward us – citizens of some future state   ('America' (*TCO*, 18))

> Her face goes green, her eyes are green;
> In the dark corner playing "The Stars and Stripes Forever".
>
> ('White Roses' (*TCO*, 35))

The key question is whether these techniques of asyntactic disjunction are sufficient to remove 'The political contaminations // of what he spoke' ('A White Paper' (*TCO*, 32)). From this perspective, the aleatory combinations of 'Europe' may be seen as a kind of revenge: they are 'written upon English paper, and English penny stamps are upon them/ ... They / mostly contain instructions to our good friends in Great Britain' (*TCO*, 73):[38]

> dying for they do not
> the hole no crow can
> and finally the day of thirst
> in the air.
> whistles carbon dioxide. Cold
> pavement grew. The powerful machine
> The tractor, around edge
> the listless children. Good night
> staining the naughty air
> with marvelous rings. You are going there.
> Weeps. The wreath not decorating.
> The kids pile over the ample funeral hill.
> has arrived from London
>   o'clock
> baited tragically
> This time the others grew.
> The others waited
> by the darkening pool – 'a world of silence'

you can't understand their terror
means more to these people waste
the runt crying in the pile of colored
snapshots offal in the wind
that's the way we do it terror
the hand of the large person falls
to the desk. The people all leave.
the industries begin
moments   puts on the silencer
You crab into the night   (*TCO*, 69–70)

The 'listless children' from 'London' are pathetic, bewildered, 'the runt crying in the pile of colored / snapshots': 'It was always wartime Britain, or some other place, / Dictated by circumstances ... / Rudeness, shabbiness' ('Litany' (*AWK*, 27)). The images of 'darkening pool', 'wind', 'rings', are repeated elsewhere in the volume, notably in 'A Last World' (*TCO*, 56–8): part of an explicit doctrine of deterrence. (The 'honey' that '*burns the throat*' in 'They Dream Only of America' can be linked up via 'arctic honey' to the 'nuclear world' of 'Leaving the Atocha Station' (*TCO*, 13, 33).)

In 'you can't understand their terror ... that's the way we do it terror', the 'we' is more expectant than denunciatory: 'the hand of the large person' which 'falls / to the desk' is both the finger on the nuclear button and the grasp of the writer himself. 'Litany' claims that 'the rite dismantles bit by bit / The blind empathy / Of a homeland' (*AWK*, 15), but it is equally possible to see the Ashberyian sublime as covertly identifying with and endorsing American power. 'Popeye sits in thunder' ('Farm Implements and Rutabagas in a Landscape' (*DDS*, 41)), 'the vengeful deity whose acts / are being recorded has all the time in the world' (*FC*, 81).

These 'gothic vignettes of the atomic age' are accompanied by a 'curious lack of anxiety' ('A Wave' (*W*, 75)): 'Violence, how smoothly it came' ('Shadow Train' (*Sh*, 48)).[39] In 'The Skaters' after a 'flame fountain' is produced by adding zinc to sulphuric acid, 'The whole surface of the liquid will become luminous, and fire balls, with jets of fire / Will dart from the bottom, through the fluid with great rapidity and a hissing noise'; but far from provoking apprehension, 'it is rather beautiful up here, / Watching the oncoming storm' (*RM*, 48, 56).[40] In 'Soonest Mended', the tone is similarly unperturbed: 'we were always having to be rescued / On the brink of destruction, like heroines in *Orlando Furioso*' (*DD*, 17); and in 'The Other Tradition',

'some wore sentiments / Emblazoned on T-shirts, proclaiming /
The lateness of the hour' (*HBD*, 2).[41] This 'weather eye on
Doomsday' (*RS*, 213) should be regarded not as an indictment of
complacency but as a boast of the power to inflict:

> ignorance
> of the law, far from being no excuse, is the law, and we'll see who rakes in
> the chips come Judgement Day.   (*FC*, 123)

> But the heavenly uproar
> is heavier; storms mean business
> in this day and age.   ('Wild Boys of the Road' (*HL*, 73))

The calm comes not before or after but during the 'storms': 'The
sound of harps is sufficient distraction / against the thunder of the
"fray" for which / Gog and Magog are said to be continually
preparing', and when 'great rains had purged the heavens / of their
terrible delight', there remain 'ruby drops of the wine / The
morning after the great storm / That swept our sky away, leaving /
A new muscle in its place' ('Litany' (*AWK*, 27, 15)). Or indeed a new
world order. 'Dust in the air' is envisaged as 'floating with a kind of
negative majesty' after the world '*implodes*': 'all is basically kindling
for the late / greater conflagration in which we think we shall see
our destiny; our fate and destiny / are one' (*FC*, 17, 158)).

> The cimmerian moment in which all lives, all destinies
> And incompleted destinies were swamped
> As though by a giant wave that picks itself up
> Out of a calm sea and retreats again into nowhere
> Once its damage is done.   ('A Wave' (*W*, 81))

> There is equanimity, even relish, at witnessing the 'cimmerian moment'
> the curiously muted register of a survivor and beneficiary:

> We may perhaps remain, here, cautious yet free
> On the edge, as it rolls its unblinking chariot
> Into the vast open, the incredible violence and yielding
> Turmoil that is to be our route.
>   ('Evening in the Country' (*DD*, 34))

One must be inside the 'unblinking chariot' rather than in its path
('our route') to possess the insouciance of 'one who naps beside a
chasm / Swollen with the hellish sound of wind / And torrents'
('Litany' (*AWK*, 25)). I now wish to examine the consequences when
Ash 'chooses to play back the tape' of the Ashberyian sublime.

For Ash, if 'Part 1' of the lesson is 'Exercises in Style', 'Part 2' contains 'Songs on the Death of Children' ('The Philosophies of Popular Songs' (*BS*, 91)). Some touches, such as the 'pile of shrimps lying in rosy death' ('Yesterday's Snow' (*D*, 43) or the 'pale dead boy, / his astonishing red hair, the shirt rumpled like sculpture' ('Poor Boy: Portrait of a Painting' (*G*, 28)), clearly invite the charge of elegant necrophilia. Nevertheless there is a cumulative power and coherence in this disarmingly casual imagery of death, violence and imminent apocalypse:

> The bombs have fallen
> harmless as walnut shells
> into the middle of the bathing party.
>
> ('American Bagatelles' (*G*, 13))

The extensive reliance upon tropes of disconnection and foreboding – 'The telephone rang in its kiosk / Unanswered on the corner' or 'The alarm keeps howling in the locked car' ('The Philosophies of Popular Song' (*BS*, 91–2)) – always risks becoming one more formal variation: 'the victim of a recent bombing / dissolved into luscious water-lights and lillies' ('Nympheas' (*BS*, 39)). This 'cool light, stopping short / of indifference' may be justified negatively, in terms of Ash's customary restraint in its use, but also positively for its historical appositeness 'to describe this new and too familiar / sense of loss with some appearance of calm' ('The Rain' (*BS*, 48)). Yet though 'the nightmares are boring' they 'will not go away' ('Street Musicians' (*BS*, 134)); we cannot forget 'our dulled anticipation / of the storm that still holds off' ('The Rain' (*BS*, 50)); 'it is increasingly difficult to disguise the general air / of "nervousness bordering on panic"' ('Accompaniment to a Film Scene' (*BS*, 56)). Ash's work captures particularly well the ambience of stagnation in the closing years of the Cold War: citizenship, the moral participation of the individual in the state, is replaced by quizzical unillusioned complicity:

> in the dull street
> beside the dirty canal
>
> no one, just now,
> is killing anyone. Why not
> we want to know?
>
> ('The Weather or The English Requiem' (*BS*, 140))

Ash's work appears to recoil from the political sphere into fantasies of nineteenth-century French bohemia, or more recently, elaborate reconstructions of an aestheticised Byzantium.[42] Yet in post-war Britain too, 'The dream of empire continues' ('Salon Pieces' (*BS*, 44)), promulgating the quintessentially romantic sentiments of 'an intolerable burden of regret' ('Telephone Nights' (*BS*, 52)) and 'a destructive nostalgia' ('Accompaniment to a Film Scene' (*BS*, 55)) for 'the burnished globes, / the toy trains, the mouldy jellies and rose-coloured maps of empire' ('Even Though' (*BS*, 25)).

> Progress has betrayed us! How commerce has declined
> and how the casinos prosper
>
> ('Finale: A Spectacle A Funeral' (*BS*, 19))
>
> Why was nothing said? Why was the court kept in ignorance
> of the loss of the colonies?
>
> ('Funeral Waltz' (*BS*, 45–6))
>
> Who could say
>
> for certain that we were not gods
> or that one day we might not
>   inherit an Empire?   ('The Bed' (*BS*, 63))

'We thought it would last much longer' ('Interlude Two: Berceuse Elegiaque' (*BS*, 18)), but now this is an 'Exploded geography!' ('Landscape and Figures' (*BS*, 32)).

> melancholy attempts at continuity were soon
> abandoned like the plans for a new Ringstrasse
> after the fall of the Empire
>
> ('The Bed' (*BS*, 65))

Despite the incessant 'recital of nostalgias' ('Orchestral Manoeuvres (In the Dark)' (*BS*, 37)), the more urgent question is that of the terms of submission to a newly ascendent power. 'The sentiment is questionable: regret for a vanished order which, if it still existed, we'd dream of destroying like any nation of the colonized' ('The Big Horse' (*G*, 18)): the syntactic ambiguity allows 'we' to harbour compensatory fantasies of aggression against the 'colonized' in order to fend off recognition of British post-war impotence as a client state.

> "My civilisation had ended,
> and I like it so much ...
>   But now it is ended,
> and *someone* must be to blame, some American, I should think ... "
>
> ('The Future including the Past' (*G*, 23))

Ash may claim to have 'embraced the violent innocence / I found in great America's heart' ('Glowing Embers: Paraphrases and Fictions' (*BS*, 57)); but the most powerful moments in his poetry emanate out of a latent hostility: 'we are forced to think of our destination – / the oppressive portals of the capitol, / the altars still smelling of blood' ('Men, Women, and Children' (*D*, 47)).

It may sound implausible to claim Ash as a poet of nuclear anxiety: 'who would choose to be the trumpeter / cracking notes all day outside a crowded charcuterie?'. Yet his apocalyptic flourishes take on a precise geopolitical location in 'The Goodbyes', when 'history / slips into a dull dream of foreknowledge': after 'the weather's wrecked the picnic' ('so English! the clouds, the downpour / as evasive terms') it is whimsically inferred, in a typically unemphatic image of incineration, that 'someone has *smoked* the landscape' (*G*, 54–5).[43] The 'goodbye of goodbyes' is given by those with somewhere left to go: 'the goodbye that leaves you ruined' refers specifically to the limited strike scenario popular with US strategists in the 1980s, an exchange confined to a European theatre of war: 'The walls are shaking. The light / is drunk. Goodbye' (*G*, 56–7). Three pages later, Ash enlarges, in 'What Remains', upon the 'goodbyes which really / too avidly anticipate the catastrophe' secreted within 'shelters against / the rising wind', exposed to a 'white cloud (burnt at the edges / by a light that has travelled further than imagination)': one finds out too late that 'the doors don't close as your fear imagined they would / in that hotel at the end of the world' (*G*, 60–1).

The close of Ashbery's 'A Last World' may be illuminatingly contrasted with Ash's variation on the same theme:

A last world moves on the figures;
They are smaller than when we last saw them caring about them.
The sky is a giant rocking horse
And of the other things death is a new office building filled with modern
    furniture,

A wise thing, but one which has no purpose for us.
Everything is being blown away;
A little horse trots up with a letter in its mouth, which is read with
    eagerness
As we gallop into the flame.   (*TCO*, 58)

The 'us' retains its collective force; an 'eagerness' is still shown for the message, the intrepid, homely, pony-express quality of the 'little horse' punctures even the giganticism of the 'rocking-horse' of the apocalypse; there is even a certain upbeat quality in its 'final gallop into the flame'. Even confronting annihilation, the verse displays 'the flowing dress of dignity and repose / with which an absolute and burdensome / mastery hides itself' ('The Death of Mozart' (*BS*, 121)). Ash's own 'idea of the End' ('Without Being Evening' (*BS*, 117)), though no less firmly situated in a tradition of romantic elegy, is wholly devoid of Ashbery's jaunty anticipation:

> Not many wish to visit
> and someone, one supposes, has to stay
>
> since the buildings still stand
> against the sky, solid and vacant
>
> as cemetery statues. Our lives
> have been folded away like a letter
>
> bearing a message of terrible
> urgency
> and never posted.
>
> ('Our Lives: a Symphony' (*G*, 20))[44]

The greater pathos of the latter passage lies in its sense of inhabiting, rather than merely contemplating, an aftermath. If the romantic expansiveness of Ashbery's rhetoric confirms that 'They have tremendous power / in their doing, these Americans' ('The Beer Drinkers' (*HL*, 140)), Ash's very failure of emulation, the 'rancid stalk' of his affected decadence, serves to remind us 'How far apart we were on most issues, and the European cooks it differently / Besides' ('Autumn on the Thruway' (*HL*, 36)).

VII

One must obviously show caution before extrapolating large-scale conclusions from the relation of two poets. Nevertheless, I hope to have established that, in so far as Postmodernism signifies the equal availability of the styles of the past, the idiom of Romanticism remains a continuous option. No causal genealogy can be established between the two movements however: instead it is more useful to transpose recent arguments directed against holistic definitions of Romanticism in order to foreground its complex ideological functions. From this perspective, it becomes apparent that there is no intrinsic linkage between formal innovation and political radicalism in Ashbery's rhetoric: instead it articulates both the seductive Utopian appeal and capacity for punitive retaliation of contemporary America. Furthermore, when transplanted to a different site of enunciation, the periphery of Britain, its communal voice displays an underlying exclusiveness. Thus to the extent that Ash fails to persuade himself that apocalypse is only for other people, his poetry confirms Ashbery's own prognosis that 'the English' are 'Probably smarter than we are / Although there is supposed to be something / We have that they don't – don't ask me what it is' ('Tenth Symphony' (*SP,* 46)). The missing term, I would suggest, the 'something' which Ashbery's poetry possesses 'that they don't', is empire.

Abbreviations

John Ashbery

AG   *April Galleons* (New York: Viking, 1987; Manchester: Carcanet, 1988)

AWK   *As We Know* (New York: Viking, 1979; Manchester: Carcanet, 1981)

CHB   *Can You Hear, Bird* (Manchester: Carcanet, 1996)

DD   *The Double Dream of Spring* (New York: Dutton, 1970)

DDS   *The Double Dream of Spring* (New York: Ecco, 1976)

FC   *Flow Chart* (New York: Knopf, 1991)

HBD   *Houseboat Days* (New York: Viking, 1977)

HL   *Hotel Lautréamont* (New York; Knopf; Manchester: Carcanet, 1992)

RM   *Rivers and Mountains* (New York: Holt, Rinehart &Winston, 1966)

RS   *Reported Sightings: Art Chronicles, 1957–1987,* ed. David Bergman (New York: Knopf, 1989)

Sh   *Shadow Train* (New York: Viking, 1981)

SP   *Self-Portrait in a Convex Mirror* (New York: Viking, 1975; Manchester: Carcanet, 1977)

SS   *And the Stars were Shining* (Manchester: Carcanet, 1994)

ST   *Some Trees* (1956; New York: Ecco, 1978).

TCO   *The Tennis Court Oath* (Middletown, Conn., Wesleyan University Press, 1962)

TP   *Three Poems* (New York: Viking, 1972)

VN   *The Vermont Notebook* (Los Angeles: Black Sparrow, 1975)

W   *A Wave* (New York: Viking, Manchester: Carcanet, 1984)

John Ash

BJ   *A Byzantine Journey* (London and New York: Tauris, 1995)
BP   *The Burnt Pages* (Manchester: Carcanet, 1991)
BS   *The Branching Stairs* (Manchester: Carcanet, 1984)
D   *Disbelief* (Manchester: Carcanet, 1987)
G   *The Goodbyes* (Manchester: Carcanet, 1982)

CHAPTER 11

Postmodernism / 'fin de siècle': defining 'difference' in late twentieth-century poetics

Marjorie Perloff

It is now more than twenty years ago that a SUNY-Binghamton professor named William Spanos, a Heideggerian student of poetics, who was bent on opposing everything the New Criticism, in which he had been trained, stood for, founded a journal called *boundary 2*, subtitled *An International Journal of Postmodern Literature*. The title is emblematic of the period: the lower-case *boundary 2* points to the desire and need for new parameters, new margins – a 'second' way to define literature. 'International' means, in 1960s or 1970s-speak, European as well as American; the first issue of *boundary 2* features an essay on Foucault by Edward Said and another on the *nouveau roman* by Bruce Morrisette, side by side with Warren Tallman's piece on William Carlos Williams's short stories, Joseph Riddel's deconstructionist essay on Wallace Stevens, and James Curtis's essay on Marshall McLuhan and French structuralism. The poetry published in the issue may also be considered 'international' since there is a 35-page portfolio of work by the Greek poet Yannis Ritsos.

But it is the word literature in the title that I find especially interesting. For, although poststructuralist theory is already much in evidence (witness Edward Said on Foucault, Riddel on Stevens via Paul de Man, and Spanos himself on the postmodern imagination via Heidegger), the journal's focus is very much on literature, it still being a given, in 1972, that 'literary' journals, published as they were by English or Comparative Literature departments, would concentrate, from however radical a point of view, on literary texts. Consider, for example, David Antin's seminal essay 'Modernism and Postmodernism: Approaching the Present in American Poetry', published in the first issue.

Antin writes from the perspective of the practising poet, who was also beginning to make a name for himself as a performance artist and art critic, having recently been appointed chair of the newly formed Visual Arts department of the University of California-San Diego. His *boundary 2* essay brilliantly dismantles what he calls the 'closed verse tradition' of late Modernist poetry from Delmore Schwartz to W. D. Snodgrass. 'What we have called the "modern" for so long', Antin declares, 'is thoroughly over'; accordingly, the recycling of the symbolist lyric (Antin dismisses W. D. Snodgrass's *After Experience* as 'an updated version of *A Shropshire Lad*'), as well as the recycling of collage (e.g., Robert Lowell's 'attenuated history collage' in 'Concord' or 'For the Union Dead'), can only be retrograde.[1] Over against Snodgrass and Lowell, Antin sets Charles Olson, the then hero of the poetic counterculture; Olson's 'disregard for metrical organization and for a poetical frame that wraps things up' (DA, 117) is considered exemplary. Indeed, following the scenario first made prominent by Donald Allen in *The New American Poetry* (1960), Antin describes the 'great explosion of American poetry' in the 1960s as the final rejection of the 'closed-verse' tradition of neo-Modernist, late New Critical poetry, in favour of a more direct and spontaneous poetry based on natural utterance, on the breath. The 'opening of the field' by the Black Mountain and Beat poets, by the New York school and the San Francisco Renaissance, so the argument goes, was animated by 'the underlying conviction that poetry was made by a man [sic] on his feet talking' (DA, 131). As such, the poetic text was to be understood less as an object than as a 'score' or 'notation' to be actualised in performance, the implication of such 'scoring' being that 'phenomenological reality is "discovered" and "constructed" by poets' (DA, 132–3). And further: postmodernist poetics meant the turn from Pound and Eliot to the neglected work of Gertrude Stein and John Cage, the poetry of Dada and Surrealism, and 'the poetry of nonliterate and partially literate cultures' (DA, 133): in the case of the latter, Antin is of course thinking of the ethnopoetics movement spearheaded by his friend and fellow-poet Jerome Rothenberg. Indeed, one of the early issues (Spring 1975) of *boundary 2* was a special issue on 'The Oral Impulse in Contemporary American Poetry', featuring the work of Rothenberg and again Antin.

To re-read Antin's 1972 essay in the mid-1990s is to become aware of how much our assumptions about Postmodernism have changed. The essay's frame of reference is, to begin with, resolutely literary, the issue being who has inherited and who should inherit the poetic mantle of the great Modernists: such neo-Modernists as Robert Lowell, who carry on, in attenuated form, the symbolist collage tradition of *The Waste Land* and the *Cantos*, or such 'phenomenological' poets as Olson and Creeley? Closed verse versus open form, the metrical line versus the 'breath', poetry as product versus poetry as process, symbolism versus immanence (as Charles Altieri put it in another important essay published in *boundary 2* in 1973),[2] and so on. But although the poem as autonomous artefact is rejected, Poetry itself remains an autonomous realm, contaminated neither by culture nor by theory nor by any of the discourses that surround it. It is also the case that just about all of Antin's poets, whether Good Guys or Bad Guys are white men. Indeed, the 'field' which is supposedly 'opening' is, at the practical level, the setting of a polite athletic contest (hockey? soccer?), where the Harvard team captained by Robert Lowell plays the Harvard team captained by Charles Olson. To put it another way: Antin, who is obviously a member of the Olson team, is theorising his own practice, telling us what kind of poetry he wants to produce (the utterance of 'a man on his feet talking') and why.

But there is another assumption Antin makes (as does Altieri in 'From Symbolism to Immanence', and the book that revised this essay, *Enlarging the Temple*, as does James E. B. Breslin's *From Modern to Contemporary*, even though Breslin is careful not to use the P word, and as does my own *Poetics of Indeterminacy*), namely the assumption that *poetry matters*.[3] Poetic discourse, in early formulations of Postmodernism, is not just a site to be contested and intersected by other discourses; for – and this is the corollary assumption – there is such a thing as *poetic value*. Not only is Olson 'better' than a member of the other team like Snodgrass; Ginsberg is judged to be better than Ferlinghetti, Denise Levertov (one of the few women poets regularly cited in the 1970s) is better than May Swenson, Frank O'Hara better than Ted Berrigan.

These twin assumptions – the value of poetry and the ability to discriminate specific poetic value – are just as central to discussions of the other arts. In 1972 art with a capital A still mattered and it mattered that Jasper Johns was 'better' than a second-generation abstract expressionist like Norman Bluhm. Merce Cunningham was judged to be more 'interesting' than Murray Feldman. And so on. Indeed, theorising Postmodernism, during the first decades of its usage, was animated by the belief – and here *boundary 2* was quite typical – that Postmodernism represents everything that is radical, innovative, forward-looking – beyond, if not contra, mere Modernism, and is thus distinguished from the mass of writing or painting or architecture, which, far from challenging Modernism, merely carries on its traditions.

It is interesting to re-read Ihab Hassan in this regard. Hassan's first book, after all, was called *The Literature of Silence* (1967), and made the case for a 'new literature' written in the wake of Dachau and Hiroshima, a literature whose 'total rejection of Western history and civilization' leads either to the apocalyptic violence and obscenity of a Henry Miller or a Norman Mailer or the silence, randomness and indeterminacy of Samuel Beckett or John Cage. By 1971, Hassan referred to this 'change in Modernism' as Postmodernism and drew up the first of his famous lists or tables, a table made up of binary oppositions:[4]

Modernism	Postmodernism
1. Urbanism	1. The Global Village (McLuhan), Spaceship Earth (Fuller), the City as Cosmos – Science Fiction. Anarchy and fragmentation.
2. Technologism	2. Runaway technology. New media, art forms. Boundless dispersal by media. The computer as substitute consciousness or extension of consciousness.
3. Elitism	3. Antielitism, antiauthoritarianism. Diffusion of the ego. Participation. Community. Anarchy.
4. Irony	4. Radical play. Entropy of meaning. Comedy of the absurd. Black Humor. Camp.
5. Abstraction	5. New Concreteness. Found Object. Conceptual Art.
6. Primitivism	6. Beat and Hip. Rock Culture. Dionysian Ego.
7. Eroticism	7. The New Sexuality. Homosexuality, Feminism, Lesbianism. Comic pornography. Repeal of Censorship.
8. Antinomianism. Beyond Law. Non Serviam.	8. Counterculture. Beyond alienation. Counter Western 'ways'. Zen. Buddhism, Hinduism, the occult, apocalypticism.
9. Experimentalism. Formal innovation. New language.	9. Open form, discontinuity, improvisation, Antiformalism. Indeterminacy. Aleatory Structure. Minimalism. Intermedia.

Hassan's frame of reference is, on the face of it, much broader than Antin's: he draws upon fiction as well as poetry, on philosophy, the visual arts, and certain well known critical texts like Lionel Trilling's *Beyond Culture*. Urbanism, for example, is exemplified by Baudelaire, Proust, Rilke, Eliot, and Dos Passos; Technologism, by Cubism, Futurism, and Dada, with a reference to Wylie Sypher's *Literature and Technology*, and the entry on Modernist Antinomianism alludes to Nathan A. Scott's *The Broken Center*. The Postmodern column is similarly eclectic, trans-urbanism (the Global Village) being represented by Buckminster Fuller, Marshall McLuhan, science fiction, and so on.

But like Antin, and like almost everyone who wrote on the subject in the 1970s, Postmodernism was where it was happening, where the excitement was. Not because the individual writers of Modernism (Pound, Eliot, Rilke, Mann) were not perhaps greater than those of Postmodernism, but because PoMo was presented as being *open, antielitist, anti-authoritarian, participatory, anarchic, playful, improvisational, rebellious, discontinuous* – and even, in Hassan's words, *ecologically active*, otherwise known as *Green*. To write from a postmodernist perspective, in these years, thus involved a romantic faith in the openendedness of literary and artistic discourse, in the ability of these discourses to transform themselves, to go beyond existing models and improve on them. As such, this Utopian phase of Postmodernism was very much an inside view, a witnessing on the part of the poets themselves (and Hassan used all manner of typographical devices and fragmentary forms so as to ally himself with the poets) that there was still a cutting edge.

Within a decade, a curious reversal had set in. By 1978, Hassan, always something of a barometer, published an essay called 'Culture, Indeterminacy, and Value', that contained more references to Foucault and de Man than to McLuhan or Cage or Burroughs. The essay is written under the sign of Nietzsche and makes much of the 'disappearance' of man as a 'concrete figuration of history' (IH*PT*, 52–3). And the 1982 'Towards a Concept of Postmodernism' begins with a catalogue of names that 'may serve to adumbrate Postmodernism', a catalogue that opens with the following: Jacques Derrida, Jean-François Lyotard, Michel Foucault, Hayden White, Jacques Lacan, Gilles Deleuze, R. D. Laing, Norman O. Brown, Herbert Marcuse, Jean Baudrillard, Jürgen Habermas, Thomas Kuhn, Paul Feyerabend, Roland Barthes, Julia Kristeva, Wolfgang

Iser, the Yale critics. The list then turns to dancers, composers, artists, architects and 'various authors' from Beckett and Borges to John Ashbery and Robert Wilson (IH*PT*, 85). But theory, specifically French theory, is clearly at the centre of the enterprise. The open form or process model celebrated by David Antin now gives way to the 'semantic instability' of Derrida, and since the construction of the text as trace structure, as a tissue of differences, can be applied to writings of any period, the examples begin to come from established writers, primarily of the nineteenth century – Rousseau and Shelley, Marx and Mallarmé, Nerval and Nietzsche. Not reading the New, but re-reading the familiar in the light of the New Theory – this becomes the order of the day.

The widespread acceptance of Jean-François Lyotard's paradigm of *La Condition postmoderne* (1979, English translation 1984) marks this shift from what we might call David Antin's pragmatics of Post-modernism (the inside view of the practising poet) to the broader cultural definition of the term as it used today. When Lyotard defines the *postmodern* as 'incredulity toward metanarratives', when he describes the 'two major versions of such narratives of legitimation', as that of the liberation of humanity (justice) and the speculative unity of all knowledge (truth), the term *Modernism* points, not as in Antin or Hassan's case, to the particular literary and art movements of the early twentieth century, but to the larger *modernity* of Enlight-enment discourse, specifically to the various progress models of the nineteenth century, which are central to Lyotard's discussion.[5] But when Lyotard declares that in post-industrial society the 'grand narrative has lost its credibility' (*PC*, 37), that 'Modernist' statements of legitimation, whether regarding truth (e.g., 'The earth revolves around the sun') or regarding justice (e.g., 'The minimum wage must be set at x dollars') no longer hold, one wonders if Lyotard's own metanarrative of delegitimation can really account for the specific changes that have occurred in Western societies over the last few decades.

Why, to begin with, 'the' not a 'postmodern condition' and why the singular form of the noun? Perhaps because *The Postmodern Condition* is itself a metanarrative, the story of how, in the face of post-World War II scientific knowledge, technology and information theory, the delegitimation of the 'grand' metanarratives has set in. Interestingly, the Lyotard paradigm continues to make the case for *difference*, for openness (the 'essay,' he says, is postmodern; the fragment, still modern), and, in a famous formulation, for the *unpresentable*, perceptible in 'presentation itself; that which denies itself the solace of good forms' (PC, 81). But in practice, respect for *difference* has now hardened into a set of norms and prescriptions that leave very little room for the free play, the anarchy, the indeterminacy and disjunctive form that used to be considered characteristic of Postmodernism.

Consider the position of Fredric Jameson, whose *Postmodernism, or, The Cultural Logic of Late Capitalism* is surely the best-known and most widely respected discussion of the subject. It is worth remembering that Jameson wrote the Foreword to the English translation of Lyotard's *La condition postmoderne* and that, although he subjects Lyotard's argument to a more orthodox Marxist spin, he too believes that we have come to an end of the 'great master narratives'. The title chapter of *The Cultural Logic of Late Capitalism*, first published in 1984 in the *New Left Review*, designates 'one fundamental feature of all the Postmodernisms', 'the effacement in them of the older (essentially high-Modernist) frontier between high culture and so-called mass or commercial culture ... The Postmodernisms have, in fact, been fascinated precisely by this whole "degraded" landscape of schlock and kitsch, of TV series and Reader's Digest culture, of advertising and motels, of the late show and the grade-B Hollywood film.'[6] And since postmodern culture (also known as media culture, consumer society, or information society) is thus 'degraded' by its capitalist economic base, its products no longer shock or offend, as did the oppositional art of the Modernist avant-garde. The 'constitutive features' (note the assurance of that term) of the postmodern are now described as follows:

a new depthlessness, which finds its prolongation both in contemporary 'theory' and in a whole new culture of the image or the simulacrum; a consequent weakening of historicity, both in our relationship to public History and in the new forms of our private temporality, whose 'schizophrenic' structure (following Lacan) will determine new types of syntax or syntagmatic relationships in the more temporal arts; a whole new type of emotional ground tone ... [and] the deep constitutive relationships of all this to a whole new technology, which is itself a figure for a whole new economic world system. (FJ, 6)

The 'new type of emotional ground tone', also called the 'waning of affect in postmodern culture' (FJ, 10), refers, of course, to the dissolution of the subject, with the consequent dissolution of 'unique style' and the replacement of parody by pastiche ('blank parody').

I don't think I need spell out here the influence this analysis of Postmodernism was to have on the theorising of the 1980s. From Andreas Huyssen's *After the Great Divide* (1986), which similarly defines Postmodernism, although less pessimistically than Jameson, as the breakdown of the Modernist 'frontier' between high art and mass culture, to Rosalind Krauss's scornful rejection, in her Introduction to the special 'High/Low' issue of *October* (Spring 1991) of what she calls the 'sublimation model' ('According to this model, the function of art is to sublimate or transform experience, raising it from ordinary to extraordinary, from commonplace to unique, from low to high; with the special genius of the artist being that he or she has the gifts to perform this function'),[7] the discourse of Postmodernism has referred, as if to a set of incontrovertible facts, to postmodern 'depthlessness', the simulacrum, the death of the subject, the non-differentiation of 'art' and popular culture, and so on.

Whether or not we adhere to these particular paradigms of the postmodern, it is interesting to note how the terminology of the early 1970s, when discussions of Postmodernism still had a quasi-Utopian cast, has subtly shifted. What David Antin and Ihab Hassan characterised as the *openness* associated with the postmodern ('Open, discontinuous, improvisational, indeterminate, or aleatory struc-tures') imperceptibly turns into 'depthlessness', with all its negative associations of mere surface, shallowness, superficiality. The erasure of boundaries between the traditional genres and media becomes the 'contamination' of all art works by the ' "degraded" landscape of schlock and kitsch', playfulness hardens into simulacrum, 'decrea-tion' into the death of the subject ('there is no longer', says Jameson, 'a self present to do the feeling' (FJ, 51)), and Derridean *différance* as deferral is gradually replaced by the very specific difference of identity politics, difference as marker or label. Indeed, despite all the talk of rupture, transgression, antiformalism, the breaking of the vessels – in Lyotardian terms, the delegitimation of the great metanarratives – there seem to be more rules and prescriptions around than ever, such familiar Modernist/postmodernist pairs as 'hierarchy'/'anarchy' and 'Master Code'/'idiolect' (see IH*PT*, 91) now being called into question, ironically enough, by the establish-ment of new hierarchies and master codes – the return, we might say, of the Law of the Father.

An important essay by Craig Owens, called 'The Discourse of Others: Feminists and Postmodernism', which appeared in the Hal Foster collection *The Anti-Aesthetic* (1983), may serve to dramatise this subtle shift. In a section subtitled 'A Remarkable Oversight', Owens apologises for the 'gross critical negligence' of an earlier reading he had performed on Laurie Anderson's well-known image, in her multimedia performance piece *United States*, of a nude man and woman (a cartoon version of Adam and Eve), in which the man's right arm is raised at a ninety-degree angle while the woman, shorter than the man and hands at her sides, faces toward him. In the performance, Anderson's voiceover (amplified to sound like a male voice) tells us, 'In our country, we send pictures of our sign language into Outer Space. We are speaking our sign language in these pictures. Do you think that They will think his arm is permanently attached in this position? Or do you think They will read our signs? In our country, Goodbye looks just like Hello' (ills. 11.1 and 11.2).[8]

Here is Owens's original commentary on this captioned image:

Two alternatives: either the extraterrestrial recipient of the message will assume that it is simply a picture, that is, an analogical likeness of the human figure, in which case he might logically conclude that male inhabitants of Earth walk around with their right arms permanently raised. Or he will somehow divine that this gesture is addressed to him and attempt to read it, in which case he will be stymied, since a single gesture signifies both greeting and farewell, and any reading of it must oscillate between these two extremes. The same gesture could also mean 'Halt!' or represent the taking of an oath, but if Anderson's text does not consider these two alternatives that is because it is not concerned with ambiguity, with multiple meanings engendered by a single sign; rather two clearly defined but mutually incompatible readings are engaged in blind confrontation in such way that it is impossible to choose between them. (*AA*, 60; my emphasis on 'he')

This passage represents Owens as quintessential Derridean: his source seems to be *Of Grammatology* or possibly *Writing and Difference*, and French feminist constructions, based on Lacan, still seem far away: witness the use of the masculine pronoun throughout. As he himself now confesses:

In my eagerness to rewrite Anderson's text in terms of the debate over determinate versus indeterminate meaning, I had overlooked something ... For this is, of course, an image of sexual difference, or rather, of sexual

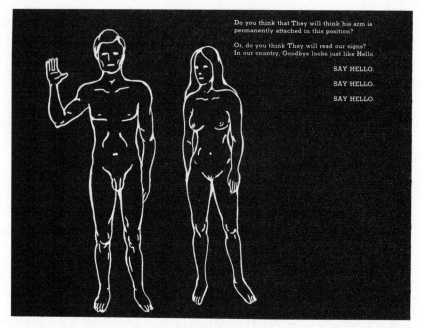

11.1   Laurie Anderson, 'Say Hello', from the book *United States*
by Laurie Anderson

differentiation according to the distribution of the phallus – as it is marked
and then re-marked by the man's right arm, which appears less to have
been raised than erected in greeting ... Like all representations of sexual
difference that our culture produces, this is an image not simply of
anatomical difference, but of the values assigned to it. Here the phallus is
... the signifier of privilege, of the power and prestige that accrue to the
male in our society ... For in this (Lacanian) image, chosen to represent the
inhabitants of Earth for the extraterrestial Other, it is the man who speaks,
who represents mankind. The woman is only represented; she is (as always)
already spoken for. (*AA*, 61)

Here is Owens speaking in his role as New Feminist. The sexual
differentiation he now notes is certainly central to Anderson's
cartoon (one wonders how Owens could have missed it the first time
around), but I am not sure its identification cancels out his earlier
reading, with its focus on the American equation of 'Goodbye' with
'Hello', an equation that parodies more than the obvious inequity of
gender roles in our culture. 'Anderson's blunt question ["Do you
think that They will think his arm is permanently attached in this

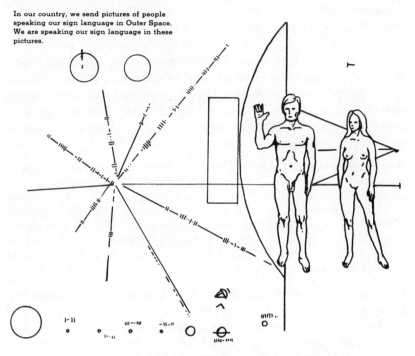

Hello. Excuse me. Can you tell me where I am?

In our country, we send pictures of people speaking our sign language in Outer Space. We are speaking our sign language in these pictures.

11.2   Laurie Anderson, 'Say Hello', from the book *United States* by Laurie Anderson

position?"]', writes Herman Rapaport in a discussion of *United States*, 'is expressionless, exposing the fatuousness of "big science", the silly presupposition that aliens are going to be able to read our "signs." She suggests that in a postmodern culture scientists are so over-specialized that when it comes to basic questions they are enor-mously obtuse. No one has noticed that saying "hello" is exactly the same as saying "good-bye", that even if aliens could read our signs, they would be confused.'[9] It is difficult to see how this aspect of Anderson's witty parody can be ignored, but Owens does ignore it in his zeal to demonstrate that his second reading 'corrects' the first: difference as signifying gap ('two clearly defined but mutually incompatible readings') thus gives way to clear-cut gender differ-ence: it is the man who speaks, the woman who is always already spoken for.

Is this then the New Enlightenment of third-stage (the first is exemplified by Antin's poetics, the second by Derridean deconstruction) Postmodernism? And if so, what has happened to Postmodernism's fabled *openness* and decentredness? For not only is Owens telling us how to read Anderson's image, telling us *what it means*, as unequivocally as Brooks and Warren once told us what the word 'design' means in Robert Frost's poem by that name, but this assertive statement ('it is the man who speaks') is embedded in a larger discourse which is not without its own coercions. Owens' essay begins as follows:

Decentered, allegorical, schizophrenic ... – however we choose to diagnose its symptoms, Postmodernism is usually treated, by its protagonists and antagonists alike, as a crisis of cultural authority, specifically of the authority vested in Western European culture and its institutions. That the hegemony of European civilization is drawing to a close is hardly a new perception; since the mid-1950s, at least, we have recognized the necessity of encountering different cultures by means other than the shock of domination and conquest. (*AA*, 57).

But even as he makes this declaration, Owens cites the following: Lévi-Strauss, Derrida, Ricoeur, Baudrillard, Foucault, Kristeva and Barthes. Seven French theorists named within the space of two pages. And on the third page (*AA*, 59), the combined authority of Lacan and Foucault advances the following hypothesis:

The *Modernist* avant-garde ... sought to transcend representation in favour of presence and immediacy; it proclaimed the autonomy of the signifier, its liberation from the 'tyranny of the signified'; 'postmodernists instead expose the tyranny of the signifier, the violence of its law ... It is precisely at the legislative frontier between what can be represented and what cannot that the postmodern operation is being staged – not in order to transcend representation, but in order to expose that system of power that authorizes certain representations while blocking, prohibiting or invalidating others.

Here is the move we have already observed from what is, so to speak, a 1970s Derridean paradigm to a 1980s Foucaultian-Lacanian one. Aside from Anderson, Owens's exempla of 'prohibited' representations include Martha Rosler's *The Bowery in Two Inadequate Descriptive Systems*, Dara Birnbaum's *Technology/Transformation: Wonder Woman*, and assorted photos and film stills by Sherrie Levine, Cindy Sherman and Barbara Kruger. But however interesting such exempla of 'gender-specific' artworks may be, it is important to note that the works of Anderson and Rosler, Birnbaum and Levine,

Sherman and Kruger remain just that: exempla, demonstrating how valid Lacan's discussion of the Law of the Father, Lyotard's notion of the postmodern 'unpresentable', and Foucault's analysis of the power system are. Ironically, then, the women artists in question continue to be victimised – if not by the patriarchy of Modernist critique and the art market, then by the French theoretical model which their work so nicely illustrates.[10] The real power, in other words, belongs not to the postmodern artist (Anderson, Sherman) but to the poststructuralist theorist whose principles validate the work.

No wonder, then, that recent handbooks on Postmodernism – and they are now legion – reduce what was once the excitement of the Cutting Edge to a list of rules and prescriptions that make one almost long for the days of *Understanding Poetry*. Take Brenda K. Marshall's *Teaching the Postmodern*, published by Routledge in 1992.[11] The Introduction opens with a page of what are evidently intended to be *parole in libertà*, as Marinetti dubbed them (see ill. 11.3). Notice that the very first word in this 'visual poem' is our old friend *différance*, but there is precious little difference in this list of the Big Names, whether of theorists (Kristeva, Barthes, Derrida, Foucault, Althusser and such American variants as Hutcheon [Linda] and de Lauretis [Teresa]), or fiction writers (Morrison, Carter, Rushdie, Wolf, Coetzee), or Big Theory Terms (genealogy, historiography, deconstruction, structuralism, ideology, intertextuality, subject position, Marxism, etc.). What is, so to speak, the poem's refrain is the word *language*, which appears four times! Language, it seems, is centrally important. But how?

Marshall begins with the Piety of the Day: 'Crucial to an understanding of the postmodern moment is the recognition that there is no "outside" from which to "objectively" name the present.' Of course not: no *hors texte*, no transcendental signified, no meta-narrative, no essentialist norms by which to judge production: 'The postmodern moment is an awareness of being within, first, a language, and second, a particular historical, social, cultural framework ... There can be no such thing as objectivity ... That does not mean that we are paralyzed or helpless; rather, it means that we give up the luxury of absolute Truths, choosing instead to put to work local and provisional truths' (BM, 3). Having made this obligatory gesture to some kind of Uncertainty Principle, Marshall now proceeds briskly to tell us what Postmodernism is all about:

Introduction

différance
       historiography   genealogy
      Morrison   context
Kristeva   deconstruction
                     ex-centric
structuralism   history
  language   Wolf
                          Barthes
           counter-memory history
   metafiction   language
        Carter   ideology
       parody   play
          de Lauretis   intertextuality
subject position   Derrida
history   Foucault
                 feminism
                         language
     Rushdie   Marxism
               critical revisiting
poststructuralism
text   work   Hutcheon
   Coetzee   language
Althusser   historiographic metafiction

11.3   Brenda K. Marshall, *Teaching the Postmodern: Fiction and Theory*

Postmodernism is about language. About how it controls, how it determines meaning, and how we try to exert control through language. About how language restricts, closes down, insists that it stands for some thing. Postmodernism is about how 'we' are defined within that language, and within specific historical, social, cultural matrices. It's about race, class, gender, erotic identity and practice, nationality, age, ethnicity. It's about difference. It's about power and powerlessness, about empowerment, and about all the stages in between and beyond and unthought of ... It's about those threads that we trace, and trace, and trace. But not to a conclusion.

To increased knowledge, yes. But never to innocent knowledge. To better understanding, yes. But never to pure insight. Postmodernism is about history. But not the kind of 'History' that lets us think we can know the past ... It's about chance. It's about power. It's about information. And more information. And more. And. And that's just a little bit of what Post-modernism [is]. (BM, 4)

Thus it is that Postmodernism enters the classroom. 'The word Postmodernism', adds the author, 'does not refer to a period or a "movement". It isn't really an "ism"; it isn't really a thing. It's a moment but more a moment in logic than in time. Temporally, it's a space' (BM, 5). If this sounds more like *The Cat in the Hat* ('It isn't really an "ism"; it isn't really a thing') than like a serious attempt to understand what is happening in late twentieth-century culture, it is unfortunately not atypical. Nor are the exercises that follow this Introduction – e.g., 'Critique of Representation and J. M. Coetzee's *Foe*', 'Critique of Subjectivity and Michel Tournier's *Friday*' – which dutifully go through the motions of reading selected contemporary novels through the prisms provided, once again, by Derrida and Foucault.

How did we ever get ourselves into this mode of critical thinking? And should we therefore, as many critics now suggest,[12] abandon the P word as useless, a word subject to the closure that everywhere threatens the demand for *difference*? If we do give up the term, moreover, can we designate our period – excuse me, moment – *vis-à-vis* earlier moments in any meaningful way? In what follows, I make some tentative suggestions, coming back to the question of a 'postmodern' as opposed to a 'Modernist' poetics.

DIFFERENCES/DIVERSITIES

The gradual but wholesale reversal of PoMo terminology between the late 1960s and the early 1990s suggests that the *fin de siècle* may well be as different from the 1960s and early 1970s as those decades were from the 1920s and 1930s. Yet the standard opposition between Modernism and Postmodernism does not take this continuing evolution into account. Theorists either push Modernism further and further back into the past, as do Lyotard and Habermas; this gives us three centuries of Modernist (Enlightenment) discourse against which to measure what is happening in the delegitimating present. Or we do the opposite: we push Modernism further and further towards the present, so as to include post-war figures like Beckett and Pinter, Georges Perec and *film noir*, Jackson Pollock and Philip Johnson, thus setting aside Postmodernism as referring to German neo-Expressionism or cyberpunk or the performance art of the 1980s.

We cannot, in short, come to terms with Postmodernism until we decide what Modernism was. 'From the Modernism that you want', David Antin has quipped, 'you get the Postmodernism you deserve.' If, for example, Modernism is equated with Enlightenment discourse from the Encyclopedia to World War II, then Lyotard may well be right to insist that Postmodernism means incredulity to the *grands récits* of progress and scientific advancement. If, on the other hand, Modernism is taken to refer to the first three decades or so of the twentieth century, then it is hard not to infer that any number of great Modernists – Kafka, Brecht, Musil, Kraus, Leiris, Celine, Bataille, Pound, Stevens, Williams – had already lost faith in those metanarratives of knowledge and social justice. Again, if Modernism is equated with Anglo-American Modernism, then the attribution of order and hierarchy, organic form and autonomy, centring and aesthetic distance may well be applicable; if, on the other hand, we focus on Continental Europe, on, say, Italian Futurism and Dada, on Apollinaire and Cendrars, or on Klee and Tatlin, the picture is quite different.

It is, I think, the drive toward totalisation and hence toward closure that bedevils current discussions of Postmodernism. Consider what we might call the Synecdochic Fallacy. In *Postmodernism, or, The Cultural Logic of Late Capitalism*, we recall, Jameson makes an extended comparison between Van Gogh's well-known painting of peasant shoes (ill. 11.4), which he calls 'one of the canonical works of high Modernism', and Andy Warhol's *Diamond Dust Shoes* (ill. 11.5). Whether we interpret the Van Gogh as an 'act of compensation', a 'willed and violent transformation of a drab peasant object world into the most glorious materialization of pure color in oil paint', or, in Heideggerian terms, as a recreation of 'the whole missing object world which was once [the shoes'] lived context', the 'disclosure of what the equipment, the pair of peasant shoes is in truth' and hence 'the unconcealment of [their] being', reading the painting, Jameson posits, is '*hermeneutical*, in the sense in which the work in its inert, objectal form is taken as a clue or a symptom for some vaster reality which replaces it as its ultimate truth' (FJ, 8).

11.4   Vincent van Gogh, *A Pair of Boots*, 1887

Warhol's *Diamond Dust Shoes*, by contrast, doesn't speak to anything beyond itself; rather, this 'random collection of dead objects hanging together on the canvas like so many turnips', functions as a set of commodity fetishes. In an 'inversion of Van Gogh's Utopian gesture', Jameson argues, 'the external and colored surface of things – debased and contaminated in advance by their assimilation to glossy advertising images – has been stripped away to reveal the deathly black-and-white substratum of the photographic negative which subtends them' (FJ, 9). As such, Warhol's work exemplifies the 'new depthlessness' and the 'waning of affect' which Jameson, as I noted above, takes to be the distinguishing features of the postmodernist 'culture of the simulacrum' (FJ, 6, 10).

What interests me here is less the specific characterisation of the respective paintings than the claim that the part ipso facto stands for the whole. Van Gogh's is 'one of the canonical works of high Modernism'; Warhol is 'the central figure in contemporary visual art' (FJ, 8). And so a late nineteenth-century painter who was one of the least appreciated and most cruelly marginalised artists of his own

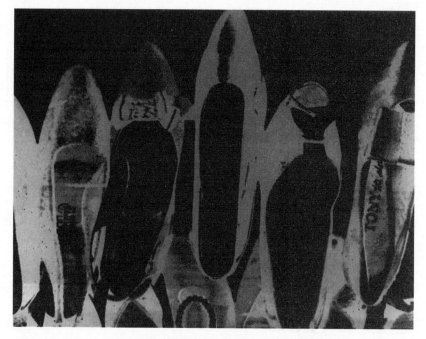

11.5   Andy Warhol, *Diamond Dust Shoes*, 1980

day is compared to an American artist who has become the icon of self-promotion, publicity, and commercial success. Is Warhol really Van Gogh's postmodernist counterpart or should we more accurately compare the former to a salon painter like Bougereau, who similarly knew how to manipulate the public and become a star? Or, to take the other side of the parallel, suppose we compare Van Gogh, not to Warhol but to Jasper Johns. The 'Modernist' 'disclosure of what the equipment, the pair of peasant shoes, is in truth', the emergence of the painted 'entity... into the unconcealment of its being, by way of the mediation of the work of art', has a perfect counterpart in Johns's paintings of coat hangers and light bulbs, beer cans and paint brushes, the various *Alphabets* and number series.

A Warhol silkscreen cannot, in any case, 'represent' the postmodern any more than John Portman's Bonaventure Hotel (another Exhibit A in Jameson's lexicon of Postmodernism; see pp. 38–44) can represent the 'new depthlessness' of architecture over against the International Style of Le Corbusier and Gropius. Common sense suggests that whatever the 'hyperspace' of the Bonaventure is or isn't, its Modernist counterpart is not a Bauhaus monument but, say, New York's Art Deco Waldorf Astoria, the grand commercial hotel of the 1930s and 1940s, even as the Bonaventure, with its revolving skytop cocktail lounge and 'reflective glass skin [that] repels the city outside' (FJ, 42), is a popular building of our own day.

Van Gogh / Warhol; Le Corbusier / John Portman: these would-be synecdoches, representing the modern and postmodern respectively also display a curious way of relating the European to the American. If Modernism is regularly considered a European phenomenon, Postmodernism is almost by definition 'born in the USA'. This means that although Van Gogh's most logical postmodernist successor might well be the Belgian Marcel Broodthaers, now recognised as a seminal figure in the development of post-conceptual art, pride of place must nevertheless be given to the quintessential American product of late capitalism, Andy Warhol. Note that neither in his discussion of pastiche nor in his differentiation of postmodern from modern architecture, does Jameson feel obliged to justify the US-centrism of his position. Indeed, despite the lipservice currently paid to multiculturalism, one often has the sense that the only thing that matters in US culture ... is US culture. True, that culture is divided up into dozens of marginalised, disempowered, and minority subsets: African-American, Chicana/o, Native-American, Asian-American, gay and lesbian, and so on. But the requisite for all these groups turns out to be US citizenship: the 'other', it seems, does not include the literatures of other nations or in other languages.

'What Postmodernism taught us', writes David Harvey, 'was that difference and heterogeneity matter, and that the language in which we represent the world, the manner of discourse, ought to be the subject of careful reflection. But it did not teach us how to negotiate differences in fruitful ways, nor did it tell us how to go about the business of communicating with each other after we had carefully deconstructed each others' language.'[13] We could take this a step further and argue that the concept of *difference*, as liberating as it seemed in the 1970s, has now been replaced by a bland *diversity* that, as the poet Charles Bernstein observes in *A Poetics*, harks back 'to New Critical and liberal-democratic concepts of a common reader-ship that often ... have the effect of transforming unresolved ideological divisions and antagonisms into packaged tours of the local color of gender, race, sexuality, ethnicity, region, nation, class, even historical period: where each group or community or period is expected to come up with – or have appointed for them – representative figures we all can know about'.[14]

Unlike difference, Bernstein argues, diversity 'presupposes a common standard of aesthetic judgment or implicitly aims to erect a new common standard. In this context, diversity can be a way of restoring a highly idealized concept of a unified American culture that effectively quiets dissent' (CB, 4–5). And he adds:

Too often the works selected to represent cultural diversity are those that accept the model of representation assumed by the dominant culture in the first place. 'I see grandpa on the hill/next to the memories I can never recapture' is the base line against which other versions play: 'I see my yiddishe mama on hester street/next to the pushcarts I can no longer peddle' or 'I see my grandmother on the hill/next to all the mothers whose lives can never be recaptured' or 'I can't touch my Iron Father/who never canoed with me/on the prairies of my masculine epiphany.' Works that challenge these models of representation run the risk of becoming more inaudible than ever within mainstream culture. (CB, 6)

A similar point is made by Henry Louis Gates, Jr in a 1991 essay for *American Literary History*. 'If black authors are primarily entrusted with producing the proverbial "text of blackness"', he writes, 'they become vulnerable to the charge of betrayal if they shirk their duty ... Representational democracy [here Gates is citing the black British film-maker Isaac Julian and the media theorist Kobena Mercer], like the classic realist text, is premised on an implicitly mimetic theory of representation as correspondence with the "real."'[15]

Which is to say that *essentialism* has by no means been put to rest and that metanarrative, far from having been abandoned, has reappeared in the new guise of an elaborate plot of ethnic amelioration. Consider the following poem by a young Chicano writer, published, like Gates's essay, in 1991:

The Willow
Las Cruces, New Mexico
Spring 1964
I loved a tree in my boyhood, a tree
In my grandfather's garden, a weeping
willow whose ancient limbs longed
upwards, then arched downwards, perfect

bows which reached so low, so low

the leaves brushed the grass as if to
sweep it clean. I played alone among
the arches of leaves, pulling the green

limbs around myself as if they were the
great arms of God. They held me tight.
I was so loved in that embrace of leaves.

And then sickness came

to the garden one spring, the old willow
wrapped in a shroud of bugs. I could only
watch, could not touch it. I shouted
at the tree, and told it to live, and

though it fought to breathe without
leaves, neither my voice nor the rain
could heal it. So the tree was chopped,
stripped limb by limb until there was

only a stump. And the stump, too
was pulled from the ground – pulled
so harshly that even the roots came up

shaking the whole garden.[16]

Ironically, nothing in the poem except its designated locale, Las
Cruces, New Mexico, identifies the poet's ethnicity or class. Its
author, Benjamin Alire Sáenz has taken on the most familiar of
Romantic models: the nature poem in which a particular speaker
remembers a particular incident that taught him a lesson – in this
case, the lesson that suffering and death are inevitable. The beloved
tree, significantly a weeping willow, predictably stands in 'my grandfather's garden'; the boy predictably plays under its 'arches of
leaves', and feels loved and protected by God. But since there is
always a serpent in paradise, one spring 'sickness came'; a blight
struck the tree and it had to be chopped down. Its dismemberment,
moreover, became the occasion for excessive human force: 'so
harshly' was the tree stump 'pulled from the ground' that 'even the
roots came up / shaking the whole garden'. The boy who has
witnessed this surgery will never be the same.

Even the quatrain form of 'The Willow' places it in the Romantic
tradition, as it comes down to us from Wordsworth to Housman,
and as it no doubt came down to Benjamin Saénz in the creative
writing workshop. Yet – in what we might take as a kind of
postmodern give-away – the poem seems ill at ease with the formal

constraint of the quatrain, the syntax being that of straightforward prose: 'I shouted at the tree, and told it to live, and though it fought to breathe without leaves, neither my voice nor the rain could heal it.' And further: the omission of rhyme and inclusion of one-line units – 'And then sickness came', and 'shaking the whole garden' – identify 'The Willow' as a contemporary poem, a poem that cannot quite reproduce the paradigm it has so earnestly chosen to follow.

To encourage this kind of writing in the name of ethnic diversity is to assume that the 'marginalised' have the right (perhaps even the duty) to use what would otherwise be considered well-worn clichés because these groups have hitherto been denied all access to poetic speech, because their voices have been suppressed by the dominant culture. But such validation is based on the further assumption that a poem like 'The Willow' is an 'authentic' representation of Chicano subjectivity, an assumption that is again an instance of what I have called the synecdochic fallacy. Indeed, the irony is that the refusal to submit the poems of the marginalised to any kind of serious critique accomplishes nothing so much as the marginalisation of poetry itself. For even as publishers are dutifully bringing out anthologies of Native American or Chicana/o or Asian-American poetry, we all know that the action has passed elsewhere. For every poetry review in the major papers and journals, there are fifty reviews of biographies, of political books, of media studies and self-help manuals. As for intellectuals, poetry as discourse cannot begin to matter in the ways that theory or cultural study matters. And theory has, as my example from Craig Owens suggests, remained almost exclusively Eurocentric, primarily French and (increasingly) German. A seminar on Bourdieu or Deleuze, on Habermas's concept of the public sphere or Judith Butler's Hegelianism will draw a lot more students than any seminar on contemporary poetry, however oppressed the constituency in question.

And yet, to tap for a moment into a more genuine and robust romanticism than the attenuated version we find in poems like 'The Willow', 'Without Contraries is no progression'. And again: 'Improvement makes strait roads; but the crooked roads without Improvement are roads of Genius.' The opposition to the bland call for 'diversity' on the one hand, and to the gloomy emphasis on the 'new depthlessness' on the other, is coming, once again, not from the professional critics but from poets, with the difference that the new poets are themselves working theorists, like Susan Howe, whose *My Emily Dickinson* and *The Birthmark* weave together poetic, historical, and critical discourse, or like Steve McCaffery, whose *North of Intention* and *Rational Geomancy: The Collected Research Reports of the Toronto Research Group 1973–82* (the latter with the late Canadian poet bpNichol) take the theorems of Derrida and Lacan, Kristeva and Althusser for a playful spin that produces fanciful and fictive verbal/ visual configurations as 'creative' as they are 'critical'. In a 1992 issue of *Raddle Moon* (no. 11), a section called 'Women/Writing/Theory' features work by Johanna Drucker, Norma Cole, Laura Moriarty, and others that cannot be categorised as 'theory' or 'poetry', the texts in question always already being 'both/and'.

Consider a recent poem by Alfred Arteaga:

The Small Sea of Europe

– At the end of the eighteenth century, Hindu law, insofar as it can be described as a unitary system, operated in terms of four texts that 'staged' a four-part episteme defined by the subject's use of memory: sruti (the heard), smitri (the remembered), sastra (the learned-from-another), and vyavahara (the performed-in-exchange).
– Gayatri Chakravorty Spivak

In Europe's small sea,
a system of exchange:
forms of life
and motion in sign.

The Case In Point –

Verkehr:
'the motion of women, of slaves,
in sleep
congested automobiles, trunks
with drugs'

Verkehr,
from the Sanscrit, (small sea),
vyavahara:
'performance traffic,
former act of transformation,
an exchange.'
Ecos escritos: Sruti, Smitri, Sastra
three sisters in myth, very
sources of Europe, Western Man
the very sounds slipping: 3Ss, sans (é)crit
3 Ss:
3Ss: ecos escritos (S grito)

Again, then,
Verkehr:
S1 in the automobile besides S2, S3
At the wheel, 'Sister...' furtive, slave-like
movements (escape? from/to/what/where?)
But who can drive? Of course, S2 remembers,
tells, S1 hears, inserts the key,
demonstrates, S3 learns, starts the motor: of
course, escape, With-Drugs o wild & steering slaves
through furtive traffic, changing lanes, exchanging
places of courses, escape:
Sruti hears, Smriti recalls, Sastra learns from an other:
S verkehr: vyavahara
a performance, vyavahara,
the S sound of abandon.

(Or) Again:
Sastra (née 'furtive slave') learned
furtive from
Sruti (née 'furtive slave') heard
furtive from
Smitri (née 'furtive slave') remembers
furtive from
the small sea of history, the big C of capital,
first squirt of legend, transcendental quill
and myth-inks, rib stain here first
no ear, no hearing, across which sheets first
defined smear.

I remember Smitri, in the dictionary
Verkehr:
'fast women in cars escape with drugs'
like Texas, but this is Berlin
to Paris, night rides hard riding off course
3 woman Ss written off across this old sad continent
fast esses, stained-fast essences, the Ss senses (S sense)
of woman defi(l/n/)ed.

Some big Dichtung
this place, ace.   London, 1988.[17]

   Cantos, in which this poem appears, is a book written in tongues
(Spanish/English). 'The Small Sea of Europe' adds Sanskrit and
German to the linguistic mix, and its epigraph from Gayatri Spivak's
well-known essay 'Can the Subaltern Speak?', together with its
locale (London), place the poem in what is a discourse evidently

quite alien to that of Benjamin Saénz's 'The Willow' – the discourse of the international theory community where Spivak is read and studied. Alfred Arteaga probably came across her work at Santa Cruz, where he received a PhD in Renaissance literature before taking a job at Berkeley.

But he is also a Chicano poet, and it is the intersection of the different (and often conflicting) forms of agency at play that generate his own poetic language. What, the poem seems to ask, is the relationship of subaltern languages (Hindi, Chicano) to the dominant discourse of 'The Small Sea of Europe', the irony being that Hindi derives from Sanskrit, which stands at the origin of the Indo-European languages, including the Spanish of the colonised 'slaves', whose images merge with those of the 'fast women in cars [who] escape with drugs', who now make the headlines. Europe is a 'small sea' in relation to the globe, hence the Conquistadors' felt necessity of crossing the 'small sea' to the New World. Then, too, the journey from Berlin to Paris to London, where the poem was written, has the shape of a 'small C' on the map, and the small sea is also the English Channel, which divides England from the Continent.

The 'system of exchange', in this context, refers not only to traffic as transportation (*Verkehr*), to the drug traffic that is part of our daily life and the slave traffic which is part of our collective memory (*sruti, smitri, sastra*), but to the exchange of phonemes and letters as well:

> Sanscrit (small Sea) . . .
> sans (é)crit . . .
> ecos escritos (S grito) . . .
> fast esses . . . [on the model of 'negresses' or 'goddesses']
> Ss senses (S sense) . . .
> woman defi(l/n)ed) . . .

and so on. The three women involved in what may be a sting operation are identified only as S1 S2 S3; they remain nameless and faceless, despite the poet's desire to endow them with the mythic weight of memory: with *sruti* (the heard), *smitri* (the remembered), and *sastra* (the learned-from-another). The 'S sound' is thus the 'sound of abandon', the invocation of the three graces or muses or goddesses ('fast esses, stained-fast essences') that can do nothing to recover the past. Not memory, but only performance-in-exchange (*vyavahara*), the 'three sisters' regarded as so many 'furtive slaves'. The 'small sea of history' is, after all, controlled by the 'big C of capital'.

Pun, paragram, double entendre: Arteaga's poem emerges as a *Dichtung* without *Wahrheit*, a journey into time and space to recapture the past (which doesn't exist). What, after all, is 'this place' which contains 'ace' within its word boundaries, 'ace' which is again 'a ce' – the small c of 'sans(c)rit'? The 'unitary system', whether of Hindu law as Spivak describes it, or of Spanish colonial history has become so many missing links – 'myth-inks' smeared on blank sheets.

Arteaga has written a complex meditative poem that interrogates and extends the current theorising on the 'subaltern' question, a question that evidently preoccupies him even as it has preoccupied a critic of a different culture and gender like Gayatri Spivak. To classify such a poem as Chicano is to elide the important *differences* between it and the neo-Romantic model we find in Benjamin Saénz's 'The Willow', a model whose tacit assumption that the lyric is a univocal and authentic form of self-expression seems oddly out of key with the discourses of the 1990s in which it is implicated.

If Arteaga's poetics have little in common with Saénz's, how do they relate to the 'postmodern' poetics of the 1960s with which I began? In one sense, 'The Small Sea of Europe' is not all that different from say, Charles Olson's 'The Kingfishers', which provided David Antin with his Exhibit A in the *boundary 2* essay. Both are poems including history; both splice together a series of seemingly unrelated cultural and mythological references; both pun on letters and numbers. The difference is that for Arteaga, poetic discourse is no longer held together by the authority of what Antin called 'a man on his feet talking' (Olson's 'I hunt among stones'). Indeed, 'The Small Sea of Europe' refuses to privilege speech over writing, refuses what the poem itself refers to as the *sans(é)crit*. The once-central Olsonian subject now occupies the interstices of the narrative, lines like 'I remember Smitri', serving as sudden reminders that the events described have actually been witnessed by someone.

This calling into question of authorial control, mimetic speech, and 'normal' syntax has been carried even further by other poets of the 1990s. I conclude with two variations on this theme. The first is a short prose text called 'Staged Dialogue with Failed Transit Actiant Opposition' by the English born Canadian poet Steve McCaffery.[18] Here the emphasis is less on the problems of history and memory that concern Arteaga, than on the on the look and sound of everyday life in the videated, Larry-King-Live 1990s:

Hello and also. Why do you live? I live because there is a house upon a street somewhere, a house I was born in. It's made of bricks. Is correct. Yes, many things are made of bricks. Bridges and walls and special cups are made of bricks. Excellent. So why do you like sport? Yes, sport is often my favourite, especially the sport of chess. That's played on boards and sometimes ice. Is ice also your favourite? My favourite is books if there's lots of them. My name is Sidney Lanier. I was once a writer. I have many books with names and sometimes thicker ones on the front porch of a house. Sometimes my house is sunny that way and once a week it will always be tuesday. Do you also like the name of Sidney Lanier? Not as a book but as a day yes. Wonderful. Now what hobbies have you got? I have the noun cooking which is my favourite. Especially some lamb and stew of lamb and chickens too that cannot fly. How do you like jetplanes? If they are eggs I like to fry them in a pan as fat as possible. Fat or flat? Yes. Either will do. The kitchen also is a place to sing. Moths sing with mouths and also beards. Precisely. I too like music especially when sometimes the songs are old. Oaktrees are old. Me too. Many days pass in which I wish to write a complete history of forests. When I say that I smile. Alders are best. Terrific. Me too. Are skies not the best? The ones that seem to be yesterday's clouds. No. We say these sounds are like a twittering pond. Ponds describe fish because today I am hungry. I know this because angles cut across my entire interior appetite. The word stomach is worse. I know a word to lead to stars and the decription of a moon as thick but wide. Excellent. Me too. What else can be known? That soup can be cooked but mud thrown is ground lost. Does each work invoke a simile? On mountains yes. Is there a fire? Perhaps. Not especially. That too is the case. Terrific. What is your name? My name is Herbert Kinsella but Abigail is best. Such difference is value. Why do they rise? Because horses are discontented by the hair. Me too. I reach a room and recognize that anything is placed to soften forms. Which forms do you like? Perhaps motion or charm or eyes soaked in wine. Yes. Tall glasses are best. The ones that have knees. Would you still like a chair? Speech yes, and a quiet bath before the ark. When true is I do not.

Here everything depends on linguistic deformation, the 'making strange' of everyday dialogue and discourse. My second example comes from the domain of the artist's book, although that name no longer quite fits the digital productions now designed to make language 'visible'. In 1994, the poet-visual artist Johanna Drucker published, in an edition of seventy copies, a book called *Narratology*. According to the colophon, Drucker first wrote the text in a child's notebook, re-worked it a number of times, and then put it on the computer together with a series of images 'culled, copied, transformed, redrawn, and then computer manipulated before being

Quarked [Quark Express is a software program] into the dummies, output on Linotronic, and then turned into polymer plates.'[19] This process allows for a variety of impositions, juxtapositions and cut-ups. After each page of text was digitally transferred to the polymer plate, Drucker then printed the book on Rives lightweight paper and handpainted the images. It was then 'handbound in die-stamped covers, Franklin Gothic and Memphis have been used throughout, but much distorted through various Quark features'.

Narratology: 'the stories according to which I thought my life would be lived, which shaped my expectations', as Drucker explains in a text appended to her book. 'Living one's life' is now 'in/through writing/representation, not outside it, inside it, or in opposition'. Thus Drucker's pseudo-romance tale, with its innocent little girl born into the perfect 1950s nuclear family, growing up, daydreaming, meeting all the wrong young men, suffering absurd mishaps, and finally encountering Dream Man, thus 'pull[ing] back', as the narrator puts it, 'from a commitment to real time and place'. Onto this romance plot, Drucker has grafted a number of conflicting discourses – economic, science fiction, Victorian romance, TV soap opera – discourses, moreover, that are intermittent rather than continuous and that are further complicated by their visual appearance: the text makes use of varied fonts, type sizes, and format (plain, bold, italic), and the 'illustrations', deliciously ironic versions of stills from the teenage and women's magazines of the period, use faces copied from old photographs (especially snapshots of Johanna Drucker herself) and submit these figures to 'colourful' hand-painting so that the 'slick' photoimages, so reminiscent of the advertising page, with its display of clothes and bodies and its catchy titles and captions, becomes something other.

No two pages of *Narratology* are quite alike. Consider the following page (ill. 11.6) about half-way through the book. The young girl in the upper left-hand corner (the face seems to be the artist's own) is a cross between Cinderella (wearing an apron and holding her dustrag) and the typical blonde young girl at the breakfast table. Above the table, another young girl (or is she the same one?) in a 1950s ballerina-length green pinafore, supports a huge console TV that is larger than herself, as if to remind us that this was the Age of Television, the first stage of seduction by the Big Box.

On the right-hand side of the page is a slinky female figure, stretching her arms as if after sleep, in a transparent, clingy night-

D O M E S T I C

His tongue protruded through the mucous membrane of her emotional **defenses**, taking the plunge which **ripped** her heart **loose** from its bearings. Pressing home his advantage he manuevered **the** lip service to contractual **arrangements** as carefully into place as **his** keys in his jeans were wedged to advertise the **other** advantages he had recently grown into. But the story on the late breaking **news** did not include the reversal of fortune she **had** suffered by being **forced** to remain after school these long afternoons without adequate transportation. Deep bitterness accumulated **behind** the dam of blocked movement as she stayed trapped between **the** seasons of vacation and the **seasons** of unrest. Splinters from a pier she'd known in the intimate proximity of **childhood** now rose to the surface of the skin, **begging to be** let free from the wounds into which they had **found** their way.

APPARATUS

TROPHY WIFE TO A CANNIBAL
Rise to the occasion little dove of my heart, and let us rejoice in the efficiency of the loaded cartridge which replays the old relief effort before our eyes. Projected on the screen it hid the house that hid our crumbling hopes and threw the global scale of the disaster back into a domestic frame while it shook the foundations of our intimate relations to their molten core.

11.6   Johanna Drucker, from *Narratology*, 1994

gown (or evening dress) that gives her the appearance of a mermaid: we can see her breasts and what looks like a chastity belt. Since this dress too is green, the woman, labelled 'Trophy Wife to a Cannibal,' may well be the young girl on the left grown up into jaded housewife. 'Trophy', moreover, fits the mermaid image: this woman has been fished out of somewhere. 'Rise to the occasion little dove of my heart', we read in the fine print beneath the title, 'and let us rejoice in the efficiency of the loaded cartridge which replays the old relief effort before our eyes.'

Indeed, the girl in the green nightgown (and pointy black pumps) is, like the girl images on the left, seen as so much 'DOMESTIC APPARATUS: **His** tongue protrudes through the mucous membrane', not of her lips or any other body part but, in perfect contemporary psycho-babble 'of her emotional **defenses**'. The lover 'maneuvered **the** lip service to contractual arrangements', and the girl's reversal of fortune comes from 'being **forced** to remain after school these long afternoons without adequate transportation' – a real fate-worse-than-death in the age of Meals on Wheels. The heroine is 'trapped between **the** seasons of vacation and the **seasons** of unrest'. Here there are no memories rising to the surface of the consciousness but 'Splinters from a pier she'd known in the intimate proximity of **childhood** [that] now rose to the surface of the skin.' And so on. The sexual and the contractual, the erotic and the economic are never far apart. Cliché follows cliché, only to move towards the inevitability of the **APPARATUS**, presented in 1½ inch boldface block letters. Meanwhile, there is a writing-through the text, produced by the boldface words read in sequence. 'His defenses ripped loose the arrangements his other news had forced behind the seasons, childhood begging to be found.' And this too fits into Drucker's scheme of things, childhood indeed regularly 'begging to be found' in the midst of those 'defenses' and 'arrangements'. To be 'found', the female protagonist would have to be 'let free', and that seems, at the moment, to be an unlikely prospect.

Are Drucker's *Narratology* and McCaffery's 'Staged Dialogue' to be characterised as postmodern artworks? Yes and no. Certainly, these texts have come a long distance from the more Utopian Postmodernism envisioned by David Antin and his fellow poet-critics in the early 1970s. *boundary 2* itself, as I remarked earlier, has long since opted for cultural critique rather than literary criticism, its 'editorial collective' (the epithet is indicative) and contributors engaging primarily in theoretical polemics, especially with regard to postcolonialism, race and gender. In this sense, the **90s** have literally inverted the **60s** ethos.

Yet if we look again at the right-hand column of Ihab Hassan's table, it is curious to note that the postmodern attributes here listed – for example, under no. 3 ('Diffusion of the ego') or no. 9 ('Open form, discontinuity . . . Intermedia') – are certainly applicable to the poetries of the 1990s: witness Arteaga, Drucker and McCaffery. In this sense, it seems quite premature to talk about the 'death of

Postmodernism'. Or, for that matter, about the 'death' of Romanticism, given that *openness* and *difference* were as central to the aesthetic
of Blake and Shelley as they are to Bernstein or McCaffery or
Drucker.

Perhaps, then, the time has come to avoid pronunciamentos,
whether pro or con, about 'the postmodern condition' and to try to
keep an open mind on the post-post days we are now witnessing,
days for which we don't yet have a name and whose postpeople we
can't quite conceptualise. In the words of Laurie Anderson, 'Do you
think They will read our signs?'

Notes

I INTRODUCTION

1 Patricia Waugh, *Practising Postmodernism/Reading Modernism* (London: Arnold, 1992), p. 5.
2 Jean-François Lyotard, *The Postmodern Condition: a Report on Knowledge*, trans. Geoff Bennington and Brian Massumi, foreword by Frederic Jameson, vol. x of *Theory and History of Literature* (Manchester University Press, 1986).
3 René Wellek, 'The Concept of "Romanticism" in Literary History', *Comparative Literature*, 1 (1949), 1–23, 147–72.
4 Pierre Macherey, *A Theory of Literary Production*, trans. Geoffrey Wall (London: Routledge & Kegan Paul, 1978), pp. 3–4; Terry Eagleton, *Criticism and Ideology* (London: New Left Books, 1976), p. 11.
5 *Byron's Letters and Journals*, ed. Leslie A. Marchand, 12 vols. (London: Murray, 1973–82), vol. III, p. 220.
6 Anne K. Mellor, *Romanticism and Gender* (New York and London: Routledge, 1993), pp. 144–69.
7 Margaret Homans, *Women Writers and Poetic Identity: Dorothy Wordsworth, Emily Brontë and Emily Dickinson* (Princeton University Press, 1980). See 'The Masculine Tradition', pp. 12–40, and 'A Feminine Tradition', pp. 215–36.
8 Marjorie Levinson, *Wordsworth's Great Period Poems: Four Essays* (Cambridge Univeristy Press, 1986), p. 10.
9 Alan Liu, *Wordsworth; The Sense of History* (Stanford: Stanford University Press, 1989), pp. 39, 501.
10 Terry Eagleton, *The Ideology of the Aesthetic* (Oxford: Blackwell, 1990), p. 409.
11 Stjepan Mestrovic, *The Coming Fin-de-Siècle: an Application of Durkheim's Sociology to Modernity and Postmodernity* (London and New York: Routledge, 1991).
12 Philippa Berry and Andrew Wernick (eds.), *Shadow of Spirit: Postmodernism and Religion* (London and New York: Routledge, 1992)
13 Waugh, *Practising Postmodernism*, p. 12.
14 Diane Elam, *Romancing the Postmodern* (London: Routledge, 1992), p. 6.

15 Ibid., p. 3.
16 Ibid., p. 50, quoting Lyotard, 'Re-writing Modernity', *SubStance*, 54 (1987), 3.
17 Clifford Siskin, *The Historicity of Romantic Discourse* (New York and Oxford: Oxford University Press, 1988), p. 12.

2 FROM SUBLIMITY TO INDETERMINACY: NEW WORLD ORDER
   OR AFTERMATH OF ROMANTIC IDEOLOGY

1 For a good discussion of chiasmus in Kantian aesthetics, see the Introduction by Wilkinson and Willoughby to their translation of F. Schiller, *On the Aesthetic Education of Man* (Oxford: Clarendon Press, 1967). Ralph Norrman is writing a book on chiasmus; see also his *Samuel Butler and the Meaning of Chiasmus* (London: Macmillan, 1982).
2 'Universal History and Cultural Differences', trans. by David Macey, in Andrew Benjamin (ed.), *The Lyotard Reader* (Oxford: Blackwell, 1989), pp. 315–16. For Lyotard's fuller, earlier discussion of the tense-logic of the sublime, see 'Answering the Question: What is Postmodernism?' (1982) trans. Regis Durand, in *The Postmodern Condition: a Report on Knowledge*, trans. Geoff Bennington and Brian Massumi, foreword by Fredric Jameson (Manchester University Press, 1984), pp. 71–82. David Ingram helpfully distinguishes 'The Postmodern Kantianism of Arendt and Lyotard' in Andrew Benjamin (ed.), *Judging Lyotard*, (London: Routledge, 1992), pp. 119–45.
3 I discuss traditions of reading Dorothy Wordsworth at greater length in the Introduction to Paul Hamilton (ed.), *Dorothy Wordsworth, Selections from the Journals* (London: William Pickering, 1992), pp. ix-xxii.
4 See the discussion of 'Georgic' in Michael Rosenthal, *Constable, the Painter and his Landscape* (New Haven: Yale University Press, 1983); John Barrell, *Poetry, Language, Politics* (Manchester University Press, 1988) and *The Birth of Pandora* (London: Macmillan, 1992); Kurt Heinzelman, 'The Cult of Domesticity: Dorothy and William at Grasmere,' in Anne K.Mellor (ed.), *Romanticism and Feminism* (Bloomington and Indianapolis: Indiana University Press, 1988).
5 Dorothy Wordsworth, *Journals*, p. 99.
6 Ibid., p. 90.
7 All references to Friedrich Schlegel's *Athenaeum Fragments* and *Critical Fragments* are from *Lucinde and the Fragments*, trans. Peter Firchow (Minneapolis: University of Minnesota Press, 1971), further references cited in the text as *AF* and *CF*, followed by the number of the fragment.
8 Peter Sloterdijk, *Critique of Cynical Reason*, trans. M. Eldred, introduction by Andrew Huyssen (London: Verso, 1988), p. xxx.
9 Ibid., p. xxxi.
10 Ibid., p. 5.
11 Ibid., p. 3.

12 C. Norris, *Spinoza and the Origins of Modern Critical Theory* (Oxford: Blackwell, 1991), p. 21-53.
13 Sloterdijk, *Critique of Cynical Reason*, p. 21n.

3 TURNABOUTS IN TASTE: THE CASE OF LATE TURNER

1 Lawrence Gowing, *Turner: Imagination and Reality* (New York: Museum of Modern Art, 1966), p. 11
2 Joseph Farington, *Diary*, 5 June 1815; quoted in Martin Butlin and Evelyn Joll (eds.), *The Paintings of J. M. W. Turner* (London and New Haven: Yale University Press, 1977), p. 130, hereafter referred to as B & J.
3 John Ruskin *Harbours of England* (1856) (see under B & J, p. 377).
4 John Ruskin, *Notes to the Exhibition at Marlborough House* (see B & J, p. 377).
5 John Gage, *J. M. W. Turner 'A Wonderful Range of Mind'* (London and New Haven: Yale University Press 1987), pp. 8-9. Gage stresses the interest taken by French artists in Turner's sketches and lack of finish at this time.
6 *Caernarvon Castle*, c. 1798 (Tate Gallery no. 1867).
7 D. S. MacColl, *National Gallery Millbank. Catalogue. Turner Collection* (London, 1920), p. 29.
8 A full listing of accession numbers is given in B & J, pp. 289-91.
9 B & J, p. 184.
10 B & J, p. 138.
11 B & J, p. 509.
12 Ibid.
13 Robert de la Sizeranne in *The Genius of J. M. W. Turner*, ed. Holmes, *Studio*, p. 1903, p. xiv.
14 B & J, p. 476.
15 E. T. Cook and Alexander Wedderburn, *The Works of John Ruskin*, 39 vols. (London, 1903-12).
16 MacColl, *Turner Collection*, p. viii.
17 J. Stryzgowski, 'Turner's Path from Nature to Art', *Burlington Magazine*, 12 (1906-7), p. 336.
18 As, for example, *Interior of a Gothic Church*, c. 1797, oil on mahogany, 28cm x 40.5cm (Tate Gallery no.5536).
19 Ruskin resigned his executorship of Turner's will before the selection of works for the national collection was made. However, he did advise on this, and published a commentary to the first exhibition of the works at Malborough House and a catalogue of the watercolour sketches and drawings shown there. See B & J, pp. xx-xxi.
20 *Burlington Magazine*, 14 (1908).
21 A. Clutton-Brock, 'The Weaknesses and Strengths of Turner', *Burlington Magazine*, 18 (1910-11), p. 23.
22 Roger Fry, *Reflections on British Art* (London: Faber, 1934)
23 B & J 509.

24 Lawrence Gowing, *Imagination and Reality* (New York: Museum of Modern Art, 1966).
25 William Vaughan, *Romantic Art* (London: Thames & Hudson, 1978), plate 42, pp. 124–6.
26 For a discussion of Schlegel's comments on these, see William Vaughan, *German Romanticism and English Art* (New Haven and London: Yale University Press, 1979).
27 Robert Payne Knight, *Analytical Enquiry*, 4th edn (London: T. Payne, 1808), chapter 'On Imagination', p. 102.

4 'CONQUERED GOOD AND CONQUERING ILL': FEMININITY, POWER AND ROMANTICISM IN EMILY BRONTË'S POETRY

1 Emily Brontë, 'The Butterfly' (wr. 1842) trans. Sue Lonoff, *Charlotte and Emily Brontë: The Belgian Essays, a Critical Edition* (New Haven and London: Yale University Press, 1996), pp. 176–9. Another very useful translation of the essay which helped me in the earlier stages of my work on it was made by Lorine White Nagel in Fannie E. Ratchford (ed.), *Five Essays Written in French by Emily Jane Brontë* (Austin: University of Texas Press, 1948) pp. 17–19.
2 Isobel Armstrong, *Victorian Poetry: Poetry, Poetics and Politics* (London: Routledge, 1993), p. 336. It is relevant to introduce a term which has been ascribed to Victorian poetry, as it is part of my argument later in this essay that Brontë's poetry, in common with other poetry written by women in the second quarter of the nineteenth century, challenges the traditional critical demarcation between Romanticism and Victorianism.
3 C. W. Hatfield (ed.), *The Complete Poems of Emily Jane Brontë* (New York: Columbia University Press, 1941). For examples of Romanticist readings of the poetry see Helen Brown, 'The Influence of Byron on Emily Brontë', *Modern Language Review*, 34 (1939), 374–81 and Jonathan Wordsworth, 'Wordsworth and the Poetry of Emily Brontë', *Brontë Society Transactions*, 16 (1975), 85–100. Robin Grove in ' "It would not do": Emily Brontë as Poet', in Anne Smith (ed.), *The Art of Emily Brontë* (London: Vision Press, 1976), pp. 33–67, compares Brontë (unfavourably) with Blake. Rosalind Miles's essay, 'A Baby God: the Creative Dynamism of Emily Brontë's Poetry', in Smith (ed.), *Emily Brontë*, pp. 68–93, draws parallels between Brontë and Coleridge, Keats and Wordsworth. C. Day Lewis, 'The Poetry of Emily Brontë: a Passion for Freedom', *Brontë Society Transactions*, 13 (1965), 83–95, compares Brontë with Blake and John Hewish's extended study, *Emily Brontë: a Biographical and Critical Study* (London: Macmillan, 1969) claims direct influence upon Brontë of Blake, Byron, Coleridge, Keats, Shelley and Wordsworth. An interdisciplinary ascription of Brontë to Romanticism is Robert K. Wallace's *Emily Brontë and*

Beethoven (Athens: University of Georgia Press, 1986) which argues that Brontë was influenced by the 'Byronic' life and work of Beethoven. Wallace alternates discussion of Brontë's work with analysis of three of Beethoven's piano sonatas.

4 Georges Bataille, *Literature and Evil*, trans. Alastair Hamilton (London: Calder & Boyars, 1973).

5 This line of thought originates in Charlotte Brontë's account of Emily Brontë's 'hero[ic]' descent into illness and death in her 'Biographical Notice of Ellis and Acton Bell'. Charlotte Brontë comments that Emily Brontë was '[s]tronger than a man, simpler than a child, her nature stood alone' (reprinted in Emily Brontë, *Wuthering Heights*, ed. David Daiches (London: Penguin, 1965), p. 35.) By contrast, Lewis, 'A Passion for Freedom', p. 95, argues that Brontë aesthetic led her to a painful awareness of her failure to transcend femininity. He comments: 'My own belief is that the source of Emily Brontë's proud recalcitrance, her preoccupation with themes of captivity, exile and freedom, was her sex; the limitation of not being a man.'

6 Margaret Homans, *Women Writers and Poetic Identity: Dorothy Wordsworth, Emily Brontë and Emily Dickinson* (New Jersey and Guildford: Princeton University Press, 1980); Irene Taylor, *Holy Ghosts: the Male Muses of Charlotte and Emily Brontë* (New York: Columbia University Press, 1990).

7 Marlon B. Ross, *The Contours of Masculine Desire: Romanticism and the Rise of Women's Poetry* (New York: Oxford University Press, 1989).

8 For example, Grove, ' "It would not do" ', p. 40, comments: 'What we seem to have is an author who gained access to her talents rarely; from time to time, and apparently at random, wrote poems of real worth ... then lapsed into melodramatics again.' Barbara Hardy's essay, 'The Lyricism of Emily Brontë' in Smith (ed.), *Emily Brontë*, p. 96 makes a similar evaluation of the Gondal poems, commenting that they contain 'fine lyrical passages in a context of weak, banal or melodramatic narrative'. Lewis, 'A Passion for Freedom', p. 93, analyses 'Julian M. and A. G. Rochelle' in these terms, praising the six stanzas describing mystical experience which appear 'in a longish, not otherwise very distinguished semi-narrative poem ... Emily Brontë sat down to write another poem about a Gondal episode, and, half way through, the thing caught fire, and we get those stanzas which are barely relevant to the story of the poem, quite out of key with it, and whose intensity shows up the rest of the poem as superficial, insipid, unreal.'

9 Bataille, *Literature and Evil*, Preface.

10 Ibid.

11 Ibid., p. 4.

12 Ibid., p. 8.

13 Ibid., p. 12.

14 Ibid., p. 15.
15 Ibid., p. 11.
16 Ibid., p. 17.
17 Ibid., p. 9.
18 Ibid., p. 7.
19 Brontë, *Wuthering Heights*, pp. 336–7.
20 J. Hillis Miller, *The Disappearance of God: Five Nineteenth-Century Writers* (Oxford University Press, 1963), p. 201.
21 Homans, *Women Writers*, p. 109.
22 Ibid., pp. 104 and 110.
23 Taylor, *Holy Ghosts*, pp. 34–5.
24 One critic who has begun to consider the implications of reading Brontë as a Victorian poet is Kathryn Burlinson. In ' "What language can utter the feeling": Identity in the Poetry of Emily Brontë', in Philip Shaw and Peter Stockwell (eds.), *Subjectivity and Literature from the Romantics to the Present Day: Creating the Self* (London: Pinter, 1991), p. 40 she remarks that 'Brontë ... exhibits a post-romantic (and Victorian) preoccupation with the legacy of romanticism, where doubts about the self and its potentiality underpin poetic articulation.'
25 For an account of the debates amongst contemporary reviewers of early Victorian poetry see Isobel Armstrong's introduction to her anthology *Victorian Scrutinies: Reviews of Poetry 1830–1870* (London: Athlone Press, 1972). Arnold's comment is contained in his preface to the first edition of *Poems* (1853), and is reprinted in P. J. Keating (ed.), *Matthew Arnold: Selected Prose* (London: Penguin, 1970), p. 41.
26 Emily Brontë, *The Complete Poems of Emily Jane Brontë*, ed. Janet Gezari (London: Penguin, 1992), pp. 3–4.
27 William Wordsworth and Samuel Taylor Coleridge, *Lyrical Ballads*, ed. W. J. B. Owen (Oxford University Press, 1969), pp. 63–5.
28 Robert Browning, *Men and Women and Other Poems*, ed. J. W. Harper (London: J. M. Dent, 1975), pp. 205–7.
29 Lord Byron, Letter to Annabella Milbanke, 29 November 1813, reprinted in Leslie Marchand (ed.), *Byron's Letters and Journals, vol. III* (Cambridge, Mass.: Belknap Press of Harvard University Press, 1974–82), p. 179.
30 Brontë, *Complete Poems*, pp. 5–6.
31 Taylor, *Holy Ghosts*, pp. 34–5.
32 Ibid., p. 39.
33 Grove, ' "It would not do" ', p. 62.
34 Brontë, *Complete Poems*, pp. 177–81.
35 Hewish, *Emily Brontë*, p. 82.
36 Ibid., p. 83.
37 Homans, *Women Writers*, pp. 157–60.
38 Patricia Waugh, 'Postmodernism and Feminism', in Stevi Jackson and Jackie Jones (eds.), *Contemporary Feminist Theories* (Edinburgh University Press, 1998), pp. 177–93.

39 Ibid., p. 184.
40 Ibid., p. 183.
41 Ibid., p. 188.
42 Ibid.
43 Ibid., p. 180.

5 A SENSE OF ENDINGS: SOME ROMANTIC AND POSTMODERN COMPARISONS

1 'A Sense of Endings' pays tribute in its title (needless perhaps to say) to Frank Kermode's *The Sense of an Ending: Studies in the Theory of Fiction* (New York: Oxford University Press, 1967). However, the indefinite article and the plural are intended to be significant transformations.

2 *Capriccio* (1942) was Strauss's last opera, self consciously so, giving its 'ending' a personal relevance. In many ways its self-refexivity and variegated intertextuality (it is a tissue of musical quotation) lend it a post-Modernist air.

3 Laurence Sterne, *The Life and Opinions of Tristram Shandy, Gentleman*, ed. I. C. Ross (Oxford University Press, 1983), p. 539.

4 See, for example, Friedrich Schlegel's 'Letter about the Novel', in *Dialogue on Poetry*, published in the *Athenaeum* (1800) trans. E. Behler and R. Struc, (Pennsylvania State University Press, London: University Park, 1968), pp. 94–105.

5 Marilyn Butler, 'Nymphs and Nympholepsy', in *Studien zur Englischen Romantik*, 1(1985), 11–31.

6 James Joyce, *Finnegans Wake* (1939; Harmondsworth: Penguin, 1992), pp. 628, 3.

7 V. Nabokov, *Ada, or Ardor: a Family Chronicle* (London: Weidenfeld & Nicolson, 1969), pp. 583–9, and the dust jacket.

8 John Barth, *Chimera* (London: André Deutsch, 1972), pp. 319–20.

9 John Barth, *Sabbatical: a Romance* (London: Secker & Warburg, 1982), 301.

10 John Barth, *The Tidewater Tales: a Novel* (London: Methuen, 1987), p. 638.

11 Richard Bradbury, 'The Development of a Postmodernist Aesthetics in the Fiction of John Barth', unpublished doctoral dissertation, University of Glasgow, 1988, p. 8 and passim.

12 Byron, *Beppo* (1817) stanza 52. All Byron quotations are from J. J. McGann (ed.), *Lord Byron: the Complete Poetical Works* (Oxford: Clarendon Press, 1980–93), further references cited as *CPW*. Here *CPW*, vol. IV, p. 145.

13 Shakespeare's elision of the distinction between theatrical imagination and 'real-life' faith, or the return of drama to ritual, produces the same paradox.

14 Byron, *Vision of Judgement* (1821), *CPW*, vol. VI, p. 345.

15 *Tidewater Tales*, pp. 644, 646, 654, for example. Here advantage is taken, however, of modern technology: 'she can spy them all the way

from her PTOR, via her highest-level keyhole'; 'our omniscopic Sheerazade'; 'in her highest resolution omniscopic mode'.

16 *Beppo*, stanza 99. *CPW*, p. 160. Byron had rather a penchant for leaving poems or cantos which had grown by accretion with the spendidly irresolute number of ninety-nine stanzas (cf. *Don Juan* XV). Laura's tirade runs fron stanza 91 to 93, *CPW*, pp. 157–8. J. Drummond Bone, 'Beppo and the Liberation of Fiction', in Bernard Beatty and Vincent Newey (eds.), *Byron and the Limits of Fiction* (Liverpool University Press, 1988), pp. 97–125.

6 A BEING ALL ALIKE? TELEOTROPIC SYNTAX IN ASHBERY AND WORDSWORTH

1 I use the term 'present-day' rather than 'postmodernist' in deference to a further complication; just as Keats or Byron would not have understood the modern term 'Romantic', so it would not be helpful to assimilate everything that chances to happen currently into a catch-all 'Postmodernism'.

2 Charles Baudelaire, *Œuvres Complètes*, ed. Claude Pichois (Paris: Gallimard, 1975), p. 11.

3 William Wordsworth, *The Thirteen-Book Prelude*, vol. I, ed. Mark Reed (Ithaca and London: Cornell University Press, 1991), p. 208.

4 Paul de Man, 'Allegory and Irony in Baudelaire', in E. S. Burt, Kevin newmark and Andrzej Warminski (eds.), *Romanticism and Contemporary Criticism* (Baltimore and London: The Johns Hopkins University Press, 1993), p. 118.

5 Samuel Beckett, *Molloy / Malone Dies / The Unnamable: a Trilogy* (Paris: The Olympia Press, 1959), p. 579.

6 John Ashbery, *Flow Chart* (Manchester: Carcanet, 1991), p. 4.

7 Christopher Dewdney, *The Secular Grail: Paradigms of Perception* (Toronto: Somerville House, 1993), p. 150.

8 As given by Dewdney, *The Secular Grail*, p. 108.

7 VIRTUAL ROMANTICISM

1 Paul Hamilton, 'Wordsworth and the Shapes of Theory', *News from Nowhere: Theory and Politics of Romanticism*, 1 (1995), 19.

2 Jerome Christensen, 'The Romantic Movement at the End of History', *Critical Inquiry*, 20 (1994), 452–76.

3 Edmund Burke, *Reflections on the Revolution in France*, ed. Conor Cruise O'Brien (Harmondsworth: Penguin, 1968), pp. 92–3.

4 Jean-François Lyotard, *The Postmodern Condition*, trans. Geoff Bennington and Brian Massumi (Manchester University Press, 1984), p. 79.

5 Jean-Luc Nancy and Philippe Lacoue-Labarthe, *The Literary Absolute: the*

Theory of Literature in German Romanticism, trans. P. Barnard and C. Lester (Albany, N.Y.: State University of New York Press, 1988), p. 15.

6 Ibid.

7 Ibid., pp. 16–17.

8 I. Csicsery-Ronay, 'Cyberpunk and Neuromanticism', in L. McCaffrey (ed.), *Storming the Reality Studio* (Durham N.C. and London: Duke University Press, 1991), pp. 182–93; J. Voller, 'Neuromanticism: Cyberspace and the Sublime', *Extrapolation*, 34.1 (1993), 18–29.

9 Lance Olsen, 'The Shadow of Spirit in William Gibson's Matrix Trilogy', *Extrapolation*, 32.3 (1991), 284; Steven Levy, *Artificial Life: the Quest for a New Creation* (London: Jonathan Cape, 1992).

10 Douglas Rushkoff, *Cyberia: Life in the Trenches of Hyperspace* (London: HarperCollins, 1994), 91.

11 Ibid., p. 84.

12 Ibid., p. 19.

13 William Godwin, *An Enquiry Concerning Political Justice*, ed. Isaac Kramnick (Harmondsworth: Penguin, 1976), p. 759.

14 Rushkoff, *Cyberia*, p. 11.

15 Ibid., p. 54.

16 Robert Markley, 'Introduction: History, Theory and Virtual Reality', in Robert Markley (ed.), *Virtual Realities and their Discontents* (Baltimore and London: The Johns Hopkins University Press, 1996), p. 3.

17 Fredric Jameson, 'Postmodernism, or the Cultural Logic of Late Capitalism', *New Left Review*, 146 (1984), 53–92.

18 Anne K. Mellor, *Romanticism and Gender* (New York and London: Routledge, 1993).

19 Steven Goldsmith, *Unbuilding Jerusalem: Apocalypse and Romantic Representation* (Ithaca, N.Y.: Cornell University Press, 1993).

20 John Whale, 'The Limits of Paine's Revolutionary Literalism', in Kelvin Everest (ed.), *Revolution in Writing* (Milton Keynes: Open University Press, 1991), p. 136.

21 J. Katz, 'The Age of Paine', *Wired*, 1.1 (1995), pp. 64–9.

22 Burke, *Reflections*, p. 313.

23 Francis Fukuyama, *The End of History and the Last Man* (London: Penguin, 1992).

24 Christensen, 'The Romantic Movement', 453, 457.

25 Ibid., 453.

26 Lyotard, *The Postmodern Condition*, p. 81.

27 Patricia Waugh, *Practising Postmodernism, Reading Modernism* (London: Edward Arnold, 1992), p. 15.

28 Neil Hertz, 'The Notion of Blockage in the Literature of the Sublime', in Geoffrey Hartman (ed.), *Psychoanalysis and the Question of the Text* (Baltimore and London: The Johns Hopkins University Press), 77.

29 Ibid., p. 76.

30 Ibid., pp. 79–80.

31 Mary Jacobus, *Romanticism, Writing and Sexual Difference* (Oxford: Clarendon Press, 1989), pp. 124, 111.

32 Hertz, 'The Notion of Blockage', p. 82.

33 Jacobus, *Romanticism*, pp. 104–5.

34 Ibid., p. 112.

35 Thomas De Quincey, *Confessions of an English Opium Eater*, ed. Alethea Hayter (Harmondsworth: Penguin, 1986), p. 103.

36 Ibid., p. 83.

37 Ibid., p. 107.

38 Ibid., p. 113.

39 Robert Young, 'The Eye and Progress of his Song: a Lacanian Reading of *The Prelude*', *Oxford Literary Review*, 3.3 (1979), 79–98.

40 Samuel Taylor Coleridge, *Biographia Literaria*, ed. George Watson (London: Dent, 1975), p. 28.

41 Ioan Williams, *Novel and Romance, 1700–1800* (London: Routledge, 1970), 162.

42 Thomas McFarland, 'Recent Studies in the Nineteenth Century', *Studies in English Literature*, 16 (1976), 694.

43 Coleridge, *Biographia Literaria*, p. 218.

44 Ibid., p. 152.

45 Jacques Lacan, 'Desire and the Interpretation of Desire in *Hamlet*', *Yale French Studies*, 55–6 (1977), 11–52.

46 Slavoj Žižek, *Tarrying with the Negative* (Durham, N.C. and London: Duke University Press, 1993), p. 209.

47 T. J. Matthias, *The Pursuits of Literature* (London, 1805).

48 Jean Baudrillard, *The Transparency of Evil*, trans. J. Benedict (London: Verso, 1993), pp. 7–8.

49 Bill Nicholls, 'The Work of Culture in an Age of Cybernetic Systems', *Screen*, 29.1 (1988), 28.

50 Ibid., 46.

51 William Gibson, *Neuromancer* (London: HarperCollins, 1984), p. 168.

52 Ibid., p. 12.

53 Ibid., p. 304.

54 Ibid., p. 309.

55 Ibid., p. 67.

56 Ibid., p. 315.

57 Ibid., p. 316.

58 Ibid., p. 173.

59 Nick Land, 'Circuitries', *PLI, The Warwick Journal of Philosophy: Gilles Deleuze and the Transcendental Unconscious* (1993), 217–35.

60 Jean Baudrillard, *America*, trans. C. Turner (London and New York: Verso, 1988).

8 THE SINS OF THE FATHERS: THE PERSISTENCE OF GOTHIC

1 See Terry Lovell's discussion of the economics of novel production in the nineteenth century in *Consuming Fictions* (London: Verso, 1989). For a useful anthology of the chapbooks and shilling shockers, see Peter Haining (ed.), *The Shilling Shockers: Stories of Terror from the Gothic Bluebooks* (London: Victor Gollancz, 1978).

2 Juliet Flower MacCannell, *The Regime of the Brother: After the Patriarchy*, (London: Routledge, 1991), p. 11.

3 Cited in A. O. J. Lovejoy, 'The First Gothic Revival and the Return to Nature', *Essays in the History of Ideas* (Baltimore: The Johns Hopkins Press, 1948), p. 138. Kenneth Clark quotes the same passage but misattributes it to Sir Christopher Wren in *The Gothic Revival*, (London: Constable, 1928), p. 7. The passage is to be found, however, in Evelyn's *Account of Architects and Architecure*, dedicated to Wren in 1697, and it is quoted as Evelyn's in the *Parentalia* (1750) which Clarke gives as his source, presumably by Wren's son who compiled its miscellaneous collection of reports and papers by various worthies of the Wren family.

4 *Alexander Pope: Selected Poetry and Prose*, ed. W. K. Wimsatt (New York: Holt, Rinehart & Winston, 1972), p. 189.

5 *The Oxford Book of Gothic Tales*, ed Chris Baldick (Oxford University Press, 1992), p. xii.

6 Lovejoy, 'The First Gothic Revival', p. 138.

7 Edmund Burke, *A Philosophical Enquiry into the Origin of our Ideas of the Sublime and the Beautiful (1757)*, ed. James T. Boulton (University of Notre Dame Press, 1968).

8 Horace Walpole, The *Castle of Otranto*, ed W. S. Lewis, (Oxford University Press, 1982), p. 3.

9 Ibid., p. 7.

10 Ibid., p. 5.

11 Lovejoy, 'The First Gothic Revival', p. 138.

12 Clark, *The Gothic Revival*, p. 110.

13 Baldick, *The Oxford Book of Gothic Tales*, p. xix.

14 Kate Ferguson Ellis, *The Contested Castle* (Champaign: University of Illinois Press, 1989).

15 Shirley Jackson's novel was made into a film *The Haunting* (dir. Robert Wise, 1963), see Patricia White's 'Female Spectator, Lesbian Spectre: *The Haunting*' in *Inside/Out*, ed. Diana Fuss (London: Routledge, 1991). Susan Hill's 'conclusion' or sequel to *Rebecca*, which has just appeared in *The Australian Women's Weekly*, October 1993, as I write, indicates the continuing attraction of the female Gothic paradigm.

16 Mary Jacobus, 'Is there a woman in this text?', *New Literary History*, 14.1 (1982).

17 John Ruskin, *The Nature of Gothic*, ed. with Preface by William Morris (London: George Allen, 1899), p. vii. For a more recent critique of

Ruskin's idealised account of medieval labour processes see John Unrau, 'Ruskin, the Workman and the Savageness of Gothic', in Robert Hewison (ed.), *New Approaches to Ruskin* (London: Routledge and Kegan Paul, 1981).

18 I owe this reference to an unpublished paper by Tony Pinkney of the University of Lancaster. See also his 'In Praise of Gothic', *News from Nowhere*, 9, (Autumn 1991).

19 Howard Dearstyne, *Inside the Bauhaus*, ed. David Spaeth (New York: Rizzoli, 1986), p. 39.

20 Letter to Wilhelm Fliess, 1 November 1896, in *The Complete Correspondence of Sigmund Freud to Wilhelm Fliess 1887–1904*, ed. Jeffrey Moussaieff Masson (Cambridge, Mass.: The Belknap Press of Harvard University Press, 1985), p. 202.

21 Jean Laplanche and J. B. Pontalis, 'Fantasy and the Origins of Sexuality', in Victor Burgin et al. (eds.), *Formations of Fantasy* (London: Methuen, 1986).

22 'From the History of an Infantile Neurosis' (1914), *The Standard Edition of the Complete Psychological Works of Sigmund Freud*, ed. James Strachey, vol. XVII (London: The Hogarth Press, 1961), p. 119.

23 Laplanche and Pontalis, 'Fantasy and Origins of Sexuality', p. 17. They distance themselves from the Freudian phylogenetic perspective as well as the suggested structuralist interpretation. In *New Foundations for Psychoanalysis* (Oxford: Blackwell, 1991) Laplanche explicitly rejects Freud's concept of primal fantasy as a genetically transmitted schema, substituting for it his theory of primal seduction and the enigmatic parental signifier.

24 *Critical Inquiry*, 13 (1987), p. 287.

25 Abraham gives as an example of possession by a parental phantom, the case of a man who acted out the fate of his mother's lover who 'had been denounced by the grandmother (an unspeakable and secret fact) and, having been sent to "break rocks" *(casser les cailloux* = do forced labour), he died in the gas-chamber. What does our man do on weekends? A lover of geology, he "breaks rocks", then catches butterflies which he proceeds to kill in a can of cyanide'. Ibid., p. 291.

26 *Standard Edition*, vol. XVII, p. 218.

27 Tzvetan Todorov, *The Fantastic*, trans. Richard Howard (Ithaca: Cornell University Press, 1975).

28 'On the Psychology of the Uncanny', trans. Roy Sellars, *Angelaki*, 2.1, 7–22.

29 *Standard Edition*, vol. XVII, P. 222.

30 Ibid., p. 223

31 For Laplanche's meditation on these themes see John Fletcher (ed.), *Essays on Otherness* (London: Routledge, 1998) (especially 'The Unfinished Copernican Revolution').

32 *The Sandman*, in *Tales of Hoffman*, trans. R. J. Hollingdale (Harmondsworth: Penguin Classics, 1982), p. 86.

33 Jacques Lacan, 'The Freudian Thing', in *Écrits: a Selection*, trans. Alan
Sheridan (London: Tavistock, 1977), p. 243.

34 *Hands of the Ripper*, directed by Peter Sasdy, produced by Aida Young,
screenplay by L.W. Davidson from a short story by Edward Spencer
Shew. Director of Photography Kenneth Talbot, editor Christopher
Barnes, Art Director Roy Stannard. A Hammer Production distributed
by Rank, 1971. 85 mins.

35 It is unclear whether they are literally husband and wife and so what a
respectable let alone aristocratic couple would be doing living in
Berners St, or whether she is his mistress and the child illegitimate. The
iconographic representation of home, hearth and the angel-in-the-
house confronting its uncanny opposite 'at home' is what matters.

36 I owe this point to John Beer made in the lively discussion that followed
an early version of this paper at the Warwick Conference in 1992.

37 'Shall I even confess to you the origins of this romance? I waked one
morning in the beginning of last June from a dream, of which all I could
recover was, that I had thought myself in an ancient castle (a very natural
dream for a head filled like mine with Gothic story) and on the upper
banister of the great staircase I saw a gigantic hand in armour. In the
evening I sat down and began to write, without knowing in the least what
I intended to say or relate.' Walpole to the Rev. William Cole, 9 March
1765, cited in Introduction to *The Castle of Otranto*, ed. W. S. Lewis, p. ix.

9 ROMANTIC IRONY AND THE POSTMODERN SUBLIME:
GEOFFREY HILL AND 'SEBASTIAN ARRURRUZ'

1 See Jean-François Lyotard, *Discours, figure* (Paris: Klincksieck, 1971); *The
Postmodern Condition: a Report on Knowledge*, trans. Geoff Bennington and
Brian Massumi (Manchester University Press, 1984), p. 79 (further
references in text cited as *PMC*).

2 The sections of 'The Songbook of Sebastian Arrurruz' were published
as follows: 'From the *Songbook* of Sebastian Arrurruz' (No. 5), *TLS*, 29
July 1965, p. 648; 'From the *Songbook* of Sebastian Arrurruz' (Nos. 1–4)
Agenda 4.5/4.6 (Autumn 1966), 34–6; 'From *the Songbook of Sebastian
Arrurruz*': '9. A Song From Armenia', *Stand* 9.3, n.d. (pub. 1968), 50; the
remaining sections of the sequence first appeared when the sequence as
a whole was published, in *King Log* (1968). The additional 'Copla by
Sebastian Arrurruz' appeared in *Stand*, 10.1, n.d. (pub. 1972), 4. The
sequence was reprinted in *Collected Poems* (Harmondsworth: Penguin,
1985), pp. 92–102 (further references in text cited as *CP*).

3 Interview in *Viewpoints: Poets in Conversation with John Haffenden* (London:
Faber, 1981), pp. 76–99. Further references in text cited as *VP*.

4 The most uncompromising statement of this view of Hill has been

made by Tom Paulin, 'The Case for Geoffrey Hill', *London Review of Books*, 4 April 1985, pp. 13–14; rev. as 'A Visionary Naturalist: Geoffrey Hill', in Tom Paulin, *Minotaur: Poetry and the Nation State* (London: Faber, 1992), pp. 276–84.

5 Peter Nicholls, 'Divergences: Modernism, Postmodernism, Jameson and Lyotard', *Critical Quarterly*, 33.3 (Autumn 1991), 4. Further references in text cited as Nicholls.

6 Hill's elegies include 'Merlin', 'In Memory of Jane Fraser', 'Requiem for the Plantagenet Kings', 'Two Formal Elegies for the Jews in Europe', 'September Song', 'Four Poems Regarding the Endurance of Poets', 'The Mystery of the Charity of Charles Péguy' (*CP*, 19, 22, 29, 30–1, 67, 78–81, 181–96) and 'Scenes with Harlequins: In Memoriam Aleksandr Blok' (*TLS*, 9–15 February 1990, p. 137).

7 The term 'flicker', meaning unsettling glimpses of alternative meanings, is used by Brian McHale, *Postmodernist Fiction* (London: Methuen, 1987), p. 32.

8 Ernst Behler, 'The Theory of Irony in German Romanticism', in Frederick Garber (ed.), *Romantic Irony* (Budapest: Akadémiai Kiadó, 1988), p. 43. Further references in text cited as Behler.

9 Bill Readings, *Introducing Lyotard: Art and Politics* (London and New York: Routledge, 1991), p. xxxi. Further references in text cited as Readings.

10 Friedrich Schlegel, excerpts from 'Athenäum Fragments' ('Athenäums Fragmente') (1798), trans. Peter Firchow, in *German Aesthetic and Literary Criticism: the Romantic Ironists and Goethe*, ed. Kathleen M. Wheeler (Cambridge University Press, 1984), pp. 44–54 (p. 49).

11 Nicholls's view of postmodern fiction has similarities with that of Linda Hutcheon, who argues that the separation of literary language from reference is a feature of late Modernism, whereas Postmodernism involves 'a world that is both resolutely fictive and yet undeniably historical'. However, Hutcheon remains somewhat closer to Baudrillard's stress on a pervasive textuality since she argues that 'what both realms share is their constitution in and as discourse'. Linda Hutcheon, *A Poetics of Postmodernism: History, Theory, Fiction* (New York and London: Routledge, 1988), p. 142.

12 Geoffrey Hill, *The Lords of Limit: Essays on Literature and Ideas* (London: André Deutsch, 1984), p. 15.

13 Geoffrey Hill, A Sermon preached at Great St Mary's, The University Church, Cambridge, 8 May 1983, p. 2. Further references in text cited as Sermon.

14 Geoffrey Hill, interview with Hermione Lee, *Book Four*, 2 October 1985, Channel Four television.

15 For example Escher's 1956 lithograph, 'Print Gallery', reproduced in Douglas R. Hofstadter, *Gödel, Escher, Bach* (Hassocks, Sussex: Harvester, 1979), p. 714.

16 'Blocking together' is defined by Readings as 'a mode characteristic of

the figural, in which two incommensurable elements (such as the visible and the textual) are held together, impossibly, in the "same" space: a kind of superimposition without privilege' (Readings, xxx).

17 'The Dream-Work Does Not Think', trans. Mary Lydon from *Discours, figure*, in Andrew Benjamin (ed.), *The Lyotard Reader* (Oxford and Cambridge, Mass.: Blackwell, 1989), pp. 29–30. Further references in text cited as Reader.

18 *Discours, figure*, p. 332 quoted and translated Geoffrey Bennington, *Lyotard: Writing the Event* (Manchester University Press, 1988), p. 96.

19 Hill himself has addressed the charge that his work is nostalgic, commenting that there are 'good political and sociological reasons for the floating of nostalgia: there's been an elegiac tinge to the air of this country ever since the end of the Great War. To be accused of exhibiting a symptom when, to the best of my abilities, I'm offering a diagnosis appears to be one of the numerous injustices which one must suffer with as much equanimity as possible' (*VP*, 93).

20 'Tradition and the Individual Talent', *The Sacred Wood: Essays on Poetry and Criticism* (1920; London: Methuen, 1934), p. 50.

21 The concept of double coding is developed by Charles Jencks in *Current Architecture* (London: Academy Editions, 1982); see p. 111.

22 'Note on the meaning of "post-"', in *The Postmodern Explained to Children: Correspondence 1982–1985*, translations edited by Julian Pefanis and Morgan Thomas (London: Turnaround/Power Institute of Fine Art, 1992), p. 93.

23 On the British Poetry Revival of the 1960s and 1970s, see Robert Hampson and Peter Barry (eds.), *New British Poetries: the Scope of the Possible* (Manchester and New York: Manchester University Press, 1993), p. 5 and *passim*.

24 On contemporary reworkings of narrative in poetry see Alan Robinson, *Instabilities in Contemporary British Poetry* (London: Macmillan, 1988), especially pp. 1–15.

25 Ernst Behler, *Irony and the Discourse of Modernity* (Seattle and London: University of Washington Press, 1990), p. 36.

26 Alan Wilde, *Horizons of Assent: Modernism, Postmodernism and the Ironic Imagination* (Baltimore: The Johns Hopkins University Press, 1981), p. 115.

27 Candace Lang, *Irony/Humour: Critical Paradigms* (Baltimore and London: The Johns Hopkins University Press, 1988), p. 195.

10 'UPROOTING THE RANCID STALK': TRANSFORMATIONS OF
ROMANTICISM IN ASHBERY AND ASH

1 Jerome J. McGann comments that Ashbery's idiom 'established in the 60s, has come to seem an early example of the postmodern style' and that 'throughout the seventies and into the eighties' he 'has been the single most influential figure in American poetry': 'Contemporary

Poetry, Alternate Routes', *Critical Inquiry* 13.3 (1987), 624–47: reprinted in *Social Values and Poetic Acts: the Historical Judgement of Literary Work* (Cambridge: Harvard University Press, 1988), 197. 'Craft Interview with John Ashbery. By Janet Bloom and Robert Losada': in William Packard (ed.), *The Craft of Poetry: Interviews from 'The New York Quarterly'*, (Garden City, N.Y.: Doubleday, 1974), p. 118.

2 See Harold Bloom, 'John Ashbery: The Charity of the Hard Moments', *Figures of Capable Imagination* (New York: Seabury, 1976); reprinted in Harold Bloom (ed.), *John Ashbery* (New York: Chelsea House, 1985), pp. 49–80; Helen Vendler, 'John Ashbery, Louise Gluck', *The Music of What Happens: Poems, Poets, Critics* (Cambridge: Harvard University Press, 1988), p. 231; and Marjorie Perloff, "Mysteries of Construction": the Dream Songs of John Ashbery', *The Poetics of Indeterminacy* (Princeton University Press, 1981), pp. 248–87.

3 See Vernon Shetley, *After the Death of Poetry: Poet and Audience in Contemporary America* (Durham, N.C.: Duke University Press, 1993), pp. 128–32.

4 For further discussion of difficulties in periodising the postmodern, see Mutlu Konuk Blasing, *Politics and Form in Postmodern Poetry: O'Hara, Bishop, Ashbery, and Merrill* (Cambridge University Press, 1995), pp. 1–29.

5 See Geoffrey Ward, 'Ashbery and Influence', *Statutes of Liberty: the New York School of Poets* (London: Macmillan, 1994), p. 105. For extended discussion, see Mary Kinzie, 'Irreference', *The Cure of Poetry in an Age of Prose: Moral Effects of the Poet's Calling* (Chicago University Press, 1993) pp. 230–46.

6 'On Postmodernism and Articulation: an interview with Stuart Hall', ed. Lawrence Grossberg, *Journal of Communication Study*, 46 (1986); cited in Andrew Ross (ed.), *Universal Abandon? the Politics of Postmodernism* (Edinburgh University Press, 1989), p. xii. Robert Von Hallberg notes that 'Insofar as an American popular taste can be identified it is imperious, exuberant, and as is clear to Europeans, expansionist ... The success of American cultural imperialism on this level is indisputable and however appalling to some, attractive to many poets', *American Poetry and Culture, 1945–80* (Cambridge, Mass. and London: Harvard University Press, 1985), p. 194.

7 See John Gery, 'The Anxiety of Affluence: Poets after Ashbery', *Verse*, 8.1 (1991), 28–35.

8 See, for example, Andrew Ross, 'The New Sentence and the Commodity Form: Recent American Writing', in Cary Nelson and Lawrence Grossberg (eds.), *Marxism and the Interpretation of Culture* (Bloomington: Indiana University Press, 1988), pp. 361–80. Compare 'It's taken on a kind of pejorative sense really. There's so much done in the name of the "avant-garde" that it's become really official, especially in art. Artists have found that anybody can be an avantgarde artist, so if everybody is one, then where is the rest of the army?': 'An Interview in

Warsaw with Piotr Sommer' in Michael Palmer (ed.), *Code of Signals: Recent Writings in Poetics* (Berkeley: North Atlantic Books, 1983), p. 294.

9 Keith Cohen, 'Ashbery's Dismantling of Bourgeois Discourse', in David Lehman (ed.), *Beyond Amazement: New Essays on John Ashbery* (Ithaca: Cornell University Press, 1980), pp. 128, 130, 138–9.

10 Compare Blasing, *Politics and Form*, pp. 118–24; Marjorie Perloff, *Radical Artifice: Writing Poetry in the Age of Media* (Chicago University Press, 1991), pp. 175–85 and John Shoptaw, *On the Outside Looking Out: John Ashbery's Poetry* (Harvard University Press, 1994), pp. 16–17.

11 Cohen 'Ashbery's Dismantling of Bourgeois Discourse', pp. 139–40.

12 Paul Breslin, 'Warpless and Woofless Subtleties: John Ashbery and "Bourgeois Discourse"': *'The Psycho-Sexual Muse: American Poetry since the 1950s* (Chicago University Press, 1987), p. 216.

13 See Alan Williamson, 'The Diffracting Diamond: Ashbery, Romanticism and anti-Art', *Introspection and Contemporary Poetry* (Harvard University Press, 1984), pp. 116–48; and 'An Interview in Warsaw', p. 312.

14 Douglas Crase, 'The Prophetic Ashbery', *Beyond Amazement*, pp. 65, 41, 54. John Bayley dubs the style 'a poetic version of "Wasp" characteristics', 'The Poetry of John Ashbery', in Bloom, *John Ashbery*, p. 203.

15 From 'The Skaters' (*RM* 44) quoted in 'An Interview in Warsaw', p. 309.

16 Compare Blasing, *Politics and Form*, p. 128.

17 'Craft Interview with John Ashbery', p. 123. Vendler ('John Ashbery, Louise Gluck', p. 241) terms this 'living a collective life'.

18 Charles Altieri astutely compares Ashbery to a neoclassical rhetorician: 'John Ashbery: Discursive Rhetoric within a Poetics of Thinking', *Self and Sensibility in Contemporary American Poetry* (Cambridge University Press, 1984), p. 150. Vendler ('John Ashbery, Louise Gluck', p. 231) notes 'long stretches of accessible table-talk'; see also Daniel Cotton, ' "Getting It": Ashbery and the Avant-Garde of Every-Day Language', *Verse*, 8.1 (1991), 3–23; and S. P. Mohanty and Jonathan Monroe, 'John Ashbery and the Articulation of the Social', *Diacritics*, 17.2 (1987), 37–63.

19 Crase, 'The Prophetic Ashbery', 34.

20 See Walter Kalaidjin, *Languages of Liberation: the Social Text in Contemporary American Poetry* (New York: Columbia University Press, 1989), p. 17.

21 David Kennedy, ' "Just the Facts, Just the": a Rough Guide to British Postmodernism', *New Relations: the refashioning of British Poetry 1980–1994* (Bridgend: Poetry Wales Press, 1996), pp. 79–119; Ian Gregson, 'John Ashbery and British Postmodernism', *Contemporary Poetry and Postmodernism: Dialogue and Estrangement* (London: Macmillan, 1996), pp. 109–23. Compare Ash, 'I guess if anybody's postmodern, then I probably am': Robert Crawford et al. (eds.), *Talking Verse: Interviews with Poets* (St Andrews and Williamsburg, St. Andrews Verse: 1995), p. 28.

22 'An Interview in Warsaw', p. 311.

23 John Ash, 'Reading New York', *PN Review*, 54 (1987), 7; on Ashbery's 'misapprehension of Webern', see 'John Ashbery in conversation with

John Ash', *PNR*, 46 (1985), 32; on nineteenth-century connections, see Robert Crawford, 'John Ashbery: a Dialogue across Time', *Identifying Territory: Self and Territory in Twentieth-Century Poetry* (Edinburgh University Press, 1993), pp. 102–19.

24 'Reading New York', 6.

25 'An Interview in Warsaw', p. 309. Vendler terms this Ashbery's 'sing-along' effect: 'A Steely Glitter Chasing Shadows: John Ashbery's *Flow Chart*', in *Soul Says: On Recent Poetry* (Harvard University Press, 1995), p. 139: compare John Koethe, 'The Absence of a Noble Presence', *Verse*, 8.1 (1991), 23–7.

26 John Ash, 'Interview with John McAllister', *Bête Noire*, 8–9 (1989), 9.

27 'John Ashbery in conversation with John Ash', 31.

28 'Interview with John McAllister', 21.

29 'The Poet's Grandmother and Other Dilemmas', *PNR*, 47 (1986), 39 [review of Christopher Reid].

30 See Kennedy ' "Just the Facts" ', pp. 104–5.

31 An unusual instance of reverse influence from Ash's 'tall songs addressed themselves to ancestors, flag-poles / and other worlds' ('According to their Mythology' (*BS*, 104)).

32 David Shapiro, *John Ashbery: an Introduction to the Poetry* (New York: Columbia University Press, 1979), p. 37. See also Perloff, ' "Mysteries of Production",' pp. 263–5; and Ward 'Ashbery and Influence', pp. 102–4.

33 Robert von Hallberg, *American Poetry and Culture*, pp. 62–92. Although, as Shoptaw argues (*On the Outside Looking Out*, p. 4), Ashbery's homosexuality may have alienated him from the McCarthyite ethos of the 1950s, he nevertheless benefited from a Fulbright Scholarship to study in Paris.

34 Max Jacob's 'Literature and Poetry' (trans. J. Ashbery in *The Dice Cup: Selected Prose Poems*, ed. Michael Brownstein (New York: Sun, 1979), p. 83) uses Naples as a frame and ends in similar disappointment: 'The meandering paths left dry by the sea had made him think of the streets of Naples'. Jacob is cited as a common source by Ash (*Talking Verse*, 30). There is also a neutral, even affirmative, use of industrial metaphor in the jacket-note to *Flow Chart*: 'a schematic diagram ... showing the progress of material through the various stages of a manufacturing process'.

35 See Norman Finkelstein, 'Still other made-up Countries', *Verse*, 8.1 (1991), 33–5

36 See Gregson, 'John Ashbery and British Postmodernism', p. 219; and Kennedy ' "Just the Facts" ', p. 118; and compare Ash's comment on Peter Porter, that 'beneath the "glitter" of his modern baroque, in a style that lies somewhere between Auden and Ashbery, we hear the pedal notes of an authentic, unsentimental sorrow' ('A Reviving Glass of Porter' *PN Review*, 33 (1983), 75.

37 A point forcefully argued by Marjorie Perloff, in response to an earlier oral version of this paper: see 'Empiricism Once More', *Modern Language Quarterly*, 54.1 (1993), 129–30.

38 In William Le Queux's *Beryl of the Biplane: being the romance of an air-woman of today* (London: Pearson, 1917), from which these lines are directly adapted, the letters contain 'secret dispatches from the German general staff to the Kaiser's spies in Great Britain' (p. 72). Compare the uncharacteristic animosity of 'An Interview in Warsaw': 'there's always been a certain animosity between England and America since the American Revolution . . . and they've never really forgiven us for being an independent country' (p. 309).

39 Ashbery, 'Frank O'Hara's Question', *Book Week* 4.3 (25 September 1966), 6.

40 Shoptaw (*On the Outside Looking Out*, pp. 94–6) offers an erotic reading of the passage (reworked from *Three Hundred Things a Bright Boy can do*).

41 Vendler 'A Steely Glitter Chasing Shadows', p. 131 acknowledges the 'fertility with which he imagined catastrophe' but posits existential 'screams from the torture-chamber' within it. Claude Rawson detects a 'feeling for violence subject to stylish containment': 'Boards, Boardrooms and Blackboards: John Ashbery, Wallace Stevens and the Academisation of Poetry', *On Modern Poetry: Essays presented to Donald Davie*, ed. Laurence Lerner (Nashville: Vanderbilt University Press, 1988), p. 190. See also Blasing, *Politics and Form*, pp. 115–24; and Herman Rapaport, 'Deconstructing Apocalyptic Rhetoric: Ashbery, Derrida, Blanchot', *Criticism*, 27 (1985), 387–400.

42 The recurrent parallel is with American ascendency rather than British decline: 'The much resented arrogance of New Yorkers is distinctly Byzantine: for most of their long history the people of Byzantium remained convinced – with some justification – that their city and its civilisation were infinitely superior than anything to be found farther to the West': *A Byzantine Journey* (New York and London: I. B. Tauris, 1995), p. x.

43 *Talking Verse*, p. 32. Ash offers the disclaimer that 'that sentiment is highly ironic'.

44 Compare also 'Uh-huh trouble brewing / the decline continuing. // towards the flame . . .' ('Seven Intervals' (*BS*, 99)).

11 POSTMODERNISM/FIN DE SIÈCLE: DEFINING 'DIFFERENCE' IN LATE TWENTIETH-CENTURY POETICS

1 David Antin, 'Modernism and Postmodernism: Approaching the Present in American Poetry', *boundary 2: A Journal of Postmodern Literature*, 1. 1 (Fall 1972), 98–99, 109–12. Further references in the text cited as DA.

2 Charles Altieri, 'From Symbolist Thought to Immanence: the Ground of Postmodern American Poetics', *boundary 2*, 1. 3 (1973), 605–41.

3 See Altieri, *Enlarging the Temple: New Directions in American Poetry* (Lewisburg, Pa.: Bucknell University Press, 1979); James. E. B. Breslin, *From Modern to Contemporary: American Poetry, 1945–65* (University of Chicago

Press, 1984); Marjorie Perloff, *The Poetics of Indeterminacy: Rimbaud to Cage* (University of Chicago Press, 1981).

4 Ihab Hassan, 'POSTmodernISM: a Paracritical Bibliography', *New Literary History*, 3.1 (Fall 1971); rpt. *Paracriticisms: Seven Speculations of the Times* (Urbana: University of Illinois Press, 1975), and *The Postmodern Turn: Essays in Postmodern Theory and Culture* (Columbus: Ohio State University Press, 1987), pp. 25–45. All subsequent references are to this collection, cited IH*PT*. Hassan lists 7 rather than 9 categories because three (elitism, irony, abstraction) are subsumed under 'Dehumanization'. For purposes of clarity, I have thought it best to break this unit up, since the subsections get as much attention as the other sections. A related essay, 'The New Gnosticism: Speculations on an Aspect of the Postmodern Mind', appears in *boundary 2*, 1.3 (Spring 1973), 547–69.

5 Jean-François Lyotard, *The Postmodern Condition: a Report on Knowledge*, trans. Geoff Bennington and Brian Massumi (Minneapolis: University of Minnesota Press, 1984), pp. xxiv–xxv, 3–8, and esp. 31–7. Interestingly, the blurb for the Minnesota edition was written by Ihab Hassan.

6 Fredric Jameson, *Postmodernism, or, the Cultural Logic of Late Capitalism* (Durham, N.C.: Duke University Press, 1991), p. 2. Subsequently cited as FJ.

7 See Andreas Huyssen, *After the Great Divide: Modernism, Mass Culture: Postmodernism* (Bloomington and Indianapolis: Indiana University Press, 1986); Rosalind Krauss, *October*, 56 (Spring 1991), 3–4. But cf. Stephen Connor, *Postmodern Culture: an Introduction to Theories of the Contemporary* (Oxford: Blackwell, 1989). Connor puts his finger on the difficulty of making definitive statements about Postmodernism, which is supposedly so undefined and open. Referring to Foucault's account in *The Order of Things* of Borges's Chinese encyclopedia as a 'structure of radical incommensurability' or 'heterotopia', Connor comments: 'The obvious problem . . . which Foucault does not here confront, is that, once such a heterotopia has been named, and, more especially, once it has been cited and re-cited, it is no longer this conceptual monstrosity which it once was, for its incommensurability has been in some sense bound, controlled and predictively interpreted, given a centre and illustrative function.' In this sense, postmodern theory regularly 'names and correspondingly closes off the very world of cultural difference and plurality which it allegedly brings to visibility. What is striking is precisely the degree of consensus in postmodernist discourse that there is no longer any possibility of consensus, the authoritative announcements of the disappearance of final authority, and the promotion and recirculation of a total and comprehensive narrative of a cultural condition in which totality is no longer thinkable' (pp. 9–10).

8 For the printed version of the performance piece, in which the voice-over becomes a caption, see Laurie Anderson, *United States* (New York: Harper & Row, 1984), Part One, unpaginated. Craig Owens's reference

is to the earlier version in *Americans On the Move*, in which the wording is slightly different. See Owens, 'The Discourse of Others: Feminists and Postmodernism', in *The Anti-Aesthetic: Essays on Postmodern Culture*, ed. Hal Foster (Port Townsend, Wash.: Bay Press, 1983), p. 60; further references in the text cited as *AA*.

9 Herman Rapaport, '"Can You say Hello?"': Laurie Anderson's United States', *Theatre Journal*, 38.3 (October 1986), 340.

10 When Owens does briefly mention Luce Irigaray, Hélène Cixous, and Monique Wittig, he refers to their work as 'the writing of women influenced by Lacanian psychoanalysis' (*AA*, 63).

11 Brenda K. Marshall, *Teaching the Postmodern: Fiction and Theory* (New York and London: Routledge, 1992). Further references in the text cited as BM.

12 In the five years since this essay first appeared, this has increasingly been the tenor of discussion. See, for example, John McGowan, *Postmodernism and Its Critics* (Ithaca and London: Cornell University Press, 1991) and Christopher Norris, *The Truth about Postmodernism* (Oxford: Blackwell, 1993). A recent essay for *Critical Inquiry* by Charles Altieri, once the proponent of a postmodern theory, begins with the sentence, 'I think Postmodernism is now dead as a theoretical concept and, more important, as a way of developing cultural frameworks influencing how we shape theoretical concepts.' See 'What Is Living and What Is Dead in American Postmodernism: Establishing the Contemporaneity of Some American Poetry', *Critical Inquiry*, 22 (Summer 1996), 764. As Altieri's title suggests, he is not averse to salvaging certain aspects of the postmodern paradigm: it is, as he suggests in his Appendix (pp. 788–9) the increasingly political definitions of Postmodernism that must go.

13 David Harvey, 'Looking Back on Postmodernism', *Architectural Digest* (1990), 12. Harvey is here rethinking some of the notions in *The Condition of Postmodernity* (Oxford: Blackwell, 1989).

14 Charles Bernstein, *A Poetics* (Cambridge, Mass. and London: Harvard University Press, 1992), p. 4. Further references in the text cited as CB.

15 Henry Louis Gates, Jr, 'Goodbye, Columbus? Notes on the Culture of Criticism', *American Literary History*, 3.4 (Winter 1991), 716.

16 Benjamin Alire Saénz, *Calendar of Dust* (Seattle: Broken Moon Press, 1991), pp. 45–6.

17 Alfred Arteaga, *Cantos* (Berkeley: Chusma House, 1991), pp. 28–31.

18 Steve McCaffery, *Theory of Sediment* (Vancouver: Talon Books, 1991), pp. 38–9. A related poetic text 'The Black Debt' is discussed in my *Radical Artifice: Writing Poetry in the Age of Media* (University of Chicago Press, 1992), chapter 4 passim. See also my '"Inner Tension/In Attention"': Steve McCaffery's Book Art', *Visible Language*, 25. 2/3 (1992) and Renée Riese Hubert (ed.), *The Artist's Book: The Text and its Rivals* pp. 173–91.

19 Johanna Drucker, *Narratology* (New York: Druckwerk, 1994), unpaginated last page.

Index